THE
Anti-Education
ERA

Also by James Paul Gee and
available from Palgrave Macmillan

What Video Games Have to Teach Us About Learning and Literacy

Women and Gaming

THE
Anti-Education
ERA

CREATING SMARTER STUDENTS
THROUGH DIGITAL LEARNING

James Paul Gee

palgrave
macmillan

To the Nine: Bandit, Bene, Bolt, Conrad,
Harley, Micah, Muffin, Rolle, Witten.

And to the One and Only: Bead.

THE ANTI-EDUCATION ERA
Copyright ©, James Paul Gee, 2013.

First published in 2013 by PALGRAVE MACMILLAN® in the United States—a
division of St. Martin's Press LLC, 175 Fifth Avenue, New York, NY 10010.

Where this book is distributed in the UK, Europe and the rest of the world, this is
by Palgrave Macmillan, a division of Macmillan Publishers Limited, registered in
England, company number 785998, of Houndmills, Basingstoke, Hampshire RG21
6XS.

Palgrave Macmillan is the global academic imprint of the above companies and has
companies and representatives throughout the world.

Palgrave® and Macmillan® are registered trademarks in the United States, the United
Kingdom, Europe and other countries.

ISBN: 978-0-230-34209-5

Library of Congress Cataloging-in-Publication Data is available from the Library of
Congress.

A catalogue record of the book is available from the British Library.

Design by Letra Libre Inc.

First edition: January 2013

10 9 8 7 6 5 4 3 2 1

Printed in the United States of America.

Contents

Preface   vii

1   Orwell's Question: Why Are Humans So Stupid?   1

PART I
HOW TO BE STUPID

2   Short-Circuiting the Circuit of Human Reflective Action   11
3   The Limits of Human Memory   21
4   Mental Comfort Stories   29
5   Lack of Context   39
6   Lack of Experience   49
7   Pitfalls along Our Search for Status and Solidarity   59
8   Words Gone Awry   67
9   Lack of Agency   75
10   Institutions and Frozen Thought   85
11   Fact-Free Stories That Sound Good   95
12   Imagined Kin   103
13   Lonely Groups of One   113
14   When Not to Trust Experts   121
15   Evading Knowledge   133
16   Flight from Complexity   141

PART II
HOW TO GET SMART BEFORE IT'S TOO LATE

17   Inclusive We: How We Can All Get Smarter Together   151
18   Big Minds, Not Little Minds   159

19 Mind Visions and New, Better Worlds   167

20 Synchronized Intelligence: Getting Our Minds
    and Tools in Synch   171

21 Interlude to Forestall Possible Misunderstandings   191

22 Getting Smarter Before It's Too Late   197

    References   217
    Index   237

Preface

AFTER MANY YEARS OF STUDYING PEOPLE I HAVE become intrigued, as have many others, by how a species named for its intelligence (*Homo sapiens:* wise or knowing man) can sometimes be so stupid. Depending on how you look at it, humans are either marvelously intelligent or amazingly stupid.

We build great cities in the desert, cities like Los Angeles and Phoenix. Then we waste and pollute the desert's already short supply of water. We pour concrete on the ground and spew carbon into the air to make the heat of the desert ever hotter.

We wage vast public health campaigns to save poor people across the world from infectious diseases. Then we kill lots of them in endless wars.

We know how to make some people richer than whole countries, people like Bill Gates, Warren Buffett, and six members of the Wal-Mart Walton family. Then we leave whole countries to starve.

In the United States, many people take the moral high ground on abortion and the sanctity of human life. Then they let a great many children and adults suffer or die in the United States because they have no health care and across the world because they have nothing to eat.

We use our financial genius and newly minted MBAs to create amazingly complex new financial instruments like derivatives and credit default swaps. Then we use them as financial weapons of mass destruction and devastate the global economy. We go on to reward those who brought on this vast destruction with bailouts and bonuses rather than punish them with jail terms.

We spend over two hundred years creating a vibrant two-party system capable of solving problems like going to the moon. Then we mire our politics in ideological and cultural debates just at the time when we face major global economic, environmental, and civilizational problems that could bring on Armageddon, problems that demand pragmatic, not ideological, solutions.

We create military technology that is the envy of the world and capable of great "shock and awe." Then we manage to wage two massively expensive and not all that successful wars in Afghanistan and Iraq and go on to decry our massive federal deficit.

We create marvelous new digital media that bring people more information about and more perspectives on the world than ever. Then people customize their media to the point where they live in filter bubbles and echo chambers where they never need hear anything they don't already agree with.

We discover the magic of how to turn plants into fuel (biofuel). But then, in a world where lots of people are starving, we actually make fuel out of food like corn, raise the price of food, and starve the poor yet more, which is all a bit like Midas turning food into gold. Perhaps we will be smart enough eventually to make fuel out of fungus rather than corn.

Humans have, of course, always been really smart and they have always been really stupid. Early human groups learned to cut down trees and hunt animals and then they sometimes cut and hunted the trees, animals, and themselves into extinction. After all, if the Native Americans had not killed off all the New World horses, they would not have been easy prey for the Spaniards on their Old World horses.

But the problem of us humans being a dumb smart species today is different: our human intelligence has now created a highly complex, fast-changing, and very risky world. The cost of mistakes in this world is now often way too high for individuals and whole societies to bear. In a fast-changing global world replete with complex interacting systems, human actions can bring on all sorts of disastrous unintended consequences. Viruses take rides on jets along with humans; a new Wall Street financial product wipes out economies throughout the world; jobs float to the lowest cost centers in the world, shuttering whole towns and cities in the United States; economic collapse and global warming send hordes of poor immigrants across the globe.

In a developed country like the United States, where inequality is high and there are a great many poorly paid service jobs, but not all that many highly rewarded "knowledge production" jobs, people face a wealth of high-risk decisions. What is worth knowing? What skills are needed for a fast-changing world? Does real education happen in school or out of it? How much of a child's fate is already determined by what has happened at home before school? How can one prepare for massive and unpredictable changes in the world? How can we keep the trains of our polarized politics, vast worldwide disparities in health and wealth, massive flows of money criss-crossing the globe as mere numbers in computers, and out-of-control environmental problems from running off the cliff?

As developed countries like the United States and emerging economies like China and India use up and pollute the world's resources, how will they face the massive flows of immigrants and worldwide wars created by shortages of water, food, and human dignity? How will developing countries ever enter the modern global economy when resources are scarce, corruption is rampant, and the developed world is awash with deficits and ideological conflicts?

Where is new thinking going to come from in a world polarized by ideology, religious conflicts, and vast degrees of inequality? We humans today have the best tools we have ever had—thanks to technology, digital media, and social media—to be smart. But these tools will not make us smarter all by themselves. Indeed, in many ways today, they are making us dumber. We need to change who we are as humans. We need to respect Mother Nature. We need to find the seeking of evidence as sexy as the trading of ideology. We need to innovate before it is too late. We need to make more people count and let more people participate.

But in this book I am not primarily interested in the fate of society and the world. That fate is too big to think about all at once. I am primarily interested in my fate and the fate of my children. I am primarily interested in your fate and the fate of your children. This is not a book about policy and statistics. It is a book about us, about you and me. It is a book about why it might be important for us to save ourselves from our own stupidity. It is a book about what sorts of creatures we humans are and how we can become better ones.

There are a lot of books today about how the human mind—designed, as it was, in our long human history for small bands of hunters and gatherers—is not well suited for the modern world. We are prone to all sorts of mental errors that can do us great harm in our modern lives.

There are lots of books today about the rising inequality in terms of wealth and health in the United States and across the globe. There is now solid evidence that too much inequality in society makes everyone—not just poor people—sicker in mind and body than they need to be.

There are lots of books today about the many crises that confront our schools and institutions of higher learning. Education at every level is expensive and it is grade inflated and dumbed down. Too often the status of a school or college counts more than what is being learned. Our colleges and universities today are entrepreneurial centers rather than institutions of higher learning.

There are lots of books today about how ideology trumps evidence in the United States and in countries across the globe where fundamentalisms of various sorts are rampant. Americans, by and large, do not seek careers in STEM (science, technology, engineering, and mathematics), but plenty of Chinese and Indians do.

There are lots of books today about how technology is changing the nature of work and institutions. Technology has made it easy to off-shore many high-level and low-level jobs. Service work has become rampant in developed countries. Unions are disappearing, along with good wages and benefits. At the same time, thanks to the Internet and other digital media, amateurs are competing with experts to produce knowledge, science, media, ads, and entertainment. Institutions and even rulers are being challenged by emergent forms of organization made possible by digital and social media.

There are lots of books today about the decline of civic participation and the ignorance of young people regarding politics and political institutions. At the same time, there are lots of books about the great increase in participation in interest-driven or cause-driven groups made possible by the Internet and social media.

This book is about all these problems and issues. But it is more about what they all have to do with each other than it is about any one of them alone.

This book is about what it means to be smart and to be a fully awake participant in our high-risk global world in the twenty-first century. It is about what parents ought to do to forestall their children becoming victims in that high-risk world. The book is about how to think about the future before we humans don't have one. We need to save our children and ourselves from the sorts of human stupidity to which we are all prone, but that are now way too dangerous to indulge in. To have a future we need to start exercising our smart side more, a side that today's schools, colleges, and media have too often put to sleep.

Video gamers have a term—"spoiler"—for something in a game review that will spoil a surprise that players could have discovered for themselves. The following is a spoiler: this is a stealth book about education.

I have spent my now long career doing two different things. One is linguistics and the other is education. Sometimes these interests have come together and sometimes they haven't. In education I have been part of our vast country-wide debates on school reform and on how we can close the equity gaps in literacy and school knowledge between richer and poorer children. These debates have taken some new turns with the proliferation of new digital technologies, but have nonetheless now gone on for a long time without much manifest improvement in schools or equity.

In fact, many of our schools have now become skill-and-drill test-prep academies, and many of our colleges have become social camps for credentials, beer, and warm bodies, not knowledge. And yet, the key place where all the problems I mentioned above—about which there are lots of books but not many solutions—intersect is in the question of what constitutes a real education for twenty-first-century citizens.

This is not a question about small class sizes and small schools, school budgets, best practices, accountability, technology in the classroom, or schools and universities as job preparation. It is a question about what would constitute a proper education for a person who wants to be a producer and not just a consumer, a participant and not just a spectator, an agent and not a victim in a world full of ideology, risk, fear, and uncertainty. What sort of education could—what would it mean for an education to—make us humans smart enough to solve our problems and save ourselves from our own stupidity?

Why a *stealth* book about education? Why stealth here? Because I am now convinced that we cannot improve our society by more talk about schools and school reform, but only by talk about what it means to be smart in the twenty-first century. I am convinced that we cannot improve our schools and colleges by more talk about practices and policies, but only by talk about what it means to be smart in the twenty-first century and what schools and colleges have to do with this question. While I will certainly demonstrate in the course of this book a good many ways in which we humans can be stupid, in the end I will argue that when we make people count and let them participate, they can be very smart indeed.

When I say this book is about education, I do not mean schools and colleges as they are. Education of the sort most people get in school and college can just as easily make people dumber as smarter. For a great many Americans, gaining more knowledge about science tends to make them even more dismissive of evidence than less well-educated people, especially if the evidence goes against their politics, ideology, or financial interests. While many educational dollars have been spent on getting American kids to learn more "STEM"—so that we can compete with the Chinese and the Indians in a global economy, it is said—it does not appear that such learning, in and of itself, leads to any respect for evidence or arguments founded on evidence.

No, by education I mean what a twenty-first-century human being ought to learn and know and be able to do in order to make a better life, a better society, and a better world before it is too late. A good deal of this education will not go on in schools and colleges in any case, and even less if schools and colleges do not radically change their paradigms.

I will talk a lot about what makes humans stupid before I get to what can make them smart. When I get to being smart rather than stupid, I will discuss digital tools. But right at the start, I want to warn that digital tools are no salvation. They can make things worse just as easily as they can make things better. They are great tools with which to become dumber just as they are great tools with which to become smarter. It all depends on how they are used. And key to their good use is that they be subordinated to ways of connecting humans for rich learning and that they serve as tools human learners own and operate and do not simply serve. Video games and social media will not make us smarter by themselves any more than books have.

This book will deal with people and institutions getting smarter and more humane in the context of growing inequality in the United States and across the world. We have always had gaps in literacy and other forms of learning between poorer and richer kids and between some minorities and the majority population. Today the gap between different classes—between richer and poorer kids—is actually larger than the well-studied black-white gap. Class is taking front stage in the United States, something that makes many Americans uncomfortable. Digital media are not making these gaps close; if anything, they are widening the gaps, especially in regard to so-called twenty-first-century skills (like innovation, system thinking, design, technical learning, and using technology for production). Inequality is at an all-time high. The evidence is replete that such high levels of inequality are bad for everyone in a society, rich or poor, in many different ways, including their health, levels of anxiety, and overall well-being.

We live in an era of anti-education. We focus on skill-and-drill, tests and accountability, and higher education as a marker of status (elite colleges) or mere job training (lesser colleges). We have forgotten education as a force for equality in the sense of making everyone count and enabling everyone to fully participate in our society. We have forgotten education as a force for drawing out of each of us our best selves in the service of an intellectually and morally good life and good society.

In the spirit of full disclosure, let me say something about my politics before we move any further. I discuss in Chapter 16 what constitutes, for me, a true conservative and liberal. True conservatives want to be cautious and incremental in the face of complex problems for fear that large changes may have bad unintended consequences. They are humble about how much better we can make an imperfect world through large-scale social engineering. True liberals see change as redesigning systems and practices that have become dangerously outdated or unfair. They do not want to "tinker" while people suffer. They are more optimistic than conservatives that we can improve our imperfect world in large ways.

Neither side is "right." These two poles are the crucial foundation for political debate and civil society. We need to save ourselves from both the unintended consequences of the arrogance of optimism and the missed opportunities of the humility of pessimism. We do this by reasoned debate, honest assessment of how good or bad, fair or unfair, things are, and intelligent voting. Many of us, in these terms, are conservatives on some issues and liberals on others. I certainly am.

Some of my examples of stupidity will strike readers as critical of conservatives. They are no such thing. Denying realities—like the reality of global warming, the possibility of rape leading to pregnancy, or that Christ did not champion wealth—is not conservative. It is just stupid. Debating what to do about global warming—how incremental or large-scale our response ought to be—is intelligent political debate.

I have lived my life in the academy. I am well aware that some so-called academic liberals believe stupid things like all reality is "discourse," truth is relative, and science is an elitist conspiracy. Such views are not liberal, they are just stupid. However, I admit that I use examples in this book that I think are impactful today on our current society and politics. Some of these are things people who claim to be conservatives say, but such people are not, in my terms, true conservatives. By and large the sort of academic "liberal" stupidity I have just mentioned has little real impact on the wider world outside the academy.

NOTE: References for claims made in this and the rest of the chapters appear at the end of the book, grouped by chapter, so as not to clutter the text with citations that tend to break up fluid reading.

1

Orwell's Question: Why Are Humans So Stupid?

IN HIS CLASSIC FUTURISTIC NOVEL, *1984*, GEORGE
Orwell raised a particularly interesting question about us humans: why do
we so often believe things that are manifestly false? Orwell had in mind the
ways in which totalitarian regimes can get people to firmly believe things
contradicted by obvious facts. But the phenomenon is by no means restricted
to totalitarian regimes. It flourishes in free societies as well. It is a human trait
easily exploited by politicians, charlatans, and the media.

Polls repeatedly show that significant numbers of people believe the
earth is less than 10,000 years old, believe that dinosaurs and humans were
once on the earth together, believe in astrology and think that the stars affect
their fate, or believe in ghosts and even think they have seen one. Currently,
many Americans believe that Barack Obama is a Muslim and isn't a citizen,
and continue to believe, well past the George W. Bush presidency, that Saddam Hussein was one of the agents of 9/11.

But the problem goes much deeper than believing in astrology. We humans are all exceedingly good at self-deception. Nietzsche said, "The visionary lies to himself, the liar only to others." I would say that we humans, all
of us, are visionaries. We are exceedingly good at believing what we want and
need to believe, even in the face of counterevidence.

Research has long shown that humans display what is called a "confirmation bias" (sometimes called a "myside bias"). This is a seemingly built-in mental bias that makes humans favor information that confirms their beliefs. Because of this bias, people seek out and remember information that supports their beliefs and ignore information that does not. The human confirmation bias is strongest with highly emotionally charged issues or deeply entrenched beliefs. For example, in reading about issues such as gun control or abortion, people prefer sources that affirm their pre-existing values and beliefs. When faced with ambiguous evidence, they interpret this evidence as supporting their belief.

The confirmation bias, because it leads to biases in seeking, interpreting, and recalling information, also leads to polarization. People who disagree about an issue like gun control or abortion can disagree ever more vehemently even though they are exposed to the same evidence. They interpret, accept, and ignore the evidence in different ways.

Psychological research has exposed a great many other mental biases that cause the human mind to rush to false conclusions. But outside of such biases (which are probably a product of the evolution of the human mind), humans hold lots of beliefs that are simply "folk theories" long contradicted by empirical evidence.

For example, the majority of people believe that human memory works like a video camera and accurately records the events we see and hear. But research on memory has long shown that human memory is fabricated, reconstructed, and transformed through use. It is not a veridical recording. We are deeply selective about what we remember. Memories can change in light of subsequent events as we replay our memories and use them to make sense of new experiences. Yet our court system invests a great deal of faith in eyewitness testimony and the belief that memory is on a par with a recording of the facts.

This folk belief about memory is just one of a great many cases in which our everyday beliefs, many of which are entrenched in our institutions and our cultural practices, are contradicted by empirical work in science. Yet science has little power, it seems, to displace such everyday beliefs. In fact, in the face of social, cultural, and institutional agendas, science has little impact. The evidence for global warming, and that it is caused in significant part by human activities, is overwhelming. This does not mean global warming is "true" in the way a mathematical proof is true (that is not how evidence works), but it does mean that the pervasive way that evidence for global warming is ignored and misrepresented is a significant indicator of how little scientific evidence counts in crucial areas of life such as government, policy making, business, religion, and politics.

All of these issues about the weakness of human thinking are well discussed in both the research literature and the popular literature on the mind. But this literature does not really get down to how deeply stupid we humans can be, despite calling ourselves *Homo sapiens.* Human history, up to today, is replete with people torturing, maiming, and killing each other in the name of religious or cultural beliefs. It is replete with greed and corruption that undermine the very societies the greedy and corrupt live in. After the 2008 recession, the largest since the Great Depression, we said the problem was that our banks and other financial institutions were "too big to fail" and had to be rescued at taxpayer expense. But then we made the banks even bigger as we allowed and even encouraged the stronger ones to eat up the weaker ones.

Across large parts of the globe, women are still virtual (and sometimes real) slaves, despite the fact that women are crucial to the success of any modern economy. On television we watch poor people across the globe starve to death from famine, war, storms, and drought—poor people who paradoxically often have a great many children—while we make fuel for our cars out of food (e.g., corn).

We demonize as traitors those who disagree with us. We call ourselves "pro-life" because we oppose abortion and yet oppose universal health care and thus let thousands of children and adults die because they lack health insurance. We claim that Jesus Christ, a dirt-poor champion of the poor and the unwashed, preached a "prosperity gospel" and wanted us all to be wealthy. We ruin the earth that sustains us in the contradictory name of endless growth in a finite world. We seek great wealth when all the evidence indicates that past a certain (pretty moderate) point, greater wealth does not lead to more happiness or well-being.

Orwell's problem was "Why are humans often so stupid even in the face of obvious or easily available evidence?" But the deeper problem is why humans care so little about evidence, truth, and the well-being of others even when, in the end, their actions undermine themselves, their societies, and their world. Why are we humans so stupid in such deep and appalling ways?

And yet, of course, humans can be very smart indeed. We have built cities, gone to the moon, made great strides in public health, uncovered mind-blowing mysteries of the physical and natural world, designed great works of art, and engaged in some grand moral and humanitarian feats.

But then again, how smart and moral can we humans really be when we have made a world in which the following things are true (this information is readily available from international organizations like the United Nations): Nearly half of all the children in the world live in poverty and a great many of them die before the age of five. We could send every child in the world to school for less than one percent of what the world spends each year on weapons, but we do not. Almost half the people in the world live on less than $2.50 a day and 80 percent of them live on less than $10 a day. Twelve percent of the world's population (none of them living in the Third World) use 85 percent of its water, as much of the world faces drought due to global warming (something many Americans do not believe in). The wealthiest nation on earth, the United States, has the widest gap between rich and poor of any industrialized nation. Yet we believe in a "trickle down" theory of economic growth, in which making the very wealthy yet wealthier will cause their wealth to trickle down and enrich the poor.

All of this might matter to you morally. But even if it does not, it should still matter to you because such a world is dangerous. Armies of dispossessed people living amid environmental collapse are not going to be good for any of us. Even in the United States, as inequality grows to ever higher rates, more and more people lose trust in their society and in their fellow citizens. They feel left out. As this number expands, the day comes when rich and poor alike will suffer, and we risk an on-the-ground civil war defined around class and lack of access to full participation in the society.

I myself do care about human stupidity on moral grounds. I care, as well, on the grounds of fear for myself, my fellow citizens, and my country and the world. But I must admit, personally, that I am completely intrigued by how stupid and venal "smart" humans can be.

I am intrigued by how often all of us—myself included—deceive ourselves. I am intrigued by how often we all do things that harm ourselves and others. I am intrigued by how readily we all ignore evidence, get bitten by the world, and continue on our way little changed and little motivated to change. We get bitten by banks too big to fail and we make them bigger. We see that corporations cheat, lie, and steal when we deregulate them, so we deregulate them further. We learned nothing from the savings and loan crisis in the 1980s: we deregulated savings and loan companies and taxpayers had to bail them out for billions, then we blithely repeated the same thing, brought on the 2008 recession, and then bailed out the big banks for even more. Yet many people (who may or may not actually be stupid or greedy) still call for yet more deregulation.

As someone who has lived a life in universities, I am deeply intrigued, in particular, by how dysfunctional and self-defeating institutions can be. We humans complain constantly about the institutions we work in or deal with, but we rarely change them for the better. We join committees where the committee as a group is usually stupider than the dumbest person on it and rarely smarter than the smartest person on it, but we call for more and more committees. We pick leaders (e.g., deans) and corporate CEOs who fail, and we reward them nonetheless with more money or promotions.

No matter how much we loathe many of the institutions we deal with, we have not heretofore been able to live without them. Institutions are essential ways to coordinate large groups of people for large tasks. However, today, digital and social media are allowing large groups of people to organize bottom-up without a formal institution.

Such media are also allowing people with no official credentials from formal institutions to become experts and even compete with credentialed experts in all sorts of domains. Indeed, ad agencies rue the day they encouraged everyday people to make ads on their home computers as a way to involve them with the products the agencies were pushing. People began to make ads that were better than the million-dollar commercials the agencies made, and some people even made counter-ads to undo the work of the ad agencies and malign the products they were advertising. Marketing consultants have called for the ad industry to rise up against amateur spots. But, of course, it is too late. In regard to digital media, the horse has already left the barn.

Now, digital and social media (just like books before them) can make us smarter and allow more people to participate and fight back against the way market-based societies marginalize them in the name of profit. But they can make us stupid, as well, and can lead to duping and manipulating people in the name of profit or ideology. It all depends, of course, on what we do with digital and social media and who controls them and how.

This book, then, is devoted to my own version of Orwell's question: how can smart people—like me and you—be so dumb? I pursue the question because, as a human being, I find it so fascinating. My own stupidity, not to mention yours, amazes me. But you will now ask, "If you are so stupid, why should we read a book you have written?" Good question. The answer is that whatever is smart in this book isn't me, or just me. It is due to my plugging myself into good tools and other people to make something bigger than myself. And this is, indeed, the way out of the perils of our human stupidity: if we plug into and play with good tools and other people in the right ways, we can be smart and moral, and we can save our world.

Like many people interested in education, I have been dismayed by our schools and colleges. I do not think that our schools and colleges prepare people to face the modern world with deep thought and problem-solving skills. I don't think they prepare people to participate in a true democracy where their votes are based on considered arguments backed by evidence. I don't think they prepare people to feel like—and actually be—important participants in society, people who count. I do not think that our colleges and universities are change agents preparing us for the future, but agents of the short-term thinking and short-term profit seeking typical of our contemporary society.

We are all, when left to our own devices and to our own desires and fears, stupid. It has to be the job of some institution or social organization to help us become smart. We don't come smart out of the box. Yes, we are capable of being smart, even wise and moral. But these virtues need to be drawn out of us; we need to be educated, but not indoctrinated. Our formal institutions of education have, by and large, given up the task of deep education for the short-term goals of test passing and tuition payments.

In the end, I do not care if people believe, for example, that high levels of economic inequality are good (and moral) or bad (and immoral), though I have my own view. But I do care that, whichever they believe, they have arguments for their position based on both evidence and a moral vision. I care that they have confronted people and texts who disagree with them and that they themselves have searched for disconfirming evidence. I hope they have also gone beyond evidence to form a considered vision of life and the world based on wisdom from the past and the present, including wisdom from outside their own local comfort zone. And, finally, I hope they remain open and committed to a public forum in which they will deal respectfully with opposing, but well-considered, viewpoints in the hope that new and better ideas can emerge out of the clash of old ones.

Whether liberal or conservative, people who do not accept these values are, in my view, mere ideologues and, if they seek to impose their views on others, thugs. The public forum in which a wide array of ideas clash and emerge, where evidence is gathered and honored and moral visions developed and sharpened, should be—should have been—our institutions of higher learning. But, if they ever were this sort of forum, for the most part they no longer are. We are all, conservatives and liberals, the poorer for it.

Being smart, especially in a fast-changing and complex world, requires people to beg, borrow, or steal new ideas. It requires that all of us, young or old, remain open to discovery and grow to be distrustful of long-held and cherished beliefs that we have not closely inspected for a long time, if ever. In the modern world our minds need oil changes every so many miles or they cease to work well. With modern media and digital technologies, including the Internet, we can all get such oil changes regularly, but we have to beware of the quality of who or what is doing the change. We need to be sure to get high-grade oil.

IN THE NEXT CHAPTER, we start Part I of this book: How to Be Stupid. We cannot learn how to get smart if we do not first understand what makes us stupid and how we can reverse it. We start Part I by discussing how the human mind, since its origins, has been tightly tied to living in, and acting on, the world. One key way to make humans stupid is to break this active tie between mind and world. This will be a key theme of the book. Respecting the world and using digital media to enhance our contacts with the world is smart and good. Disrespecting the world—by disrespecting facts, for example—leads not just to stupidity, but to being bitten, sometimes badly, by the world.

PART I

How to Be Stupid

2

Short-Circuiting the Circuit of Human Reflective Action

EVOLUTION HAS SHAPED THE HUMAN MIND TO BE good at some things and not at others. Our minds were not shaped by modern conditions, but by those in earlier ages when humans lived in small hunting and gathering bands. We humans bring to modern society a mind and body shaped by times and conditions that bear little resemblance to those in which we live today.

The most important step taken in the evolution of higher intelligence was the development of the ability of an animal to think and plan both before and after taking an action. Before acting, such an animal can think about what might happen and devise an effective plan of action. After the action, the animal can reflect on what happened and think about whether the results of the action were good or bad. Then the animal can plan a more effective action if necessary.

How do the animals that can do this, including us, do it? Such animals have evolved the ability to project images in their heads. They can "act in their heads" and not just in the world. They can recall what happened in a similar situation. They can also recombine elements of former experiences in imaginary scenes to speculate on what might happen and what the consequences might be. What these animals can do is essentially run simulations in their heads. They do so in order to think about possible contingencies and outcomes based on prior experience and extrapolations from prior experience.

These simulations in our heads are rather like video games. We play a role in the simulation. We act in the simulation as if the mental simulation were a sort of virtual world. Not only can we humans act out our own roles in our mental simulations; we can even play the roles of other people. We can role-play the minister at a wedding, the possible actions of our opponents in a game or war, or the feelings of a person we have wronged. By simulating other people's actions, motives, and feelings, we can get inside their heads while staying inside our own.

We can even get inside the heads of things that do not have heads. We can simulate things that happen in the natural world. We can imagine a river flooding a town and simulate the damage in our minds. We can reflect on the effects of one car hitting another going in a certain direction at a certain speed. A scientist can imagine that he or she is an electron and try to see the world from the electron's perspective. We are at our best engaging in such imaginings when we are using them to prepare for actions in which something really matters to us.

So, humans are good at learning from experience and using it to engage in simulations that prepare them for action. Of course, when we think before we act, we are not always successful. Indeed, we can readily fail when we have no prior experiences that are relevant to a new situation, not even experiences that can help us make intelligent guesses about what might happen.

A good deal of our success in acting depends not just on how we reflect before we act, but on how we reflect after we act. When we have taken an action toward a goal, we get an outcome. Now we have to assess this outcome in our minds. We have to think about whether it was what we wanted and whether it is a good or a bad outcome for achieving our goal. If it is not good, we need to consider another action that might bring us closer to our goal, or we need to rethink our goal. Of course, it is very hard to assess an action—and adjust or correct it if need be—if one does not have a clear or coherent goal.

We humans are very good actor/simulators. We have language, and language allows us to think about things in a more complex way than other animals do. It allows me, for instance, to simulate what will happen if I wait until the day after next to do something I should have done two weeks ago. No other animal can manipulate time in this symbolic way.

So as actor/simulators we humans can be smart. But certain conditions have to be met for us to be smart. First, we must have had a good deal of prior experience, experience that we can use as "fodder" for simulations. Second, we must have a clear goal in terms of which we can assess our actions and plan new and better ones on the path toward our goal (or rethinking the goal to get a better one).

There is a third condition. It turns out that humans think and act well only when they care about what they are doing. Caring, here, means feeling that something is at stake for us—that something really matters to us—when we act. Thus, emotion is crucial to thinking and simulating because it helps us to manage attention, persist past failure, and assess outcomes in terms of what we care about.

So the three conditions for smart action are: (1) lots of prior experience; (2) clear goals; and (3) something being "at stake" (mattering emotionally). You can now see a paradox here. If we cannot think and act well without prior experience, how do we ever think and act the first time, before we have some experience in a certain area of thought and action?

This paradox is resolved socially. In our initial experiences in a new area, we need mentorship. People more expert than ourselves have to help us and share their experience with us. They need to help us see what to pay attention to, how to assess the outcomes of actions toward our goal, how to adjust our actions in corrective ways, and how to progressively reframe our goals if we need to. This process is sometimes called "scaffolding." We initially act collaboratively with a mentor who supports us and shows us how to think about a situation and how to proceed toward a goal in a new area. The mentor gradually withdraws support (like taking down scaffolding) as we are progressively able to act and think on our own and thus gain new experiences on our own.

Of course, we can act all alone in new situations with no prior experiences and no way to properly assess the outcomes of our actions. We have all done this at times. On Darwinian grounds, however, a good many people who did this regularly in the past died in the attempt, a form of learning from experience that has no transfer to new experiences. Better to have a mentor initially show you what to pay attention to in new experiences.

So let's restate the conditions for smart human action, adding mentorship. The conditions are: (1) initial mentorship to get us prepared to learn from experience in specific areas; (2) lots of prior experience; (3) clear goals; (4) something being "at stake" (mattering to us emotionally); and (5) the opportunity to act. I have also added the fifth condition, the opportunity to act. No matter how much experience you have had and no matter how well you can use it to build simulations, it does little good unless you are an actor and not just a spectator of other people's actions.

When these conditions are met, humans are "smart." But what does being "smart" mean? I have just described a specific multipart process:

1. the process of building simulations based on experience to think before acting;

2. acting;

3. assessing the outcome of the action in terms of how well it works toward accomplishing our goal;

4. choosing a new action or an adjustment of the old one; and

5. then acting again. I will call this process "the circuit of reflective action."

When the five conditions for smart human action above are met, we humans are good at the circuit of reflective action. However, this circuit is not primarily devoted to determining what is "true." It is devoted to determining what "works," what is adequate for our purposes, values, and goals.

This is not to say that truth is irrelevant to the circuit of reflective action. It is just that truth alone is not enough. Things need to work toward the accomplishment of goals. The circuit of reflective action is a type of interactive conversation with the world. We act and pay attention to how the world reacts. We then reflect on what the reaction from the world (the outcome of our action) means or augurs for what we should do next—what we should change or adjust—in order to accomplish our goals. Then we act again and the world answers back again. You need a world with which to play the game of reflective action.

The world that answers us back in response to our actions is a stern taskmaster. It does not care about us. It can bite back if we do not pay attention to its responses. The world resists human ideologies and desires. Fire burns you and certain uncooked plants kill you, regardless of your values, desires, politics, religion, or ideology.

Early humans lived right up against the world. There were harsh and possibly dire consequences when people did not listen to the world's responses or respond to them intelligently. Those who jumped off a mountain because their "religion" told them they could fly died. So eventually did their "religion."

The world is so important to the circuit of reflective action that we need, one last time, to modify the conditions for smart human action. The conditions are:

1. initial mentorship to get us prepared to learn from experience in specific areas or domains;
2. lots of prior experience;

3. clear goals;

4. something being "at stake" (mattering to us emotionally); and

5. the opportunity to act in a way that elicits a meaningful response from the world.

I have changed the fifth condition to get our conversational partner, the world, in there. We need to get responses to our actions and responses that are meaningful.

I have not spelled out what "meaningful" means here. However, it is clear that the responses from the world need to be not so overwhelming that we die or tremble in fear, nor so weak that we cannot make out what they are, nor so ambiguous or vague that they are of no help in determining what to do next. We humans need to learn how to elicit useful responses from the world. Good mentors can help with this, as can the stored knowledge of the social groups to which we belong. Right now, though, the main point I want to make is that you cannot elicit useful responses from the world if the requisite parts of the world are not present or if you do not know how to elicit useful responses from the world.

There is a lot more to say about the circuit of reflective action. It is what made and makes us smart. It is interesting that the conditions for reflective action are often not met in formal schooling.

Consider these features of much formal schooling, especially when that schooling is oriented to standardized tests:

1. Much of formal schooling is devoted to listening to and reading language, not to taking actions in the world that are relevant to that language (say in history, civics, or physics).

2. Often students can see no clear and compelling goal for learning in formal classrooms beyond grades and graduation. They often do not care about the material in any deep way.

3. Many students have had little or no prior experiences of actions in the world relevant to the often technical language they hear or read in school.

4. Some students have had mentorship in the subject area prior to or outside of school, mentorship about what to pay attention to and how to act and assess action toward goals in the area. Others have not. Nonetheless, we pretend they are on a level playing field.

Labs in areas like chemistry and physics can work better in terms of actions and goals, though lack of prior mentorship, prior experiences, and caring is often still a problem. Worse, in many labs the goals are not all that clear beyond "getting the right answer." Further, the students are often not deeply aware of what makes the world's responses to their actions in the lab meaningful, in part because they do not have any clear goal or purpose of their own save, perhaps, getting a good grade.

School is often based not on problem solving, which perforce involves actions and goals, but on learning information, facts, and formulas that one has read about in texts or heard about in lectures. It is not surprising, then, that research has long shown that a student's doing well in school, in terms of grades and tests, does not correlate with being able to solve problems in the areas in which the student has been taught (e.g., math, civics, physics).

Now there is an objection to my complaints about formal schooling. It is this: School is about abstract textual knowledge (reading, writing, theories, and factual knowledge). The circuit of reflective action is about practical knowledge in the sense of learning what is adequate to our goals in action and problem solving. School is not meant to be practical in that sense. Unfortunately, this objection—though it sounds good—is nonsense. The sorts of practical knowledge we produce through the circuit of reflective action are what give meaning to words, concepts, abstractions, and facts.

To see that it is the circuit of reflective action that gives meaning to words and abstractions, consider the following passage from a high school science textbook:

> The destruction of a land surface by the combined effects of abrasion and removal of weathered material by transporting agents is called erosion. . . . The production of rock waste by mechanical processes and chemical changes is called weathering.

Note that this text appears to be about abstractions like "destruction," "abrasion," "removal," "agents," "erosion," "production," "mechanical processes," "chemical changes," and "weathering." But in reality it refers to actions in the world: something *destroys* land, something *abrades* material, something *weathers* material, agents *transport* something, processes and changes *produce* rock waste, rock *wastes* away, and more. You can really understand this text if and only if you can simulate in your mind the "named" actors and actions and see the effects of the actions. It is all the better if you are simulating this in order to take an action to accomplish a goal yourself or if you have done so in past experiences. You need to be able to see in your mind's eye how things like water and wind can abrade a rough surface and why this would matter to anyone, especially you.

Now, to tell the truth, I cannot do this. I have not had the requisite prior experiences. I know what the words mean, but I cannot see in my mind how the things they refer to in the world actually act and effect change. For example: I have no idea what the difference is between "abrasion" and "removal of weathered material by transporting agents," which I would have thought was one form of abrasion. What's a "transporting agent"? What's a "mechanical process"? I am not really clear on the difference between "mechanical processes," especially in regard to weather, and "chemical changes." And what chemicals are we talking about here—stuff in rain?

Since the first sentence is about "erosion" and the second about "weathering," I suppose these two things are connected in some important way—but how? They must be two forms of "destruction of a land surface," given that this is the subject of the first sentence. But then, I would have thought that producing "rock waste" was a way of building, not just destroying, land, since rock waste eventually turns into dirt (doesn't it?) and thus, I would have supposed, eventually into potentially fertile land. But this is a geology text, and geologists don't care about fertile land (or do they?). The word "land" here has a different range of possible contextual meanings than I am familiar with.

So in giving me the text in the absence of prior experience, mentorship, clear goals, actions to be taken, and caring (having something at stake) you have ensured that I cannot use the circuit of reflective action to learn and succeed. You have taken away what I, as a human being, am potentially good at. In turn, you have made me stupid. Good teaching does not do this, of course. It places words like those above inside mentorship, experiences, goals and actions, and caring.

One way the human mind connects to the world is through memory. We think of human memory as an accurate record of experience. But it is not. In the next chapter we turn to how treating memory as a fixed fact rather than an actively changing story can make us stupid and even dangerous.

3

The Limits of Human Memory

IN THE LAST CHAPTER I ARGUED THAT HUMANS ARE smart when they use the cycle of reflective action under the right conditions. They can be stupid when these conditions are not met. Let's turn to another way in which humans can be stupid.

To us moderns the word "memory" means one of two things. Either it means accurately storing past experiences in our minds or it means accurately storing information ("facts"). Such storage is something computers and books are good at. However, humans are, for the most part, bad at both of these things.

In the sense of memory as the passive and highly accurate storage of experiences or information, we humans (save for a few exceptions, like *idiots savants*) barely have a memory. It is true that humans can learn to memorize lots of disconnected information, such as strings of numbers, but, by and large, they do this by arduous tricks (tricks known since at least the Middle Ages, if not long before), like assigning each number a meaning (e.g., "76" = revolution) or a specific location in a well-known room.

With computers, we think of memory as information stored on the computer's hard drive. The operations that store information in a computer's memory are separate from the operations that retrieve it. When the information is retrieved by a user, this process does not change the information as it is stored. If the information was accurate when it was originally stored, then it is accurate thereafter, unless and until the user deletes it or saves new information over it. This may very well be your image of how human memory works. Nonetheless, this is not how human memory works.

For humans, memory and retrieval (recall) are closely connected. And retrieval—and the uses we make of what we retrieve—can and does change our memories. Even if a memory was accurate when we originally stored it in our heads, the material we store in our heads does not always stay accurate. In fact, it is often not all that accurate when we originally store it.

To see how human memory works, let's consider our memories of experiences we have had. We are capable of storing an almost limitless number of experiences in our heads. When we "store" any experience we have had (made up of persons, objects, places, and events, as well as emotions), we "edit" the experience first. We don't store everything, but only what was salient and relevant to us in the experience. At least, we store stuff that is salient and relevant more vividly, so to speak, than stuff that is just background to us.

What determines for humans what in an experience is salient and relevant? Well, lots of things. Some of these are: the context we are in; what has happened to us recently; how we feel at the time; what we value; what we have been taught to pay attention to; what fits well with our goals; what is connected to other experiences we have had; and our interests and desires. So, if you and I have had the same experience, have, for example, had dinner together, we will have different recollections of the event. We will each store a highly edited version that includes some things and leaves out others and that foregrounds some things and backgrounds others. So what we store in our heads is not "the truth," but a version of reality as we see it and sometimes as we wish it to be.

There is an additional problem with human memory. We cross-reference or cross-index the memories of our experiences. Elements that are similar in two or more experiences are associated with each other. This helps us place our memories into "families" of related memories. It also associates related things with each other, making us think of one when we first think of the other. For example, I have had lots of experiences birding (bird watching). I group together my experiences of birding in America versus birding in Australia, birding at sea versus birding in forests, birding with friends versus birding with real experts who were teaching me.

I also associate seeing bobolinks with when I have seen meadowlarks, since I have often, when I am birding in grassland, seen both of them on the same trip, though I have seen more meadowlarks than bobolinks. So when I see a meadowlark, I expect that I might eventually see a bobolink. When I think of one, I think of the other. Our memories of experiences are linked through a massive number of such associations. These associations constitute a massive but ever-changing database. These associations also key us in to what to expect when we are acting. Unfortunately, they also contaminate one memory with others.

If I am recalling one memory, all the others associated with it will activate. The memory I am recalling will make me consciously or unconsciously think of related memories. When this happens, I can sometimes think that what was true of one memory was true of another. I can think I saw a bobolink that time when I was birding in Wisconsin on my birthday and saw meadowlarks, when, in reality, I did not see a bobolink on that trip.

This contamination process is actually helpful in many cases. It helps us fill in information that is missing. For example, if I have often experienced large men with leather vests and tattoos riding motorcycles, these elements are all strongly associated in my mind. When I am in a bar next to such a guy, I may guess or infer that he came on a motorcycle. Since I also associate such men and motorcycles with biker gangs, I may infer that this man is a gang member and that maybe this bar is a gang hangout and maybe, too, that I ought to get myself out of there.

Just as we can make guesses about what elements might come next in what we are presently experiencing, we can fill in elements of our memories based on just such associations and come later to remember, even quite vividly, that the man at the bar had a motorcycle and was a gang member even when there was no "real" evidence at the time that such things were actually true.

Our memories, unlike those of computers, are often updated and changed when we recall or use them. Perhaps I did not actually think the man at the bar had a motorcycle, since, say, he had no "in your face" tattoos and his leather jacket had no patches with logos connected to gangs. But later, when I am again in the same bar, and this time it is filled with Hell's Angels, I recall having talked to the man. I may now add motorcycle and gang member to my memory of him, even add angrier tattoos and different patches based on what I have seen in this newer experience. I have updated my memory of the man and the time I was with him. In the future, when I recall this new updated (and possibly false) memory, I may really come to think I actually saw a row of bikes out front, as well as his gang tattoos and patches.

Of course, the problem is that while this is how human memory actually works, it is not how we humans think it works. And it is not how it feels to us that it works. We strongly believe that our memories are "real" and "true." They just feel that way. We would "swear to it" and sometimes do in court. We think of memory as a stable store, like things written down on paper and only in need of being read out loud for us to recover the truth of what happened. Nonetheless, recalling experiences is not like passive reading. It is active and continual interpretation, editing, and rewriting. The memory keeps changing based on when and where we recall it, what we experience later, and how we make use of the memory in storytelling or other sorts of accounts and activities.

Human memory for information works much the same way as memory for events. Related pieces of information are associated with each other. And each piece, when it comes to mind, makes us think (consciously or unconsciously) of the others with which it is associated. Thus, I may well associate all sorts of facts because they are all part of the Civil War era. I know the Civil War started in 1861 and ended in 1865. This information is stored in my head with lots of other associated information about the war.

I also know that in 1866 railroad companies run by robber barons went to the Supreme Court and tried to argue that corporations were "persons" and thus had all the rights that (real) people have. This 1866 case is called *Santa Clara County v. Southern Pacific Railroad.* Ironically, the railroad argued that it was the Fourteenth Amendment to the US Constitution (the amendment that freed the slaves and gave them equal protection under the law) that made them a "person" and gave them "equal rights."

The Southern Pacific Railroad argued that this amendment applied to both "natural" persons (humans) and "artificial" persons (corporations). Since Santa Clara County was taxing Southern Pacific differently than it did real human beings, it was not granting Southern Pacific equal protection under the law, as required by the Fourteenth Amendment. This was a ploy, one that worked later in history (but not in the 1866 case per se) and that stands in place today, to free corporations from regulations and restraints on their active pursuit of profit. This piece of information I store in my mind with related information about corporate greed and power. Ironically, of the 307 Fourteenth Amendment cases brought before the Supreme Court between 1866 and 1910, only 19 dealt with African Americans; 288 were suits brought by corporations seeking the same rights as natural persons, i.e., human beings.

It is now hard for me to recall the Civil War without thinking of early corporate greed and power seeking, a topic about which I happen to care, because I have linked or associated the dates 1861–1865 (Civil War) to 1866 (Supreme Court case) due to their proximity and sequence. I have made these associations, in part, because when I learned about the 1866 court case, I was struck by how close it was to the Civil War. I was struck, too, that the amendment that had freed the slaves was used then—and has been ever since, including today—to protect corporations.

I had always thought (incorrectly) of corporations manipulating the court system as a "modern" thing (possibly starting in earnest with Ronald Reagan in the 1980s) with no connection to something as "early" and "primitive" as the Civil War. Now, having associated the two, I see that the Civil War was more "recent" and "modern" than I used to think, and I see corporate greed as less recent and less modern than I used to. I see the empowerment of African Americans after the Civil War as something stolen by corporations. Indeed, thanks to Jim Crow and racism, the Fourteenth Amendment often worked better for corporations than it did for African Americans.

Obviously such links and associations can be good if they lead to seeing new and true connections in the world or history. But they can be bad if they just lead to conspiracy theories or seeing coincidences as more meaningful than they are. The trouble is that we humans (including me, of course) often have a hard time saying which is which.

So why does human memory work this way? Why is it something flexible, changeable, and full of associations? The reason is that human memory was not built (by evolution) to be accurate, fair, objective, or fixed. It was designed to help us make sense of the world, see connections, and find patterns, all in the service of accomplishing goals, surviving and flourishing in the world, and fulfilling our needs and desires. Being true can sometimes be a very important property of making memories and their recall effective for action and the accomplishment of goals. But truth is not the sole—and sometimes not even a—purpose of human memory. Human memory is, like the circuit of reflective action, "practical." It is not a disinterested search for truth, but a search for effective action in the world.

You might very well have guessed by now—and quite correctly—that human memory and recall work very poorly in court where witnesses have to say what "really happened" or who "really did it." Unfortunately, courts—at least modern ones—rely on human memory as if it were an accurate recorder of data and not what it really is, an active manipulator of data.

It is really too bad that we use the same word for both human memory and computer memory. Humans can use memory very effectively to interpret the world, make sense of things, fulfill needs, and get on with the work of surviving and, hopefully, flourishing. They cannot use it very effectively to store and recall neutral and objective information just because it is "true." Human memory might better be called ever-transformable "mental associations."

Formal schooling tends to demand that humans use their memories the way computers do, rather than the way humans do. This, too, can make people seem stupid. School treats memory as a "bank" that can be filled with accurate information. In turn, this information can be withdrawn from the bank without changing it in any important way to be written down on a test. Memory, in this sense, is meant to be uninfluenced by human feelings, needs, and purposes (beyond, say, being a good student and getting a good grade).

Now there happens to be one condition under which humans are good at retaining accurate details. If a detail, say the date of the 1866 *Santa Clara* case, is embedded in a larger story that matters to a person and is crucial to that story's having the meaning it does, then the detail can be retained unchanged for a long time. For me, the 1866 *Santa Clara* case is so tied to the Civil War and my realization that concerns of today (e.g., corporate greed and the Fourteenth Amendment) were equally relevant back then that the 1861–1865, 1866 sequence is important and meaningful to me. My story of the Fourteenth Amendment and my account of America, racism, and corporate greed both rely, for me, on the Civil War's having ended just the year before the court case (a court case that, by the way, happens to involve the California County in which I was born). So these dates (1861–1865, 1866) are not likely to drop out of memory or get changed.

That said, I must admit that I have often gotten the 1861 start date of the Civil War wrong and said that it began in 1860. The reason for this is that I have long been struck by the fact that the Civil War happened only

100 years before the 1960s, a decade that I lived through and thought of as a time of "revolution" in the name of equality and human worth against corporate greed. So, saying the Civil War started in 1860 brings out the nice 100 symmetry between 1860 and 1960.

My point then: if you want accuracy in dates and details from humans, they have to have meaning inside a story the human really cares about. And even then, dates and details can have different meanings in different stories and they can interfere with each other. When I think strongly about the *Santa Clara* case, I tend to get 1861 right as the start of the Civil War. When I think of the 1860s/1960s 100-year symmetry, I "remember" that the Civil War started in 1860. In school and on tests it matters, but I am not sure it does otherwise.

At any rate, human memory is what it is. It is poor on meaningless or disconnected details, strong on meaningful stories and accounts. It is poor for things we do not care about and strong for what we do care about.

Humans prefer stories to hard facts. We find comfort in stories that evade facts in favor of fantasies. Such comfort often leads to the sorts of stupidity that makes life worse for all us. To such mental comfort ("comfort food") stories we turn in the next chapter.

4

Mental Comfort Stories

HUMANS ARE SMART WHEN ENGAGING IN THE CY-
cle of reflective action for practical ends. They are smart when using human
memory for what it is good at: making associations and filling in information. Humans are smart at yet a third thing: telling stories.

There are a number of reasons why humans are good at telling stories.
Before I get to these, though, let me make a distinction between "narrative"
and "story." A narrative is any use of language in which specific events are
said to have happened one after the other. Thus: "The king died. Then the
queen died" is a narrative. The human mind has an interesting and important tendency to understand narrative (that is, events happening one after
the other in time) as meaning that one event caused the other. Though this
little narrative does not literally say so, we humans tend to interpret "The
king died. Then the queen died" to mean that the queen died *because* the
king died. Our minds have the urge to turn the little narrative into a story.

A story is a narrative with a "plot." To interpret sequence in time as
causation (X happened, then Y happened, or X caused Y to happen) is already to begin to give a plot to a narrative (a sequence of events). A plot is
a framework imposed on a narrative that gives the narrative a beginning, a
middle, and an end. A story gives meaning or significance to events. It tells
us not just what happened, but why it happened or what these happenings
meant to or for us or others.

If "The king died and then the queen died" is interpreted as just a temporal sequence and not as one event having caused the other, there is no plot to make a story. However, by saying, "The king died and then the queen died of grief" (beginning: the king died; middle: the queen grieved; end: the queen died from grief), the writer has provided a plot line for a story. A plot is a causal sequence of events with an overt or implied significance in terms of why things happened as they did or what they portended. Even if some event turns out to be a coincidence in a story, that event usually turns out to have a larger meaning or "purpose" in terms of what it set in motion in the story.

Stories help humans banish arbitrariness and meaninglessness. So, why are humans so into "storying" the world? When I discussed the circuit of reflective action in chapter 2, I mentioned that it is like a game played with or against the world. The world is a demanding taskmaster. It does not care about us and often gives us answers we humans do not like. Suffering and death, as well as coincidences, inexplicable events, and unintended consequences, are some of the answers from the world. The human mind cannot accept this. It needs to find pattern, purpose, and hope in the world. It will supply these in story form if they are not forthcoming directly from the world.

What is it about us human beings that makes us want to find meaning and purpose in the world even when they seem not to be there? There is an enormous amount of evidence that human beings become sick (in mind or body or both) when they feel no sense of control, when they feel that anything they do will be ineffective, and that nothing really matters. Stories can be a kind of self-medication.

Stories of an afterlife are a good example. This world (especially for the vast majority of humans who are now, and have been through history, poor) seems imperfect, harsh, and unfair. Thus, we tell a story that there is another world, a perfect one, where we will live later. This world will make up for the imperfections of the current world and give these imperfections meaning and purpose. Religion, in its origins, is composed of stories and rituals that connect humans and the imperfect world they live in to another, better world or one that helps explain why our world is as it is.

There is an interesting fact about human beings' need for a sense of meaning and control in their lives. Humans often find this meaning and sense of control not in individual terms, but as members or representatives of some group. A human can find meaning and purpose by believing that he or she is acting out the history and contributing to the future of a family, social group, culture, race, or nation. His or her sufferings can be seen as contributions to the group. The group, rather than the individual, can be seen as the truly effective and in-control actor on the world's stage. This, it turns out, can actually become a quite dangerous process, but more on that later.

Humans are very poor indeed at telling the difference between correlation (two things just happen to be associated with each other in some way) and causation (one thing causes another to happen). They regularly take simple correlations to be causation and impose structure on events—beginnings, middles, and ends—that do not always come that way in the real world. For example, when marriages go bad, they rarely go bad all at once. Many things happen over time. If we want a neat end point—and we often do—we story our marriage to have one. When did the 2008 recession actually start? We can make up a starting date or even just say 2008, but the world gave many a warning signal before that.

We Americans fight all the time about what the "true" story of the United States is. Is it a march toward democracy and freedom that started in Athens long ago? Is it the formation of an empire determined to dominate the world and its resources that began with our defeat of the British Empire? Or is America different things at different times, none of which add up to a coherent story? Some right-wing commentators say we have already lost the "real" United States and need to recover it. So, for them, something has ended and needs to begin again. Others say we have yet to find the "real" United States in terms of what its best hopes and dreams appear to have been at its "founding."

The stories we tell to comfort ourselves are often not stories in any very formal sense. We humans can mix and match forms of argumentation with story elements to do the work of storying the world. For example, consider a young woman from Philadelphia defending her belief in fate:

I believe in that. Whatever's gonna happen is gonna happen. I believe that y'know it's fate. It really is. Because my husband has a brother that was killed in an automobile accident, And at the same time there was another fellow, in there, that walked away with not even a scratch on him. And I really feel—I don't feel y'can push fate, and I think a lot of people do. But I feel that you were put here for so many years or whatever the case is, and that's how it is meant to be.

Because like when we got married, we were supposed t'get married like about five months later. My husband got a notice t'go into the service and we moved it up. And my father died the week after we got married. While we were on our honeymoon. And I just felt that move was meant to be, because if not, he wouldn't have been there.

So y'know it just seems that that's how things work out.

This talk mixes generalizations, forms of argumentation, and narrative events. But it is doing the work of storying for comfort, meaning, and a sense of purpose in the world. It is a perfect example of finding patterns and relationships in the world. These patterns and relationships give events significance so that things seem to have happened "for a reason" and "for good." The teller does not want to feel like the victim of the whims of pure chance. This story, though small, is akin to the larger stories of religions and myths that have existed since the dawn of humanity.

There are, of course, many types of stories we humans tell, ranging from dinner-time conversation to books and movies. The human mind's capacity to make up and believe stories that supply our need for control, meaning, and purpose, whether they be claims that "everything happens for a purpose," the myths of a long-ago culture, or today's religions of the book, gives rise to what I will call "mental comfort stories."

The stories we tell for comfort arise because we do not understand the real reasons that things happen as they do. Ancient people had no idea why lightning happened, even less an idea about why someone just died from a bolt out of the blue. They had few ideas about the causes of diseases or how humans arose or why they were split into often warring groups. Stories about gods throwing thunderbolts, dreamtime animals creating landscapes, and gods granting humans immortality were not based on evidence. People had none and in most cases could not get any.

This capacity to tell comforting stories in the absence of evidence or knowledge of reality is deeply rooted in how the human mind works. Our minds/brains are made up of many modules, each of which (at lightning speed) analyzes stimuli from the world, attributes meaning, forms motives and responses, and creates feelings and attitudes. For the most part, the internal workings of these modules and how they reach their results are not open to our conscious minds. We just feel and know their results, the outcomes of their otherwise hidden inputs and decision-making processes.

There is a module in the mind that has been called "the interpreter." The interpreter makes meaning of the results that the unconscious modules have reached based on their hidden analyses and computations. Since we do not consciously know how these results were arrived at, the interpreter makes up a good story or rationale for the results, one that makes sense to us and makes us feel in full control of our decisions and actions.

You are feeling blue, unbeknownst to your conscious mind, because you have just been momentarily, but unconsciously, reminded of a long ago lost opportunity. Your interpreter needs to find a reason for why you are feeling blue and it does not know that some other module gave rise to this feeling because of a brief reminder of things lost. It just knows that feeling blue was the result. Your interpreter spins a story in the absence of any real evidence of why you are feeling blue. Perhaps, you tell yourself, while watching your spouse read the newspaper at breakfast, it is because of how mundane your marriage has become. You may or may not need to work on your marriage, but if you choose to do so now, it may be because of the story your interpreter has just spun, based on no relevant evidence other than the fact that you're feeling blue and see your wife reading a newspaper at the breakfast table. This is an example of correlation being mistaken for causation.

The interpreter works the same way in the absence of evidence for why things have happened in the world whose "true causes" we do not know. We fail to get a promotion at work because, the boss tells us, the economy is bad, there are fewer open positions, and Joe has done a better job in the areas the business now needs most to pay attention to. We are not privy to all our boss's motives and the data on which he based his decision, nor are we privy to all the complex politics and institutional realities of our workplace. Furthermore, our ego is hurt. So we spin a story that makes us the "wronged one," a victim of our boss's jealousy and Joe's selfish cunning. We appeal to reasons and data that are partial and self-selected in order to make our story compelling to us and to others. We ignore data that do not fit with our story and all the data to which we are simply not privy.

My point here is not that we humans cannot reason when we have evidence. We can. My point is that we can also reason when we do not have evidence. In the absence of evidence, especially when we feel a loss of control, meaning, or status, we can spin elaborate stories or arguments that comfort us, right our sense of failure and loss, and render the world lucid, even if unjust.

The interpreter is the conscious part of the mind. When it has evidence, it is the part of our mind with which we reason "rationally" and "logically." But when we don't have evidence, or enough of it, it is also the part of our mind that can spin good stories for mental comfort if we need it. And it is often hard for humans to tell the two apart.

Another way to put this point is to say that humans are experts at post hoc reasoning. After something happens, no matter how complex all the interacting causes were that gave rise to it, we can always find a good story for why it happened just as it did. The problem is that if something different had happened, we would have constructed an equally good story about what happened and why it was "inevitable."

If someone succeeds, we can always, after the fact, find traits that explain why that person succeeded. He or she was "smart," "hard working," or "came from a rich family." But if the person had failed—or if similar people fail—we can just as easily find traits that made them fail. He or she was "too smart for his or her own good," "worked only to impress the boss," "had it too easy earlier in life." No matter what happens, thanks to the brilliance of our interpreters, we humans will have a satisfying and convincing story, analysis, or argument. All forms of telling stories for mental comfort are unempirical, not because we do not appeal to evidence, but because, even if we do, we self-select it and fail to acknowledge that we are missing a good deal of it.

Humans engage in storying not to tell the truth or even to attempt to discover it, but for comfort. This human skill is often very good for us. But it can be—and has historically been—dangerous. When people, especially groups of people (tribes, ethnic groups, cultures, and nations) tell comfort stories, these stories lose a lot of their force for comfort if others do not believe them or if they have opposing stories. Humans have a tendency to enforce their stories if they can and to demonize people who hold opposing stories. In part, this is because telling stories for mental comfort is often a form of self-deception, and self-deception does not work well when others are around to disabuse us of our deceptions.

Historically, people in power (shamans, priests, nobles, elites, dictators, and politicians) have used stories for more than mental comfort. They have used them for control, telling and enforcing stories that validate their power and sustain it. Often, they have used the enforcement apparatus of the group or state to keep people from challenging their stories about why the world is as it is and why they and not others should have power and influence in it ("naturally"). Stories can dupe people. But people can also know that stories are untrue and still keep silent out of fear.

People are rarely offended when you say that other people's comfort stories are not based on evidence or truth, but on a desire for comfort or power. But they become offended when you say this about *their* stories, especially if these stories are part of their "religion" or "culture" or "national heritage." For example, what I have said above may offend many religious people.

I readily acknowledge that comfort stories, including religious ones, can have power for good and can have a kind of truth of their own. If they empower us to survive, flourish, and do good for our neighbors and our environment, they make their own truth by making the world a better place. And such stories can most certainly yield kinds of spiritual truths about what it means to be human in the face of suffering and death. And, yet, comfort stories, most certainly religious ones, have led to war, oppression, and death as people kill or harm others in the name of their god or gods or the principles incorporated into their stories.

I do not myself know a great deal in depth about any religion save Christianity, though this does not mean I know nothing about other religions. But let me only comment here on Christianity. Saying that the different Christian sects tell themselves stories for mental comfort and, at times, for power and influence, will be offensive to many Christians. It would have been offensive to me earlier in life when I was a devout Catholic.

In my view and in that of some biblical scholars, if one reads the New Testament, it is crystal clear that Jesus Christ stood for radical poverty and a complete lack of regard for status. He told the rich young man not just to do good, but to give away all his money. Jesus had no home of his own and entered the homes of the wealthy and poor alike. In his account of the Last Judgment he made it clear that people would be judged on how they had treated the poor and prisoners.

A Christian would live a life of poverty, disavow all status, and serve others, especially others who are poor, of low status, sick, and in need. And

I don't mean just give them money; I mean actually *be* with them. In that sense of Christian, the sense in which it has to do with Jesus Christ as depicted in the canonical Gospels and as Christ has been depicted in research on the historical Jesus, there are actually next to no Christians. The stories in the four Gospels bear little or no comfort for people who want wealth, power, status, or even a "middle-class lifestyle." As John Dominic Crossan has said, it is just too hard to be a Christian. So perhaps, in reality, there is next to no one actually to offend here.

The comfort stories that work best, including myths and religious doctrines, are ones that cannot easily be disputed based on clear evidence. Good religious stories stay clear of making easily falsifiable claims. Their events occur in a time and place long ago, populated by larger than life people and gods. Prior to the rise of modern science, many stories about nature were not falsifiable. Who was to say that Zeus was not throwing thunderbolts to cause lightning or that "bad air" or the "evil eye" were not the causes of sickness and death?

But, of course, now science has given us access to previously inaccessible causes and mechanisms in the world. Now we do know what causes lightning, drought, and lots of diseases. When someone claims that, based on the Bible, the universe was formed in seven days or the earth is less than 10,000 years old and takes these claims literally, we now know perfectly well that they are false. If we want to pay attention to science—and some people don't—certain stories will become less comforting. However, there is always the option of reading the stories metaphorically and retaining both science and religion. In any case, comfort stories are more comforting, sometimes, the less we know. That is why they often comport badly with education, provided that that education is not itself full of comfort stories (e.g., political, ideological, or religious ones).

Stories can be richly metaphorical and deeply meaningful. At their best, they do not compete with science; they extend, enhance, and supplement it. Science can give us rich meanings by giving us access to the wonders and even the challenges of the world. But good stories and good science are tightly tied to human experiences in and with the world. It turns out that the human mind works well when dealing with meaningful experience, but works poorly indeed when forced to deal with meaningless abstractions. In the next two chapters we turn to an ideal way to make people stupid in and out of school: ensure they don't care.

5

Lack of Context

many different cultures problems like this one: Here are pictures of a hammer, a saw, a log, and a hatchet. Pick the one that does not belong. The "correct" answer is the log since it is the one that is not a tool. However, some people, especially people with little formal schooling, saw the hammer as the odd item in the group. They looked for a story that connected things and viewed the hatchet and saw, but not the hammer, as good for working with the log.

It has been argued that people who picked the log as the odd man out in a problem like this were engaged in abstract thinking. They were thinking in terms of classificatory schemes like "tools." People who picked the hammer were said to be engaged in contextually bound thinking. They were unable to free their thoughts from specific contexts they had experienced.

It is interesting that the results of tests like this are very sensitive to whether someone has had formal schooling of the Western sort or not. Researchers had earlier thought that the different sorts of responses (log, hammer) correlated with literacy or the lack thereof. However, it was later found that they correlate more with formal schooling (which gives one a specific type of and orientation to literacy) or the lack thereof. It has also been claimed that people who respond in terms of tools are "modern" and people who respond in terms of the functions the items can serve in contexts of use are "not modern."

The contrast between abstract thinking and context-bound thinking is appealing. It seems that the former is a sign of intelligence and of education. The latter seems to be the fate of those who are "trapped" in a world from which they cannot sufficiently generalize.

However, there is something wrong about these claims. In one way, there is no such thing as abstract thinking in the sense of thinking that is context free. We humans, no matter how smart we think we are, are all bound to context. But we are bound in different ways.

In fact, humans are good at thinking in context. They are good at relating their thinking and problem solving to specific situations. They are not good at thinking outside of specific contexts in terms of pure generalities and bare abstractions (despite how readily educated people can name tools). To see an example of this, consider the problems below:

CASE 1

There are four cards in front of you. Assume that each card has a letter on one side, and a number on the other. Rule: *If a card has a D on one side, then it has a 7 on the other.*

TABLE 5.1

D	F	7	5
Card #1	Card #2	Card #3	Card #4

In order to check whether the rule is true of these cards, which cards do you need to turn over? Don't turn over any cards that are not absolutely necessary.

CASE 2

Teenagers who don't have their own cars usually end up borrowing their parents' cars. In return for the privilege of borrowing the car, the Goldsteins have given their kids the rule, "If you borrow my car, then you have to fill up the tank with gas." Of course, teenagers are sometimes careless and irresponsible. You are interested in seeing whether any of the Goldstein teenagers broke this rule. These cards represent four of the Goldstein teenagers. Each card represents one teenager. One side of the card tells whether or not a teenager has borrowed the parents' car on a particular day, and the other side tells whether or not that teenager filled up the tank with gas on that day. Which of the following cards would you definitely need to turn over to see if any of these teenagers are breaking their parents' rule? Don't turn over any cards that are not absolutely necessary.

TABLE 5.2

borrowed car	did not borrow car	filled up tank with gas	did not fill up tank with gas
Card #1	Card #2	Card #3	Card #4

These two problems are both "logical" problems. They are asking people to understand what in classical logic is called a "material conditional," that is, statements of the form "*If* this, *then* that." The answer to both problems is: turn over cards 1 and 4. From the point of view of logic, these two problems are the same problem in different words. Nonetheless, most people find version 2 much easier than version 1. Many more people get version 2 correct than get version 1 correct.

Why is version 2 easier for humans? There are a number of possible reasons. Version 2 is less abstract and more familiar as a situation. There is also another interesting possibility. Lots of experiments have shown that tasks like those above are particularly easy for people if the rule to be tested is a rule one needs to follow in order to obtain a benefit and the test subjects are asked to police the rule. Evolutionary psychologists have argued that the human mind has evolved to be particularly good at solving problems involving social interactions where things are "at stake." In particular, they argue, humans are especially sensitive to and good at catching cheaters. They are good at looking for and discovering when people are cheating, taking unfair advantage, or getting benefits they do not deserve.

But the basic point I want to make here is that there are two ways to approach tasks like the two above. One way is to approach them in terms of a formal and abstract rule. In this case, this rule would be a rule of classical logic that defines the material conditional ("*if* X *then* Y") as: "*if X then Y" is false if and only if both X is true and Y is false.* The details of the two problems, what they are about (their "content"), does not matter in classical logic. All that matters is the formal relationships between categories ("sets"). It does not matter what "X" and "Y" actually name. One just follows a general rule. In this case, there should be no advantage for problems that are concrete or about catching "cheaters." This would be an example of abstract decontextualized thinking.

The other way to approach these sorts of tasks is to consider our own experiences and contexts with which we are familiar. In this case, we do expect content details to matter and we do expect an advantage for concrete problems over abstract ones. This would be an example of context-bound thinking. However, for problems like the two above, even highly educated people often find version 2 considerably easier than version 1.

So to return to the point from which I began: humans are good at thinking in terms of specific contexts and their details. They are less good—often bad—at thinking in more purely abstract and formal terms not tied to experience and contexts and not tied to "interests" (like catching "cheaters"). In answering questions like those in the two tasks above, most humans do not follow a general rule, but think in terms of experience, contexts, and interests.

Of course, we can learn to think in terms of general rules (in school, for instance), but we do need to learn this. In everyday life, it is not always useful to think in abstract and general terms. Furthermore, people do not usually learn to think in terms of general principles and rules by being taught the rules directly. Rather, they learn best to think this way by first learning lots of concrete cases or examples. Then, having experienced and learned about a great many different concrete cases in which the rule or generality applies, albeit in somewhat different ways, they are prepared to generalize and to think in a more abstract way, when need be. Abstraction and generality usually grow bottom-up from experience.

There is, however, one big and common flaw in human contextual thinking. Because the human mind is so good at associating things and finding patterns, when we humans think and learn in terms of specific situations or contexts, we often generalize too quickly, without enough examples. We experience several different contexts where swans are white or some group of people has been rude to us and we too readily assume they all are. But there are black swans in Australia and probably most people in the group we find rude are perfectly polite. We humans jump to judgments based on too little evidence. We need to realize that before we can make generalizations that have any hope of being correct, we need to have tested out a large number of different contexts relevant to the generalization. In many cases, we also need to have purposefully sought out potentially falsifying examples.

There is, on the other hand, also one big and common flaw in thinking that uses general rules or principles. Even when we have drawn correct generalizations from lots of experience or have created abstract systems like logic and mathematics, humans commonly do not realize that if they are going to apply these generalizations to the world as matters of policy or problem solving, the generalizations most often have to be modified to allow for somewhat different effects in different contexts. That is, people using generalizations and abstract reasoning to effect change in the world have to be sensitive to how these generalizations and abstractions are affected by specific contexts where they are applied. For instance, it may well be a true generalization that people are motivated by money, but how this motivation works, or even if it does work at all in specific contexts, depends on many other factors.

Rushing to generalizations based on too few contexts or too little experience can be dangerous. So can applying generalizations to the world with little regard for the influences and effects of different contexts of application. So, contextual thinking and general thinking both have their dangers. They often work best when they interact with each other.

But, as I mentioned above, the terms "abstract thinking" and "decontextualized thinking" are problematic. The logical rule we saw above, the rule for the material conditional *("if X then Y" is false if and only if both X is true and Y is false)* certainly looks context free. It looks as if it applies anywhere and everywhere. But it is not, in fact, context free. It applies only in contexts where we are using the rules of classical logic, and we do not use these rules in all contexts.

In everyday language, linguists have long known that the words "if" and "then" do not mean what they are defined to mean in classical logic. Even in the two card tasks we saw above, people have trouble with version 1 because they must use a logical rule (the logical meaning for "if-then") that they usually do not use in everyday language. In version 2 they have a familiar context and their practice at catching cheaters to fall back on.

In reality, if and when we use the logical rule for material conditionals to solve both of the card problems above, we are thinking contextually, but the context is classical logic, which some of us have learned in school and some of us have not. Humans always think in terms of contexts because that's the way language works.

What does "language" mean here, when I say that language works via associations with specific contexts of use? All humans have one or more "natural" (human) languages that they speak, barring severe problems. But humans have also invented a number of special languages or language-like symbolic systems for special purposes. They have invented the language of classical logic, the languages of many branches of mathematics and science, and the language of law, for instance. No one learns these languages as their first language at home, even though some of them use words from our everyday languages like English, sometimes with their everyday meanings and sometimes not. So I want to use the term "language" broadly for things like everyday English, the language of algebra, and the technical languages of lawyers and engineers (which mix everyday words and phrases with technical ones).

The words or symbols in any language get their meanings from context, not in a completely context-free way. The "if-then" statement in classical logic gets its meaning from the context of the historical formulation of classical logic (there are other types of logic). There are rules about how to use logical symbols and there are contexts or practices (e.g., solving certain sorts of problems) in which such rules and symbols are used. The same is true of the technical parts of the language of law. The meaning of "if-then" in everyday language gets its meanings (actually a variety of them) from the contexts and practices in which these words are used in everyday life, which are different from the contexts and practices in which classical logic or formal legal procedures are used.

To say that someone is "illogical" because they did not know they were meant to apply the rules of classical logic in a given case or have had no experience doing so is silly. Beyond classical logic, mathematicians have developed a number of other logical systems that seem much odder to most people (because they are even further removed, in some cases, from the meanings of everyday language), for example, fuzzy logic, intuitionist logic, linear logic, and modal logic. It is pretty clear to anyone that if someone had difficulty with linear logic, having had no experience using it and no real idea of it as a system (a "language"), we would certainly not think that person "illogical" or "a poor thinker." And it is clear that such systems apply only to certain situations or contexts of application for which logicians and mathematicians have designed them.

In reality, all thinking is context bound because all language and symbol systems are. And language and symbol systems are what give us access to people's thinking. Why am I belaboring this point? Because a common way to make people look stupid is to present them with something that is claimed to be general, clear, and explicit in and of itself, without any appeal to context or past experience, and then tell them they are stupid if they do not understand it.

Some will say: If you can just read, surely you can understand, for example, "Hornworm growth displays a significant amount of variation." If you do not know what a hornworm is or what "significant variation" means, you can just "look it up" or read about it. You do not need to have had any special experiences here or know about any specific contexts. All you need is to be able to read. Unfortunately, all of this is not true.

To understand what "Hornworm growth displays a significant amount of variation" really means, you need to know about the contexts in which biologists use statistical measures of "significance," why they use them, how they use them, and what sorts of meanings they give to claims of significance in the different contexts in which biology operates. If you attempt to learn this just by reading but have no experience of what biologists do in contexts of problem solving, you will just run into more and more words and phrases tied to the practices of biologists and statisticians, practices you have not experienced and don't really understand.

As I said earlier, any generality you gain about what things like "statistical variation" mean (how it applies across lots of different contexts though, of course, not all) must, in general, grow "ground up" from lots of experiences of the application of this concept to specific situations and problems. Trying to get people to learn the meanings of such terms without experiences of situations in which they are applied and problems that they are used to solve is one good way to make people look stupid. When people fail to think "abstractly" or to see generalizations, the reason is almost always that they have not been introduced to and have not experienced the contexts in which a particular language and form of thought tied to it are used.

We have concluded that humans are good at thinking in terms of specific contexts, though they often try to generalize too early (the source of stereotypes). They are poor at thinking in more general terms unless they have been introduced to the contexts from which the relevant generalizations can be drawn, often over time with lots of experience. Even when they have become adept at drawing useful generalizations, they are not always adept at applying these back to the world with due regard for the ways in which the details of specific contexts can affect how they work and what their outcomes will be.

Unfortunately, it is not uncommon in school to hand young people textbooks in science, social studies, or art when they have had little or no (certainly not enough) experience that would give the words in the texts meaning in terms of the contexts to which they apply (and often a bit differently in different contexts). What they need is ample experience to allow them to draw generalizations across those contexts, but generalizations still tied to these contexts as insights about how to solve problems efficiently in different contexts and for different purposes.

Such learning experiences will typically also require that students work across traditional subject area boundaries. One illustrative example is the

Artist as Chemist curriculum, which uses a problem-based learning approach to teach introductory high school chemistry concepts as well as give students insight into the chemistry behind common artistic creation. The curriculum requires students to create a work of art and related museum display that documents the techniques utilized in creating the artwork, including the underlying chemistry. Students learn about the physical properties of the materials used, such as metals, clay, paints, glass, and dyes; how these materials interact; and related processes such as the effects of weathering on outdoor artworks. They learn from each other's work about how different materials vary in their properties when combined with others, and how the aesthetics of particular pieces of art are affected by such combinations.

We have now seen that the human mind is filled up with experiences through which it thinks and plans and acts. While experience is essential, it can also be dangerous. In the next chapter we look at how associations that we pick up in experience can run wild in the human mind.

6

Lack of Experience

HUMANS THINK THROUGH THEIR EXPERIENCES.
They learn to generalize—sometimes too fast—by finding patterns across experiences. People give meaning to words and to the world based on their past experiences and in terms of the specific contexts they are in. We often think words have meanings in terms of definitions, definitions that are themselves words. But they do not. Definitions are just helpful guides to the possible range of meanings words can take on in different contexts of use, something that can and does change across time.

A word has meaning based on the contexts in which we have used it in the past and in which we have heard or seen it used. Furthermore, the meaning of the word is always open to change as it is used in new or different contexts. Consider the word "love." We can use this word in many different ways, sensitive to different contexts of use. We can say all of the following: I love my wife, I love my cat, I love all cats, I love pizza, I love my new rocking chair, I love even my enemies, and I love God. Obviously, we love these things in quite different ways. And we cannot say, for instance, that "love" means "like something a lot," since I do not just like my wife a lot (nor my cat, for that matter) and I may not actually like my enemies at all. And we can perfectly well assign a meaning to the sentence "I love you but I don't like you."

The meaning of "love" for anyone is the word's associations with a variety of past experiences of loving something and of using, hearing, or reading the word in different specific contexts. We can certainly say things like "I did not really know what love was until I met my wife" or even "I didn't really know what love meant until I met my wife." For humans what a thing "is" and what it "means" are often the same thing or closely related. We connect the concept of love and the meaning of the word with experiences we have had or can imagine.

If we hear a word used in a new way in a new context, we can use our past experiences with the word to make a guess about what it means in the new context. If it is used enough in such contexts, it grows a new meaning along with its older ones. For example, imagine that I say, "These flowers love the sun" or "The waves lovingly caressed the beach." We can readily figure out what these sentences mean based on analogies with our past experiences. We can say that "love" has a metaphorical meaning in these sentences. However, with words, it is often hard to know where literal meaning stops and metaphor begins. Are "I love pizza" or "I even love my enemies" metaphors? What about "I love my cat"?

Because word meaning is based on the contexts in which a word has been used and our experiences of those contexts, two people can have different views about what a word actually means in a given context. This is because they have had different experiences with which to give meaning to the word as well as, sometimes, different value systems. For example, I do not accept that the United States is a "democracy," since we do not directly elect the president and because, in my experience of American politics, money buys votes and, very often, elected representatives represent only corporations and the rich and not all the people who elected them. Others will disagree with me. There are some in the United States who refer to universal health care as "socialism." I would not, since this is not how I have experienced the word and not how I have experienced countries with universal health care. Again, others can disagree.

Well then, how can we communicate? Sometimes we can't. We just fight and disallow other people's language. Sometimes, though, we can debate how the word ought to apply based on arguments about how people ought to view their experiences, say, of Scandinavian countries with universal health care or of electoral politics in the United States. We can also debate how the word ought to apply based on arguments about what new experiences people should seek out as a route to learning new insights. These are ways in which people try to make their experiences and their judgments about them compatible enough to agree on what words (should) mean and, therefore, what the situations to which they apply are "actually" like.

When you assign a meaning to a given word in a specific context, such as "love" in "I love my cat" or "I love even my enemies," what you do is imagine, based on your past experiences, situations in your head that you associate with such sentences. You imagine, for instance, the ways one would interact with and treat a cat one loves and, perhaps, how this compares to loving a person. On the other hand, for a sentence like "I love pizza," you imagine situations where one readily chooses one thing over another as a sign of strong desire. And, I must admit that I myself cannot really assign any real meaning to "I love even my enemies," since I have little experience to go on here and have experienced this sort of claim only in religious contexts that I guess I never really internalized, for all sorts of reasons. Perhaps you can do better.

The fact that we assign meanings to words, concepts, and things in the world based on our experiences immediately raises, as we have seen, the problem that different people have had, or certainly could have had, quite different experiences. If two people's experiences are too disparate from each other, as can certainly happen across cultures and social groups, there is a real danger that they will assign quite different meanings to words in specific contexts and thus fail to communicate. Words like "love," "friend," "honor," "democracy," and many others tend to vary in their meanings and how they apply in different contexts across different groups of people with different experiences in life and different value systems.

It is best to think of words (or concepts) as having complex webs of meaning based on their associations with other words and phrases. Take the word "ice cream." What do you associate this word with? I associate it with "cold," "creamy," "soft," "cones," "sugar," "comfort," "fat," "childhood," "melting," "hot days," "frozen yogurt," "custard" (because this is a type of ice cream in Wisconsin), "flavors," "making a mess," "dessert" (and, sadly, "desert," since I cannot spell well and constantly confuse the spellings of the two words), and many more things. Some of these associations are stronger than others. Furthermore, some of these associations operate in a much stronger way in some contexts than they do in others. If I am eating pizza and think about ice cream as another "comfort food," I also strongly think of "getting fat."

Obviously different people have different webs of associations for different words, based on their experiences and how these are shaped by their cultures and social group memberships. The associations you make with "ice cream" or "pizza" are probably not all that important (though they could become so when you are trying to relate to people who associate "ice cream" and "pizza" with weak-willed and un-health-conscious slobs). But things can matter deeply when people have quite different webs of associations for words like "government," "embryo," "democracy," "social services," "social justice," "wealth," "women," "men," "gender," "justice," "religion," "evolution," "science," and on and on.

Many associations are value laden and emotionally laden. Since I partially associate "ice cream" with comfort and childhood, it carries a certain emotional charge for me (and for many others). When I associate "government" with social order and a social contract among fellow citizens, I give it a positive charge since I value social order and co-citizenship in a common cause. When I associate government with red tape and corruption, I give it a negative charge. And, of course, different contexts trigger one or the other (or some other) set of associations. Which chain of associations is being triggered when someone votes can make a difference in how he or she votes and, indeed, more generally in the outcomes of elections.

The association webs in people's heads have some interesting problems. Associations get stronger the more they are triggered or used. However, it is hard to delete an association even when one becomes aware that it is false or meaningless. For example, many people, thanks to movies and books, associate Native Americans in the nineteenth century with living in tepees in the wilderness. Yet many lived in houses and towns (from which they were forcibly evacuated in some cases). Even though I have learned this, it is still hard for me not to think of tepees and wilderness (and "wildness") when I think of "cowboys" and "Indians" in the "old days."

Another problem is that the associations in our webs of associations are sometimes based on reality and evidence and sometimes on fantasy or on what we have heard or been told. Yet we have a hard time telling one from the other. We do not, it seems, typically recall why we associate one thing with another, though if we think consciously and reflectively about particular associations (something we do not often do), we can sometimes make pretty good judgments about how much real evidence we have for them or where they might have come from. An association triggered by media or talk often seems to be just as strong as one triggered by evidence and actual personal experience, unless we really do think hard about the matter.

In the debates about public health care in the United States, some elderly people said, "I want the government to stay out of my Medicare," despite the fact that Medicare is a government health care program. These people so strongly associated "government," "bad," "public health care," and "socialism," thanks to politics and the media, and yet so valued their Medicare, that these associations overrode their knowledge (or their willingness to gain that knowledge) that Medicare is something the government "gives" them.

Of course, if you want people to get carried away by their associations this way, you want to see to it that they do not actually think about and reflect on the matter or get new information that would trigger them to make different associations or think about matters in a different way. Reflection can sometimes break the hold of old associations and even cause people to form new associations or try to delete old ones (which we have seen is not always easy).

For example, many people associate religion with peace and video games with violence, but there is a great deal of violence (and sex) in the Old Testament, and both the Bible and the Koran have led to a great deal of violence across the ages (as well as to good deeds, of course). At the same time, there are thousands of non-violent video games, and video games have led to much less violence (and also to fewer good deeds) than has either the Bible or the Koran.

Reflection can make us think again, perhaps gain more experience (or read more, one way to gain experience), and then make some new associations or weaken some old ones. (I am not advocating, by the way, that people should associate religion with violence alone, but rather that they should realize and reflect on the fact that religion has been associated with both great good and great evil in the world throughout history and today.)

The human mind evolved at a time, early in the history of humanity, when there were no books, no media, and no PR firms. There were, however, already lies and liars. Even chimpanzees can lie. So humans have always been subject to the possible manipulation of what they associate with what and how strongly they do so. It is certainly possible that some early shaman harped on the idea that people should associate drought with an unhappy god and pay the shaman for a rain dance. And, given that they had no good explanation for drought, this association probably got formed since it was better than having no understanding or hope at all. By the way, the shaman may have been lying or he may have believed his "lie" (i.e., engaged in self-deception), which is the most effective way to "lie."

However, the human mind was not formed at a time when it could ever have experienced the massive reach and number of lies, self-deceptions, and manipulations possible with today's books, radio, television, films, and digital media. The shaman has grown into the PR firm. At the same time, the PR firm faces the challenge of actual evidence against its claims coming from science, something the shaman did not really face. This, however, does not appear to be much of a challenge for politicians, ministers, or PR firms.

Most people make the associations they are manipulated to make (by politicians and the media) without any real investigation of the matter, even though such investigations are today, thanks to digital media, often easier than they have ever been in the past. This failure is partly because politicians, ministers, and PR firms know how to tie the associations they want us to make to what we called in an earlier chapter "mental comfort stories."

We have seen that the meanings attached to language are based on experiences we have had, contexts in which we have been, and associations and patterns we find in and across those experiences, some spurious, some real. However, today the "real world" is only one source of our experiences, and an attenuating one at that. We get a good deal of our experience secondhand from media like books, movies, television, videos, video games, and the Internet. There is a problem here.

The human mind is made in such away—thanks to the fact that there were no screens when it was being formed (evolving)—that it sometimes has a hard time telling media apart from reality. It also has a hard time remembering where it learned something, whether from a conversation, media, or actual experience in interaction with the world. We have all had the experience of forgetting that what we saw long ago in a movie or television show did not actually happen. This, indeed, was even a well-discussed problem for former President Ronald Reagan. We tend to meld all our experiences together, both first- and secondhand experiences, and draw conclusions from that bank of experience, as well as making associations and finding patterns based on it. Unfortunately, some of our experiences are tainted by media that want to manipulate us or downright lie to us.

We are all aware that humans can and do react emotionally to things in books and screens as if they are real. They cry at movies, for instance, or get scared playing a horror video game, or they get a warm glow from a happy ending. Our minds respond to book and screen images and actions as if they were real. Some people even accost actors who have played villains as if they really were the character they played.

Responding to media with emotions and even sometimes with belief as if what they depict were real is, of course, part of what makes them give us so much pleasure (sometimes referred to as "vicarious pleasure" and the "suspension of disbelief"). In the act, we make associations and come to believe in connections and generalizations that are not true. Of course, we can stop ourselves from experiencing a movie, say, as real by engaging our conscious minds reflectively (as we do when we say "It's just a movie. It's just a movie" while shaking in our seat at some unseemly violence).

I myself long ago went to a Catholic all-male boarding school that was straight out of the Middle Ages (the school is now itself long gone). After years of gender-segregated Catholic schooling, I had no idea whatsoever how to deal with girls when I left that school and went to a beautiful public college on the beach. This college was filled with surfers and beautifully tanned boys and girls, all of whom had had tons of experiences in high school with boy-girl relationships. I did not fare well, having no experiences with which to seek out associations and patterns that led to successful action. For example, I was stupid enough not to realize that when a girl asked you, day after day, what time it was when she was wearing a functioning watch, she was trying to pick you up, as a surfer dude later told me. I did not even know girls "picked up" men. I thought it only went the other way round.

By the way, if you will excuse this excursion into life's baser pleasures, I did not know how sex worked. In college I bought a book that told you how it worked and how female bodies operated. It had line drawings, unfortunately. I have always been challenged by maps and still could not really get it. I have argued ever since that people need to get "situated meanings" from actual images and experiences that render their words, and, in this case, their line drawings, meaningful for action.

But I did go to a lot of movies (I had time on my hands). I used movies as my experiential gender database and then went into action in the real world. It did not work all that well, at least initially. Later, as I watched more movies and gained some actual experience, I had (amid many failures) a few successes. My crowning movies-to-life moment is still a flashbulb memory these many decades later (it was based on the movie *The Heartbreak Kid*), though the failures are painful memories as well. In the end, I recommend not using media as one's sole source of experiences for reasoning and action, though I must say, in the age of cable television and talk radio, many a person does (and you have seen how well that works).

In the state of nature, when our ancestors lived in small bands as hunters and gatherers, each person in the group had pretty much the same experiences. They all shared a great deal of knowledge. They rarely met "strangers." Further, the world they lived in, though harsh, stayed pretty much the same for long periods of time. The complexity to which modern tools, technologies, communication systems, and human interventions in the world (e.g., cities, industries, and environmental destruction) have given rise did not exist. Today, however, we regularly meet "strangers" with whom we share little experience, and the pace of change is fast and furious.

One reason humans can be "stupid" is that in a complex and ever-changing world they have each had only limited experience. They have experienced things only from their place and situation in life. Others have experienced other things, with different limitations. Yet we sometimes come into contact with these others where our different assumptions and values, based on our own experiences, can clash or cause miscommunication. This can even happen in a marriage. In the modern world, people can marry others with whom they share much less background than did people in earlier times or in less cosmopolitan places today.

Pooling experience across diverse people with diverse experiences can be a powerful force for correcting errors and discovering new and better associations and patterns. It is, in fact, the basis of a phenomenon called "the wisdom of the crowd." On the other hand, groups of people without sufficient diversity of experience can often just entrench their errors and prejudices by pooling information based on their own limited shared prior experiences, associations, and pattern recognition.

Imagine a technology that would allow individuals who are engaged in discussion or debate to offer not just arguments, but experiences to each other. They could let the other person experience how the world looks, feels, and works from the viewpoint of different people. These demonstration experiences could be drawn from a bank of recorded or simulated experiences had by a great number of socially, intellectually, and culturally diverse people. After undergoing each new experience, each person in the debate could reconsider their own opinions. They could now form their arguments based on a wider sample of experiences, testing them again later against new experiences and new arguments from their fellow discussants. Perhaps they could reach agreement, discover new alternatives, correct a plethora of old errors, and move forward to make a world in which everyone has better and more humane experiences.

This fantasy is, perhaps, a greater possibility now with digital media and virtual realities, though people have often sought to achieve it through stories. But, beyond technology, it would require humans to risk seeing their views and themselves as limited when they inhabit a diverse world.

While sharing diverse experiences with each other can lead to better debate and wiser policies in society, other social forces can divide us and limit our ability to learn from others. These forces are status and solidarity. They can be good (honor and bonding) or bad (exclusion and in-group-ism). They can quickly lead to stupidity and even violence. We turn to these social forces in the following chapter.

7

Pitfalls along Our Search for Status and Solidarity

THE HUMAN MIND DOES NOT ALWAYS WORK WELL in the modern world because the human mind is not modern. As noted, it was shaped by the conditions when humans were hunters and gatherers and nature was much less "tamed." For example, in those earlier times, humans would only occasionally have had access to sweet things like fruit and only in perishable quantities. It makes sense that when they found sweet things, they would eat their fill. There was little danger that the sweets would make them fat (they got lots of exercise anyway). Not so today. Sweets are plentiful. When we give in to our strong desire to eat them, we now get fat.

This story about the human mind is true, as far as it goes. But there is also something wrong with it. What makes humans truly special—different from any other animal—is how adaptive they are to new conditions. This is due to the fact that humans invented culture. Culture allows humans to store knowledge, learn a good deal from each other, and partially protect themselves from the whims of nature, chance, and natural selection ("the survival of the fittest").

So why can't we humans stop doing stupid things like eating too much sugar? If our "old mind" tells us to eat and eat more, why doesn't culture (or the "good sense" it is supposed to impart to us) tell us not to? The answer to this question is usually that humans have a hard time with delayed gratification. They know getting fat will be bad, but they are faced here and now with a luscious piece of cake that they really want. Yet it isn't true that humans always have trouble with delayed gratification. Exercise clubs are often full, and many teens even delay a short-term pleasure to get into an elite college.

So questions remain: When are humans good at delayed gratification and when aren't they? When can they stop doing what they want in the short run to get what they want in the long run?

The answer to these questions is, I think, fairly simple in theory, though not in practice. It has to do with how culture works. If I want "X" now (say, a piece of cake) and I also want "Y" later (say, being thin), I will choose "Y" over "X" only if my desire for "Y" is stronger than my desire for "X" and sufficiently stronger to overcome the hold "X" has on me by being immediately present and available (a powerful force on humans). What makes something more desirable than something else and desirable enough even to create delayed gratification? The answer to this question resides in the workings of two powerful cultural forces: status and solidarity.

Humans are social beings in the sense that they strongly orient toward others. In all cultures, all humans can have two different orientations toward other people. Sometimes they orient toward others in terms of status and other times they orient toward others in terms of solidarity. On the one hand, we want status and respect for ourselves and we also want to offer status and respect to those we admire or fear in some fashion. On the other hand, we want solidarity with others, a sense of bonding and belonging with people we think or hope are "like us" and will count us as "one of them."

Of course, status and solidarity are in the eyes of the beholder. Someone has high status because others cede status or give respect to that person. One and the same person can be viewed as high status by some and low status by others. Someone is bonded to us, and we to them, because we treat that person and they treat us as "one of us," equals, peers, or even intimates. We humans create status and solidarity by how we think, value, and behave.

A person can orient toward the same person or group in terms of both status and solidarity in different situations. Status and solidarity can be relative to context. Years ago I knew a number of families who had sons who were priests. They treated their sons in some cases in terms of solidarity and intimacy, as a family member, and in other cases in terms of status and deference as a "man of God."

When we orient toward someone in terms of status, either because we feel they are higher status than we are or because we feel we are higher status than they are, we engage in relatively formal talk and behavior. When we orient toward someone in terms of solidarity, because we feel we are equals and alike, friends or intimates, we engage in relatively informal talk and behavior. How we treat people can be negotiated. Sometimes we engage in mixtures of formal and informal talk and behavior with people whom we want to orient toward somewhere between solidarity and status (this is one way that some cultures orient toward strangers).

For each of us, there are not just individuals we treat as high status (or low status); there are also groups of people we orient toward this way. And, for each of us, there are not just individuals we treat as equals, friends, or intimates, but groups we orient toward as being "like us," with whom we feel or want solidarity and bonding (for example, for many people, family is one such group, and for some, an ethnic group is).

Let's refer to groups that we feel are high or low status as "status reference groups." Let's refer to groups that we feel connected to in terms of equality, friendship, or intimacy or some other form of belonging as "solidarity reference groups."

Status reference groups and solidarity reference groups affect our behavior. We want to imitate the behaviors, styles, and values of our high-status reference groups (and, remember, these are often different for different people). We want to do this to show and, perhaps, gain respect. But we also want to imitate the behaviors, styles, and values of our solidarity reference groups. We want to do this to show and gain belonging and bonding. Thus, we can behave in different ways in different contexts, depending on how we orient toward status or solidarity. Sometimes we feel conflicted. Should I order beer to show solidarity with my buddies or wine to show my appreciation for the "high life"? Should I date women I like or women who make me look important? Should I listen to country music in deference to my roots or classical music in deference to my education and refinement (at least in front of "refined" people)?

Let's return to why we eat sugar and get fat, even when we "know better." The desire to be thin requires me to see a reference group that values thinness as more important for my actions than either a reference group that does not (if I have one) or just the immediate desire to eat. That reference group could be a status one ("upper-class people are thin") or a solidarity reference group ("my family values hard work and moderate habits").

They key point here is that it is not the "truth" of claims like "Being fat is bad for your health" that drives humans to engage in delayed gratification. Rather, it is a desire to achieve solidarity with or status among a reference group that values thinness or concentrates on a "healthy lifestyle" as a value.

It is our desire to be like those we feel bonded to or, on the other hand, those whom we view as high status that drives us. It is not "truth" per se. And, again, we can feel torn both ways. All my drinking buddies have beer bellies and I want to be one of the boys, so I should order another beer. But I also want people to view me as attractive like the beautiful people in the magazines, so maybe I should forget the beer and even the boys.

Some people spend time in the sun even though they know it can cause cancer because, down deep, they believe tanned people look better and thus have a certain status. Nonetheless, people readily stay out of the sun when they are aligned with a reference group that wants to live longer or thinks "pale is beautiful."

I have, like lots of Americans, gained and lost weight many times in my life. When I gain about fifty pounds, my alignment with the status of being thin is triggered and I go on a successful diet. Until then, my alignment with people who don't stress "lifestyle" and the media hype around thinness is stronger, abetted by the pleasure of immediate gratification. So I bounce back and forth.

We humans bounce around like billiard balls bouncing off the edges of a pool table, buffeted by different orientations toward different reference groups with different values and ways of being in the world. Further, the modern world gives us humans more possible reference groups and more ways to define status and solidarity than ever before in history.

So this is yet another example where "truth" takes a back seat for humans. The truth of claims like "Being fat is bad for your health" or "Going out in the sun can cause cancer" is not irrelevant to us, of course. But it does not move us as deeply as do the forces of status and solidarity, as well as the power of immediate gratification. Furthermore, untrue claims can work just as well if they play into the workings of status and solidarity. Believing that lots of exercise will make us look like a movie star is motivating, even if we know, down deep, it really isn't true.

So humans can be perfectly good at delayed gratification if their desire to orient toward a particular reference group is strong enough. Rich kids put off immediate gratification because everyone in their family and setting has gone to college (solidarity). The poor kids do so because no one in their family and setting has done so and they want to achieve something like the "important" people they see in the media (status). Or, perhaps, the poor kid doesn't want to go to college because he or she fears it will rupture solidarity with family and friends.

We humans have a built-in desire to show solidarity with family and local communities even if they do not deserve it. We do not, after all, choose our families. We have a built-in desire to gain respect and try to achieve status, even if the high-status people and groups we aspire to be like do not deserve our respect. But we don't always make good choices about either whom to bond to or whom to respect and whose respect we seek to earn.

Status and solidarity are forces that the media, politicians, PR firms, and ad agencies seek to manipulate. They try to convince small-town Americans to feel solidarity with other "real Americans" (a group that, in reality, does not exist). They try to convince people that corporate CEOs who abuse their employees and trash the environment are high status and worthy of respect. They claim that working-class whites and blacks should not feel solidarity and common cause with each other. They try to tell Americans that we are "exceptional" and superior to others, even when more Americans die for lack of health care than people in any other developed country. They even try to tell us that we Americans have the "best" health care system in the world, without bothering to mention that for those with no access to it, it is one of the worst.

If we wanted to avoid being duped, if we wanted to orient toward "truth" (or, at least, evidence), then we would have to be able to make good judgments about the worth of our (perhaps many) different status reference groups and solidarity reference groups. We would have to ask questions like: Who should I really feel bonded to and why? Who should I see as worthy of esteem and why? Should I feel good about being "one of the boys" at the bar or "one of us" as a professor? Should I esteem working people or corporate board members or both? Should I, as an American, feel solidarity with other Americans as co-citizens or not? What about solidarity with others across the world as fellow global citizens? Should I always place kin over strangers? Is my social group or culture really higher status or more worthy of respect than someone else's?

Such questions are the sorts we will later call "complex questions." Answering such questions requires access to lots of data and access to the workings among many variables that most people most of the time have no access to. Such questions are very hard to answer minus a research project that most people don't have the time or resources for. Even then they are hard to answer. For example, though I myself hold corporate CEOs in low esteem, I have no access to any wide sample of their daily behaviors, let alone the complex causes of their behavior (other than greed). Faced with an inability to answer complex questions about who deserves our solidarity and who our esteem, we fall back on our mental comfort stories, where and when we were born, the always-limited experiences we have had, and the groups to which we have access, if only via a magazine.

But the real issue arises when our allegiance to a status or solidarity group ends up taking our lives in directions we later regret or even regretted as we took them. It is hard for us humans to make decisions in these domains. For humans, status and solidarity are strong forces. They are what allow us to place different choices (e.g., have cake or be thin) into hierarchies and sometimes engage in delayed gratification. We have to orient toward *some* groups. We have to make choices about what sort of people are worthy of solidarity or status; otherwise we would always just engage in immediate pleasure and have no real value system at all. We are damned if we do and damned if we don't.

In the modern digital global world, we "moderns" are faced with a great many groups to bond to or to view as high enough in status to want to join or to respect from afar. Facebook and other such sites often list people as "friends," a term of solidarity, when some of them, in reality, barely know each other. Magazines and other media call for us to admire faux celebrities with no visible talents other than shameless self-promotion.

More and more complex questions arise: Should I feel more solidarity with people in other countries who share my lifestyle or values or with fellow citizens who do not? Should I aspire to join or respect high-status groups whose values badly conflict with people with whom I feel solidarity? Should I retain solidarity with people or groups whose values conflict with high-status groups I have joined or aspire to? How many of my decisions are "my own"—if any—and how many are the outcomes of the ways I am jostled by people and groups demanding solidarity or status?

People in some countries see themselves as "individuals." They believe that it is not groups that shape what they do and who they are. It is just themselves as individuals loyal to their own sense of self, marching to their very own drummer: "I gotta be me," "I did it my way." But imagine for a minute that there were no people or groups whom you oriented toward in terms of either status or solidarity. How would you determine who you were and how you should act? There would be no reference points, no points of comparison and contrast, nothing to be for or against. You would be nobody doing nothing. If you have done it your way, and no one else's way, then you are probably in a padded room. Or, at least, you are very lonely.

For us humans, there is no asocial starting point, no asocial ending point. The English word "idiot" is derived from the Greek word *idiōtēs* meaning "individual," itself derived from *idios* (private, one's own). It's interesting that our English word for stupid comes from the Greek word for a person viewed just as an individual apart from the social body. It is the push and pull of status and solidarity that make people "public," visible, and what they "are."

In the next chapter we turn to the power of naming. Words and language are the very foundation of human intelligence. Yet words can make big trouble for us humans.

8

Words Gone Awry

WORDS CAN MAKE HUMANS SMART AND THEY CAN make them stupid. Perhaps it is better to say words make humans "cunning." Take someone who is opposed to abortion, but supports the death penalty, opposes universal health care (leaving thousands of people without access to care), and opposes poverty programs that would keep young children from suffering and dying. Such people often call themselves "pro-life." But, in reality, they are not pro-life. They are "pro-embryo."

This example shows an important fact about how humans use words. We use them, for the most part, not to orient toward truth, but to orient toward persuasion (of others, as well as ourselves). When the mujahidin fought the Russians in Afghanistan, Americans called them "freedom fighters." When they fought the Americans in Afghanistan, Americans called them "terrorists." Their tactics had not changed, only their enemy.

We do not try to "name" things in ways that lead to fairness or potentially helpful arguments that might lead to compromise. We tend to name them to benefit our causes, desires, and beliefs. We usually use words not to say how the world is, but to say how we would like it to be. We use terms like "clean coal" for dirty and polluting coal that may (or may not) be produced in a bit "cleaner" way than "dirty coal." We talk about the glories of "free markets" when our markets are controlled by monopolies and policies that downplay competition (like subsidies). We call public health care "socialism." And we call people "Christians" who preach a "prosperity gospel" arguing that Jesus wanted people to be rich, though the historical Jesus would have been appalled by such a thing.

In many cases, people are just lying. But not in all or perhaps even most cases. They are often, sometimes quite appropriately, advocating or simplifying for the sake of accomplishing their goals. They are being, in this sense, "practical," focused not on truth, but on "work," on getting things done, on remaking the world in their image.

Naming things is, however, just the tip of the iceberg as far as language goes. Language, like painting or musical notation, is, in actuality, a tool for making "art." It is not primarily for telling some literal truth and/or giving each other unvarnished information. Why do I use the term "art" here? I use this term because art is supposed to move people emotionally by getting them to imagine certain things in their minds. It is not, primarily, about literal descriptions of the world as it is. Art, even so-called realistic painting, says, "Here, look at this in this way and it will open up for you some new ways of thinking and feeling about things." Art is about perspectives, how things can be viewed in order to open up new possibilities, cause emotions, or get people committed to new lines of action or ways of living their lives. So, too, is language as we use it in our everyday lives.

Language, whether spoken or written, is always designed by the speaker or writer to help (or encourage) the hearer or reader to interpret it in certain ways and not others. It is always designed to attempt to get the hearer or listener to respond in certain ways and not others. Of course, we do not always successfully manage our recipients' responses. But we try.

As an example, consider how we talk about teachers, pupils, and schools. Some people choose to call students "consumers" or "clients" and talk about "auditing," "inputs," "outputs," "performance indicators," and "efficiency gains" in schools. This is the language of business. Applied to schools, it asks us to view schools as being like factories or stores that make and sell things. In other work, I myself have talked about teachers as "resources" for students' active and collaborative problem-solving experiences and compared teachers to video-game designers. The traditional language of teachers as "instructors" and students as recipients of "instruction" is based on a model of teachers as conveyers of information and students as containers into which the information is placed. So here are three different ways to talk about teachers and schools.

Note some things that are typical of language here. First, there is no neutral way to talk about teachers, students, and schools. We have to take some perspective simply by choosing certain words over others. Second, there is really no way to distinguish among how we want to talk about teachers, students, and schools, what we think they are or should be, and what we value or advocate (or at least accept) in regard to them. These three things are all mixed up together.

Before a joint session of Congress on September 20, 2001, President George W. Bush said of the 9/11 attacks: "On September the eleventh, enemies of freedom committed an act of war against our country." Traditionally, it is countries that declare war, not a group of people from diverse countries. So this was a new way to look at things. One could have said, "On September the eleventh, a small group of religious fanatics committed a serious crime on American soil." Others, less sympathetic to the United States, might have said, "A group of young men opposed to American foreign policy attacked symbols of that policy." Or one could have said this: "A group composed largely of young men from our ally Saudi Arabia attacked the United States." There were other ways to put the matter, as well. Our president could have called for a war, a police action, international cooperation, or critical reflection on some of our allies.

There is no one "right" way to put the matter. Complex events can be correctly described in many different ways, each of which captures only part of their complexity. How we put the matter depends on how we view it, what we want to do about it, and how we want others to view it. Whether we call out the army, the diplomatic corps, or the New York police department depends on how we see things; and how we see them, in turn, partially determines and depends on how we talk or write about them. Without certain words—or without thought about other ways to look at and talk about matters—our options are limited. We can expand our options by expanding our language and our thinking.

The norm is that we use language to design a "picture" (philosophers use the fancy word "representation" here) of how we see the world and the way we want others to see it. We paint on the canvas of people's minds using language as the paint. Like Monet we play with perspective, with "light" and "shadows" (foregrounding some things, and backgrounding others), in order to get others to see things differently, sometimes anew. We do this sometimes for narrow self-interest, sometimes for higher purposes—and often we cannot tell which is which.

When we experience "reality," we have to edit what we have seen and felt in order to store it in our minds. Then we edit it anew when we put it into language for others (and even for ourselves). We stress certain things as foreground (important, focused on) in what we have experienced and how we have experienced it. We relegate other things to background status or leave them out altogether as not important or relevant.

I can refer to the United States as a "democracy," thereby foregrounding voting and representation. I can refer to it as a "republic," thereby foregrounding the ways in which voting (one person, one vote) is limited by the Electoral College and the equal representation that small states get in the Senate. I can refer to it as a "plutocracy" and thereby foreground the role of money and wealth in determining elections and policies. I can refer to it as an "oligarchy" and thereby foreground the fact that the wealthy ruling class is small, compared to the numerous many who are not rich and have less impact on policy. Since the combination of both plutocracy and oligarchy is called "plutarchy," I can also refer to the United States in this way.

As wealth pools into fewer and fewer hands in the United States, people who think of the United States as a democracy might change their view and thus how they talk, though this would happen at different points for different people and never for some. How far can we go in making the rich richer and fewer and the poor poorer and more numerous before we change terminology and viewpoints?

Consider the two quotes below:

... thoroughgoing restrictions on economic freedom would turn out to be inconsistent with democracy.

... high quality public pedestrian space in general and parks in particular are evidence of true democracy at work.

If the word "democracy" just means "voting for representatives," then neither of these quotes really makes any sense. Parks seem irrelevant and it is not at all clear why people in a democracy cannot vote to limit economic freedom if they so choose. It might (or might not) be a bad thing to do, but it certainly does not seem to render a democracy not a democracy.

In reality, each quote is foregrounding, drawing attention to, focusing on, what the author views as a relevant or important defining feature for democracy and, thus, for "democracy" (the word) too. In the first case, the focus is on the freedom not to have voters take away one's property (because otherwise, people, especially the better off, should not agree to be in the so-called democracy). In the second case, the focus is on the ways in which everyone should benefit from the results of a democracy, not just the rich or the few (because otherwise, people, especially the less well off, should not agree to be in the so-called democracy). The second also stresses that the voters in a democracy are not just people, but "the public."

The Supreme Court of Israel, in the case *The Public Committee Against Torture in Israel v. The State of Israel,* ruled against torture, saying "That is the fate of democracy, in whose eyes not all means are permitted, and to whom not all the methods used by her enemies are open." The US government under President George W. Bush and Vice President Richard Cheney did not seem to believe this of democracy, or perhaps they foregrounded different aspects of what they thought was and was not torture.

Again, it is hard to say what things are apart from how we choose to talk about them and hard to know how to talk about them apart from how we take them to be or want them to be. Language, thought, and the world constantly interact with each other. They get harder and harder to disentangle after they have been at it for a while. Limitations on words are limitations on thoughts and on options in the world. Limitations on thoughts set limitations on words and on options in the world.

All this makes it sound as if we humans cannot use language to argue and discuss with each other on the basis of evidence instead of desire. But humans can seek truth and not just persuasion. However, such "truth seeking" is a type of "language game" in the sense that it requires a commitment to using words in certain ways. Many people are not willing to make such a commitment when their cherished beliefs or mental comfort stories might be at stake.

What does this truth-seeking game look like? It looks a lot like what we called in the first chapter the "circuit of reflective action" carried out collaboratively. In the circuit of reflective action, we formulate a goal (and the goal could be answering a question) and then we take an action in the world. We see how the world responds to the action, ask ourselves whether this response was good or not for the accomplishment of our goal, and then, if need be, act again on better information or a redefined goal. The circuit of reflective action is an interactive conversation with the world.

In a truth-seeking game we agree to engage in the circuit of reflective action collaboratively with others with a goal of reaching truth and not just persuasion or the fulfillment of our desires and interests alone. To play this game requires that we formulate our claims in ways that are "falsifiable," that is, open to disconfirmation by ourselves or others (who need not have our interests and desires at heart) based on how the world responds (and not just how opinion makers, media pundits, experts, or ministers respond).

Some questions are not open to this game. A question like "Is an embryo a human being?" cannot be played in a truth-seeking game. The world has no definitive response here. How we characterize an embryo is based on our values and desires, not on any fact we can discover in the world. The question "Is an acorn a tree?" is equally unplayable, since nature does not care whether these two things (acorn and tree) are placed in the same category by humans or not. It "cares" only that it can make a tree out of an acorn in the right circumstances. So, of course, questions like "Is an embryo potentially a human being?" or "Is an acorn potentially an oak tree?" are answerable. We have now stated them in a way that the world answers. We can, after all, plant an acorn and see what happens.

Some questions are not directly and in one fell swoop open to the truth game, because they are too complex, too big. We have to break them down into many sub-questions, which the world will then answer. But then it can sometimes be quite difficult to put all the many answers to the sub-questions together to get a coherent and plausible answer to the big question. This enterprise—putting the many sub-answers together into a coherent and plausible answer to the big question—is called "theory building." Humans regularly confuse theory building (a larger and more adventurous form of the truth-seeking game) with telling themselves mental comfort stories, which is not a truth-seeking game, but a comfort-seeking game.

The truth-seeking game is a way to use language to interact with others and the world. It need not give rise to anything like "deep meaning" or "master narratives" or "eternal truth." What it gives us humans is just our "best bets" when we want to act successfully in the world without damaging ourselves and others too much.

The world renders "true" judgments in the truth-seeking game provided that we have tried and failed so far to falsify a claim and have garnered lots of evidence for the claim. Before anyone knew about Australia, if they had searched the world for black swans and found only white ones, they would have been entitled, based on the truth-seeking game, to say "All swans are white" (and, indeed, they all were in their "known world"). But once having been to Australia, they have to modify their claim and say, "All swans are white, except some of them in Australia."

So we see here that "truth" as an everyday concept, not a deep philosophical one, is "tentative" and can be revised. In fact, the truth-seeking game, since it is based, in part, on efforts to falsify claims, pretty much demands this. It demands that human beings keep open minds, while at the same time being willing to close them enough here and now to get on with the work of surviving and flourishing in the world. But they need to keep asking and keep searching. They need to keep respecting the world. This is not an attitude most humans are all that comfortable with. They usually want certainty, and their comfort stories give it to them in feeling, if not in reality.

The truth-seeking game cannot answer many questions humans care about. When we debate questions the game cannot answer, either because we are using unfalsifiable claims or because we are asking questions that are too complex and have not been properly broken down and adapted to theory building, then the "debate" is not really a debate about truth. It is about what to value or it is about power, comfort stories, desires, or bargains we will make with each other in order to live together. There is nothing wrong with this per se. It can lead to good or bad results. But confusing such "debates" with debates using the rules of the truth-seeking game can lead to stupidity.

So far we have talked a lot about the human mind and its ties to the world of experience. But minds are actually brains and parts of our bodies. Human minds/brains/bodies do not work well when they are sick. Perhaps the deepest human sickness is a lack of agency, a lack of the feeling that one counts and matters. Such a sickness is now an epidemic in our society and it makes both us and our society stupid. To this crucial issue we now turn.

9

Lack of Agency

HUMANS, LIKE ALL ANIMALS, ARE DRIVEN BY NEEDS. They have basic needs for food, procreation, and safety. When these are not filled, humans will focus on them intently. For many people in the developed world, these needs are filled, though not for all, and not for many in other parts of the world. When these needs are basically taken care of, another set of needs takes the foreground for humans. These are needs for control, belonging, respect, meaning, and agency. All humans have these needs, seek to fill them, and suffer when they are not filled, though if a person is starving, food tends to take first place.

We saw in an earlier chapter than when humans feel no sense of control, they can become quite sick, physically and mentally. They feel trapped. We also saw that humans seek solidarity with others, a sense of belonging and being accepted. They also seek status in terms of respect from others. We have seen, as well, throughout this book so far that humans desperately want to find meaning in the world and that they cling to mental comfort stories.

This leaves us in this chapter with the human need for agency. By this I mean that people want to feel they are effective actors in the world, not just spectators of other people's actions. They want to feel that their actions have their intended consequences and will lead to success in accomplishing their goals (this is a large part of what feeling a sense of control is about).

In a small hunting and gathering group everyone had to pull together and act in ways that were effective for the survival of all. They could not pay others to do things for them and they could not easily opt out of tasks they didn't like. Furthermore, each person got plenty of mentoring and practice in mastering the tasks that had to be accomplished for survival and flourishing as a group. Everybody needed everybody else. The same is true for soldiers at war.

By and large, none of this is true any longer in modern cities and countries. Many people feel that their voice (as in voting) and their actions count for little in the face of so many people and so many formal institutions and so much complexity. They feel that some people count much more than others because of their wealth, influence, power, or good luck.

At the same time, modern media bring us all sorts of powerful, beautiful, and famous people strutting across the stage of life where it seems everything they say and do, no matter how trivial, counts and bears rabid attention. We come to feel like watchers of life, rather than livers of it. Our lives seem small, common, and mundane. For some reason, there are no klieg lights shining on our deeds.

Part of the problem here is caused by the "winner-take-all" nature of our modern global world. Before high fidelity recording, every town had its own local best singers. But with masterful recordings, all people everywhere had ready access to the world's best singers, and the locals came to seem minor. Even if you want to see performers in person, with modern transportation you can easily and often hear the best on tour.

We can buy the best coffee from around the world, shipped in a day to wherever we are. No need for the local stuff. The same goes for our food, clothes, and a myriad of other products. We do not even need local friends, since we can interact with others wherever they are via digital media and fast transportation. Many people do not even need local jobs for they can telecommute to work from anywhere to anywhere.

In any area of life today, there are a small number of winners (the best singers, designers, coffee makers, actors, financial advisors, and renowned surgeons) who take most of the rewards. Then there is the vast "everyone else" competing for the remnants. If I am stuck with the local surgeons in my county hospital for non-routine surgery and cannot make my way to the elite surgeons at a major clinic or hospital, perhaps far from home, I'm in trouble. Pity the poor kids stuck at home in their local college with its minor professors when they could have gone across country to attend Yale or Princeton, if they had just had the "smarts" or the money.

Of course, this change is still in progress. Imagine the day when we record (as we are already beginning to do) the best lectures and digitize the best instruction and assessment in every area of education and make them readily available to everyone. We will not need well-paid teachers and professors locally, only aides to help people access "the best" from wherever it comes.

Imagine the day when surgeons direct surgery via digital media and tools that scan and operate on the body. Much surgery (e.g., laparoscopic surgery) is already carried out on screens. We will not need well-paid local doctors, just helpers to monitor the process and change the patients' bedpans and sheets. Of course, some people will always have to settle for what is available locally, but this will more and more become the sign of either poverty or resistance to the modern world.

In "olden days," peoples' accomplishments were, by and large, known locally. People sought respect locally or regionally. Twenty-four-hour cable TV channels did not exist to broadcast fame far and wide, even fame for trivial things like good looks or accidental sex tapes. It is harder now for people to feel they can get recognized for being good at something if these efforts stay local. I live in a small town (Sedona, Arizona) sometimes called the "New Age Capital of the World." It has lots of New Age gurus. I have coffee every afternoon in a coffee store where the local gurus gather, a sorry lot compared to the gurus with bestselling books or national tours. In the long-ago past, the local shaman was a really big deal, but today the local guru is hard pressed to get any attention at all.

There is, in our modern digital global world, a principle that captures well the winner-take-all phenomenon. It is called the Pareto principle.

According to the Pareto principle, in any modern group endeavor (whether this be scientific research, inventing, investing, photo sharing on an Internet site, or designing virtual clothes for The Sims), 10 to 20 percent of the participants produce 80 to 90 percent of the results (e.g., research papers, inventions, investments, photos, virtual clothes) and 80 to 90 percent of the people produce 10 to 20 percent of the results.

This is also how wealth tends to work in developed capitalist countries if forces are not in place to stop it. As of 2007, the top 1 percent of households owned 34.6 percent of all privately held wealth. The next 19 percent had 50.5 percent. This means that 20 percent of the people owned 85 percent of the wealth, and 15 percent of the wealth was left for the bottom 80 percent of the people. This is also the way markets work. The first companies on the market with a new product take the lion's share of the profits; indeed, the first takes most.

In most activities in developed countries today, a small number of people, through talent, practice, or luck, come to dominate. The rest of us are part of a long tail composed of "minor" contributions that garner us little fame and fortune, save among our families, friends, and the "locals" if we still know any.

Now it is tempting to believe that this dominance by the few is the result of a sort of social Darwinism in which the "best" have survived through hard work and struggle, a sure sign of their talent or merit. However, research has clearly shown that this is, in fact, not true. The winners tend to win because they were in the right place at the right time to gain the experience, practice, and the leg up required for success. They may, of course, have had talent, but many equally or more talented people were not there at the right time and place. Success is a product of effort, some talent, and circumstances, as well as pure luck.

There is an interesting theory of success called "the kick theory." According to the kick theory, small initial advantages ramify into large later advantages. One person gets into a better college than another person based only on a very small difference in grades or based on where they live (they receive a small kick forward). But then that person has added one extra advantage (another kick) for getting into a better graduate school. That kick gives the person a better advantage to get a good job, and that job leads to more opportunities to publish, and, thus, a better chance to get tenure, promotion to full professor, a high salary, and, eventually, some fame and fortune.

Two people who looked close at the beginning are far apart at the end, one working at a prestigious university or think tank and the other laboring at a local campus of the state college. This theory can apply in nearly any area. It has been used to explain why women do less well in science careers than men (gender discrimination is an initial small disadvantage but through the further kicks men get based on that initial discrimination, it grows into a major disadvantage).

You may feel important at the end and slap yourself on the back for your talent, but initially you might have had a small—and even arbitrary—advantage over others. Nonetheless, thanks to your success, you feel a greater sense of agency (importance as an actor in the world whose actions "count") than does the person who in the beginning was so close to you. Perhaps they even feel like a failure.

There is a fascinating phenomenon in public health called the "status syndrome." In any country, if you line up people, one after the other, from first to last, in terms of status, this status hierarchy correlates very well with their health. People higher in the line are healthier than people lower in the line; people lower in the line are less healthy than people higher in the line. And the really interesting thing is this: it really does not matter how you define status. You could define status in terms of income, job status, education, or even the size of one's house.

The status syndrome appears in all countries but is worse in some than in others. It is fairly weak in Japan and quite strong in the United States. Why should one's status make one, all things being equal, healthier than people who are lower in status? The answer is not just access to better medical care, since people relatively high in the hierarchy still have less good health, on average, than those above them, though all have adequate access to health care in terms of income.

The answer, it has been argued, is that the higher your status in a society, the more you believe that your actions count and that you are participating in and contributing to the society. The lower your status, the less you feel that you and your actions count and contribute. Feeling that you matter is good for your health. Feeling that you don't (or don't much, or not as much as others) is bad for your health. People have a need for agency, for mattering as actors. In highly hierarchically stratified societies (like the United States and many other countries to different degrees) and in a winner-take-all world, many people do not feel a sense of agency, or, at least, not a very robust one. And, of course, if you are poor and just trying to survive, things are worse, since you are still trying to fill your basic needs and are, by definition, at the bottom of the status hierarchy.

Have you ever played a game, like a board game, with someone who does not care about the game or feels they cannot possibly win? They do not take the actions seriously or think much about them. They look stupid or silly. When people don't believe their actions will make a difference or when they don't know how to act, they appear stupid. They do not make good team members. When games are set up so that there is only one winner or a very few out of a great many players—and when winning begins to feel like a long-shot lottery—lots of the players give up or don't put in much effort or they never get in the game.

Formal schooling is often like this. People are placed in hierarchies where small differences often translate eventually into big ones. There are a few winners and lots of losers in the middle and at the end of the hierarchy. Many students do not think their actions really matter or do not understand how to act so as to make them matter. So they put in less effort, sometimes even give up, and we tell them it's their fault, that they just weren't smart enough or did not work hard enough. In reality, different forms of organization for learning might well have had different outcomes. Currently, school creates a situation in which many people feel a loss of agency, and thus school performance may not be a very good indicator of their potential for agency in other realms.

To be agents, people need both opportunities to be an agent and models of effective action. They need to see that taking action can really matter, and they need to see what successful action looks like. For this, they need two additional things. First, they need to trust that the system is not rigged or unfair. They need to believe that their effective actions can have successful outcomes and that the outcomes of the game are not already predetermined by the actions of a select few. Second, they need to be members of a community or social group that models for them what counts as an effective action and that demonstrates to them that the actions of the community or group can be effective and will not be undermined by others with special privileges or access.

For many people such conditions are not met. Modern media readily show them that the outcomes of actions are often the products of caprice, power, ideology, or money untethered to truth, evidence, practicality, or argumentation. Perhaps it was always so, but it is far easier today to see it and to be rendered immobile.

There is another important force that diminishes people's sense of agency. In the first half of my life, people thought that companies were meant to make profit, churches were meant to ameliorate society spiritually, and universities were meant to improve society by promoting knowledge. Churches and universities were not, at least in theory, up against the market, judged by the bottom line of profit. Furthermore, business was, in theory at least, meant to achieve long-term success, not just short-term profit, by serving its stakeholders well. Stakeholders were all those people on whom the business impinged, not just its stockholders, but also its employees, customers, and the people who lived in the community where the business resided.

None of this is true today in our global, high-tech "new capitalism." Today all institutions, such as churches and universities, not just businesses, are up against the market. They must focus on making money and competing with others to succeed. States will no longer, for example, substantively subsidize public universities. Businesses can no longer focus on long-term goals and success, since they are now judged on how well their stock price does each quarter. If the stock price goes down, or does not meet expectations, mutual funds sell the stock and punish the company. Furthermore, companies are not judged by the quality of what they produce or do, but by the track record of their stock price, with an emphasis on the latest figures. Finally, corporations are now viewed as having moral and financial obligations only to their stockholders, even if this means harming employees, customers, or communities.

Today, wealth is pooling into fewer and fewer hands. Inequality in wealth in the United States is as bad today as it was in the 1890s, the age of the robber barons. Only one-fifth of the jobs in a highly developed economy reward people well, usually for producing new ideas, products, and services. Another one-fifth of the jobs involve technical skills, but pay less well, though they may have bonuses and something approaching a living wage. The remainder are mainly in the service and manufacturing sectors or involve manual labor (Wal-Mart, a company famous for paying its employees poorly, is the largest employer in the United States). With the significant diminishment of unions and benefits, these jobs have low wages and often involve little sense of agency and control.

In such a world, it is impossible for most people to get a sense of dignity, mattering, belonging, and agency "on market" from their job. Yet our society tends to judge people by their jobs and wealth, that is, in terms of success "on market." A society in which close to three-fifths of the people feel no real sense of dignity, agency, or participation is not a "civic society" of involved citizens.

More and more, people must—and, thanks to digital media and technology, can—seek dignity and agency outside markets in often virtual communities on the Internet that share and produce knowledge and designs around a myriad of interests or passions, whether these be health, cats, citizen science, video-game design, fan fiction, political activism, or a great many other things. They engage in these spaces usually not for money, but for a sense of belonging and contributing as effective knowers and actors. They seek dignity "off market," outside their jobs or the market-based (and often class-based) judgments of a capitalist society driven by short-term goals and profit seeking detached from values beyond stock prices.

For those who cannot find dignity "off market," there can be a sense of a loss of one's full humanity in the face of a world where the rich get ever richer based more on bets and speculation than on real work or long-term investment in high-quality goods and services that actually make people's lives better. Many people who don't seek refuge "off-market" simply watch TV when they come home, become stupidified, and generate a massive "cognitive surplus" of possible human energy and agency that sits unused, wasted, and atrophying.

For a long time formal institutions have been a great force for unleashing human agency and collaboration. They have, however, too often crimped agency and led to dysfunctional human interactions instead. Institutions are particularly dangerous when they freeze thinking and fail to face new realities. Today they are being challenged by everyday people as producers and collaborators.

10

Institutions and Frozen Thought

INSTITUTIONS AROSE AMONG HUMANS TO SOLVE A particular problem. That problem was how to coordinate the actions of lots of people to accomplish a common purpose. Institutions are simultaneously one of the greatest and one of the worst inventions of human beings. They can make us extra smart or extra stupid.

An institution is a set of rules, procedures, conventions, and structures of authority that govern how a group of people will work to accomplish a purpose. If a small group of people want to erect a building or engage in a hunt, they do not need an institution. But if a large group wants to build a city or engage in the mass production of food, they need one or more institutions. An institution is meant to get everyone on the same page and coordinate a complex set of interacting activities toward a complex set of goals. Of necessity, it involves rules, even legal ones, and a system that distributes and enforces roles and authority.

Institutions are "frozen thought." They exist in part to "think for us." In any complex set of tasks involving lots of people, there are a great many things to think about, make decisions about, plan for, and reflect on. Institutions take some of these things and "freeze" them into set procedures that we do not need to think about and make decisions about. These procedures lower the cognitive load for people in the institution.

For example, in a school, rules or conventions determine that students will sit in rows, follow the authority of a teacher at the front of the room, divide up time into certain periods, and be judged ("assessed") in certain ways. Lines of responsibility and authority are clear. People do not need to think about where to be when and how to get down to work. Lots of decisions are removed so that they can concentrate on what is most important to the institution's purpose.

Standardization is an important part of any institution. In a court, the language, procedures, documents, and practices of law are highly standardized. This does not mean that they are identical from performance to performance. It just means that they are highly consistent with well-known precedents, models, and parameters for getting things "right." The judge does not sit in the back of the courtroom, lawyers do not wear shorts, juries do not telecommute, arguments are not made in rap, and witnesses cannot question the judge or attorneys. All this removes a great many decisions from individuals, who usually just follow along without any thought about these matters. They simply take them for granted as "natural," when they are, in fact, just conventional. Court systems in different countries operate by different conventions, though there are some conventions that are pretty common given the purpose of courts to make judgments about crime and punishment.

Institutions, of course, end up with large buildings and built environments designed in certain ways to facilitate their work. They can spread across countries and the world. They can be composed of a vast network of people, roles, places, and procedures. They can come to seem like "super people"; they can come to seem to be actors in their own right, to have agency beyond the sum of the people who compose them. We come readily to talk about them as actors: IBM did this, Harvard did that, schools act this way, and courts act that way.

It is not really clear what such talk actually means if we think about it, which we usually don't. In any case, such talk has been enshrined in law in the United States where corporations (a type of institution) count as "people" and have free speech rights and the other rights the Constitution once appeared to reserve for real, live, individual human beings. And, alas, I, too, will use such talk here. But we should keep in mind that when we say an institution did something or wants something, it is, in reality, people in the institution who did it or want it, though it is not always easy to say who exactly these people are. And, surely, we should realize that corporations are not people, no matter what US law or courts say about the matter.

Institutions arise in history for a specific purpose. They often live a long life, sometimes long enough to have outlived their original purpose or at least to have entered times in which the original purpose means something quite different. For example, colleges in the United States and England were originally meant to train religious thinkers and leaders. Colleges and universities were, by and large, religious institutions—not churches, but training grounds for churches. Though they remained structured in much the same way, later in history many universities saw themselves as training secular thinkers and leaders who were to be some sort of "secular priests," saving society not through spiritual truth, but through empirical knowledge. Today, in the United States, at least, universities are confronted with many students who are more interested in beer and bodies or "getting a good job" than in salvation or knowledge. At what point should the institution die or radically change?

Until the advent of digital media, as we will see below, humans had no way to coordinate the activities of large groups of people other than via formal institutions with their structures, rules, and often top-down chains of authority. Yet those of us who have spent our lives in and around institutions, which is virtually all of us, know that humans think of institutions as "vexed" things. We complain about them and often find their procedures silly, stupid, or counterproductive. I most certainly do.

After nearly forty years as an academic, I am appalled at many of the practices and proceedings of colleges and universities. Why is this so? Why do institutions, which were meant to make people smart and effective, so often seem to make so many individuals stupid and ineffective? For example, I am simply amazed at how often even smart people seem stupid when they are on a committee. I am even amazed at how often I am stupid when I am on a committee.

The truth is that institutions often function, more or less, to do what they are supposed to do, not perfectly, nor even always well, but as well as can be managed in a complex world where until recently there were not really alternatives that were any better. Like democracy, institutions were a poor solution to a problem whose other solutions seemed even worse. That said, institutions often function in dysfunctional ways. There are many reasons for this, but I want to focus on two important ones.

First, since institutions are frozen thought, they often freeze a solution to a problem. The solution was good originally but gets to be less and less good as circumstances (and the problem) change. Once a solution is frozen, it takes lots of work to unfreeze it, to get people to rethink it and refreeze ("institutionalize") a different solution. Even if it can be unfrozen, it unfreezes slowly and only with much effort and controversy. People become used to the frozen solution. They take it for granted. Sometimes they have invested a lot of time and effort in learning to follow it. Sometimes they feel it was sanctioned by "higher authority" that ought not to be challenged.

The QWERTY keyboard is often used as an example of frozen thought that is impossible to unfreeze, though it is now a solution to a problem that no longer exists. In the "old days," mechanical typewriters had keys that would jam if you typed too fast. So the keyboard was purposely laid out in such a way as to discourage fast typing. Keys that were often typed together were placed far apart on the keyboard. With electronic devices, like computer keyboards, there is nothing to jam, and we can type as fast and furiously as we wish. Yet we still lay out the keys on the keyboard in the worst possible way for fast typing. So why don't we get rid of the QWERTY keyboard?

We do not get rid of the QWERTY keyboard because each generation puts effort into learning it, gets used to it, and comes to see it as "normal" and "natural." People do not want to invest in undoing what they have learned, confront an "odd" and "unnatural" layout of the keys, and learn something new. Furthermore, and equally important, there is no institution that can initiate the change on a grand scale and force people to follow along. The QWERTY keyboard is a once-good thought/decision/solution that is now a bad one, frozen in time, with a life of its own without its original function.

Institutions of all sorts are full of their own QWERTY keyboards. They are full of rules, procedures, and structures that have frozen solutions into forms that are now dysfunctional or irrelevant. Being frozen, however, they discourage any active human thinking about them, thinking that might lead to new decisions. We humans should often think about, reflect on, and make new decisions about institutionally frozen solutions, but mostly we do not. People who have long followed and are well practiced at the frozen solutions often have a vested interest in not unfreezing them. Newcomers may want to change them, and see more clearly the need to do so, but, in an institution, they almost always lack the power and authority to do so. Indeed, they often get accepted as a true "insider" within the institution only when they stop questioning the institution's frozen thoughts, decisions, and solutions.

Why do we have to arrange the seats in a classroom all in a row and stare at one person, the teacher? Why should every course meet for the same amount of time and get the same amount of credit? If you ask questions like this in a school or college, you had better have the authority (or gumption) to make changes and push against the inertia of the college before you lose your job. And, indeed, enough people are asking such questions now that change is beginning to happen, though slowly and unevenly. Change is also happening here, as in so many other places today, due to digital media offering us new and better solutions to problems for which many an institution has only old and frozen solutions.

The second reason that institutions are often dysfunctional is built into the nature of human beings. An institution is founded for a purpose. The purpose can disappear or it can change over time, even when the institution does not itself disappear. At any time, however, an institution has goals of its own. These are goals that the people in the institution are supposed to carry out for the good of the institution. Sometimes, such goals are part of an institution's mission statement.

However, humans always have their own local goals. In fact, they have two sorts of local goals. They have personal goals. These goals are what they want to accomplish for themselves, based on their own needs and desires and their own assessment of them. And they have social-interactive goals that involve interacting with other people. In face-to-face communication (and now in its digital forms) they have very human needs for solidarity with others and for respect from them. They have desires to maintain contact and not lose face or threaten other people's face in social interaction.

These local goals, of both sorts, can and often do conflict with the more global goals of the institution. People gossiping around the water cooler at work can interact in ways that undermine the goals or mission of a business, for example. In face-to-face talk around the water cooler a person may encounter a conflict between showing support for the institution and validating his or her interlocutor's griping about the institution. This validation is a form of social bonding and conflict avoidance. Humans are built in such a way that when they face a conflict between global goals and the local goals of social interaction, they almost always choose the latter over the former. The power and "gravity" of social interaction is very hard to overcome.

Universities want their professors to teach well so that they can keep their tuition-paying undergraduates happy. They also want their professors to publish because this brings the university status. However, professors often find the latter goal more personally rewarding (in status and money) than they do the former goal. Universities abet this conflict by rewarding publishing more than good teaching. Humans are built in such a way that when they face a conflict between global goals and local goals based on personal needs and desires, the latter almost always win out over the former. Personal goals are a powerful force, powerful enough to overcome institutional strictures and commitments. This is not simply a matter of greed or selfishness. It is a survival instinct, not just for one's life, but also for one's dignity as a person. People are willing to sacrifice only for groups whose survival seems synonymous with or deeply connected to their own (part of what makes it meaningful).

This conflict between local goals and wider institutional goals is problematic for any institution. Institutions have to do something to mitigate this conflict. They have to get members to serve institutional goals, sometimes even at the expense of personal and social-interactive goals. Accomplishing this requires building into people real loyalty toward an institution's goals, mission, and values. This is not easy to do, especially if and when people see that aspects of an institution's "frozen thought" have become dysfunctional or meaningless (save as ritual). It is not easy to do when an institution's goals, mission, or values seem opaque or vague or inconsistent, as often happens when different aspects of an institution's ways of proceeding become frozen on different and inconsistent goals and values.

For example, newly empowered undergraduate consumers in colleges (students who now pay more and have more choices) have come to demand better teaching and better services. In response, a college introduces policies to accomplish this, but leaves in place the now outdated procedures that heavily reward publication over teaching, thereby sending an inconsistent message to both faculty and students. Another example: facing a new high-tech economic environment that more and more demands collaborative project-based teams for success, a company reorganizes its work force into so-called cross-functional teams, but leaves in place its old winner-take-all merit system that pits workers against each other, thereby contradicting the value of cooperation and collaboration.

When people see contradictions, mixed messages, and a lack of lucidity around goals and values in an institution, they revert to privileging their local goals over the institution's goals. They may give lip service to the institution's goals and "talk the talk" (at least in front of bosses), but they don't "walk the walk." As we have said, humans are built in such a way that they will almost always favor their local goals over institutional goals unless something works to mitigate this conflict.

Humans have certain personal needs and goals that will invariably trump wider institutional goals. They need a sense of belonging, as well as a sense of being respected. They need to feel like agents whose actions matter. And, as we saw in an earlier chapter, humans are particularly sensitive to cheating and unfairness. They need to believe that arrangements are fair. If institutional procedures fulfill these personal needs and goals, there can be a good marriage between people's personal goals and the institution's goals and mission, since people now feel committed to the institution.

However, such marriages are getting rarer and rarer in institutions in many countries today, especially in the United States. In our global economy, the bottom line comes to matter more and more. People's needs are regularly sacrificed in the name of efficiency and income or even just survival in a fast-changing, highly competitive environment that is often focused mostly on short-term gain.

So two of the key reasons institutions so often seem dysfunctional are their inability to quickly unfreeze no longer useful or functioning aspects of their frozen thought and their inability to mitigate conflicts between local (personal and social-interactive) goals and more global institution-wide goals.

These problems for institutions are particularly pronounced because they now face competition. Today, thanks to digital and social media, institutions face a competing solution to one of their main purposes, that is, the efficient and effective organization and coordination of large groups of people. Via texting, Twitter, websites, and mobile devices, people can organize themselves quickly and democratically to respond to immediate problems and then, often, disperse. They can show up in a city center, protest, and disappear, only to reappear somewhere else.

Via websites and digital design tools, people can organize themselves into large "knowledge communities" and produce products, knowledge, and designs of all sorts. They can create an effective "amateur" cat-health sharing site, competing at times with professional vets on issues of cat health and breeding. Substitute anything else besides cat health and you will probably find a large group of "amateurs" producing competitive knowledge and solutions around it. Such knowledge communities produce, for example, art, video games, digital stories, digital movies, music, legal advice, robots, political and environmental activism, citizen science, and a great many other things. They need no institution to organize them or to assess them. They do this for themselves, sometimes even in opposition to institutions as they school themselves and compete to design things that were heretofore "owned" by corporations (including making ads or even counter-ads or gathering their own news).

Such self-organizing knowledge communities also freeze thought. They have their own standards and conventional ways of proceeding, often built bottom up and democratically to some extent. But they seem to be able to unfreeze decisions and solutions faster than formal institutions can. And they very often meet people's personal and pro-social goals and needs in very deep ways while simultaneously allowing them to contribute to a larger group in a meaningful way.

It remains to be seen how formal institutions (including governments) will fare in the face of this competition. Perhaps they will co-opt it for their own ends. Perhaps they won't be able to. We will see.

Sometimes it is not institutions that freeze thought, but minds themselves. We humans sometimes fear thinking—it might lead to results we don't like—and, as we have seen, soothe ourselves with comfort stories. But for some people comfort stories are not enough. They make up facts so that they can convince themselves that what they hope is true is true in a literal, non-metaphorical way. We turn now to one of the most fascinating aberrations of the human mind: Pseudo Empirical Stories.

Fact-Free Stories
That Sound Good

IN THIS CHAPTER AND IN THE NEXT WE WILL DIS-
cuss two mental "pathologies." One is a pathological version of what we
earlier called mental comfort stories. The other is a pathological version of
the human need for solidarity with others whom we see as "like us." Here we
will discuss pathological mental comfort stories. In the next chapter we will
discuss pathological solidarity.

Telling ourselves a comfort story like "Everything happens for a reason"
(which usually means a good reason, however hidden at the time) can make
life more livable. It can even get people to make lemonade out of the lemons
life hands them. This story is not open to empirical falsification. No fact
could show it to be wrong. People can always say that some hidden purpose
was present, perhaps only in the mind of God or in the hands of fate, neither
of which are open to empirical inspection.

The type of pathological story that I want to discuss here is different.
People who tell these pathological stories attempt to recruit "facts" (evidence) to support them. But these facts are simply fictions dressed as facts
inside nice-sounding, but blatantly stupid arguments. I will call these sorts
of stories Pseudo Empirical Stories. Such stories seek to sound fact based, but
all they do is sound good to those who want to believe them anyway. They
recruit "facts" that even a little thought and effort could show are false. This
leaves behind the deep mystery as to why anyone would believe them.

Many people believe that the earth is less than 10,000 years old because they think the Bible tells them this. Confronted with the vast geological evidence that this is not so, some of them claim that God put that evidence there to test our faith, to see if we would trust Him even in the face of what seems irrefutable proof of a very old earth. This is not a Pseudo Empirical Story because the "God is testing us" line makes it un-open to empirical falsification. This is just a good old mental comfort story.

However, when creationists use the second law of thermodynamics in physics to argue against Darwinian evolution by natural selection, they are engaged in a Pseudo Empirical Story. The second law predicts, according to creationists, that any system will, in the course of time, move toward greater disorder, not greater order (this is not actually how the law is stated in physics, but it is how it is commonly stated in creationist literature). Since, in the course of evolution, things move from being less complex (less order) to more complex (more order), evolution is said to violate a fundamental law of physics.

The problem is that the second law of thermodynamics applies to isolated objects or systems into which no energy is input. But if I freeze a glass of water, the water will indeed turn into ice. To do this requires the input of energy into the system (the glass with water in it) from outside it (e.g., from a freezer run by electricity), which means that the system is no longer isolated. While order (complexity) is increased in the glass, disorder increases outside the glass because heat is released into the atmosphere as the water and the glass freeze. Order is increased in one place (in the glass) at the cost of disorder being increased in another (the environment around the glass). The balance sheet equals out. The second law is not violated. Indeed, this is a textbook example of how it works.

Furthermore, evolution does not actually operate to move organisms from less complexity to more (as in the move from worms to humans) in any simple sense. It operates at an entirely different level. Evolution operates in small steps. A species with fur can evolve less fur or even no fur over time if its environment turns warmer. A species with little or no fur can evolve fur over time if its environment grows colder.

The first evolution, from lots of fur to little or none, seems like a move from more complexity to less, but in reality it is hard to say which state is "more complex." They are just different. Indeed, breeders of cats and dogs can do this "fur trick," playing the role of the "selector" in natural selection (a role usually played by "nature" as it doles out life and death). Blind cavefish that have lost their eyes in an evolutionary process also seem to have moved from more complexity to less. It is true, in some sense, that over long stretches of time evolution gives rise to more complexity, but this issue is complicated, because evolution really gives rise to diversity.

Creationism is, at least when it engages in arguments like the one above (and then it is often called "intelligent design theory"), a Pseudo Empirical Story. Such arguments are specious, built on misunderstanding, fantasy, or even lies. How dangerous "intelligent design theory" is I do not know. It can surely retard the growth of scientific literacy, but obviously it has not had anything like the bad effects of, for example, the eugenics Pseudo Empirical Stories of the sort peddled by Hitler and his ilk. Perhaps it has even had some benign effects if it has made its believers seek to make their behavior more humane, though I know of no evidence for this. Nonetheless, it seeks to play an empirical game it cannot win. The best mental comfort stories do not do this. They stay out of the empirical domain (the domain of falsifiable facts) altogether.

Before we take up the question of why people believe Pseudo Empirical Stories, sometimes passionately, we need to turn to an example of a Pseudo Empirical Story that is more audacious than intelligent design theory. It will give us insight into why people are attracted to Pseudo Empirical Stories.

Our example here is a Pseudo Empirical Story that I will call the Anglo-Israel Story. The Anglo-Israel Story states that the ten lost tribes spoken of in the Bible are actually the Anglo-Saxon race. Thus, Anglo-Saxons are the true

Israelites and the true chosen people of God, the real heirs to His covenant. The people who are living in Israel today are imposters. They call themselves "Jews" and they think they are Israelites, but they are, in fact, the descendants of Judah, not Jacob/Israel. They are not God's chosen people. They are not part of God's covenant as laid out in the Old Testament. They have no right to the Holy Land.

The Anglo-Israel Story is not new. It has been around for quite a long time, at least since the nineteenth century, and in some forms even before that. It was aggressively advocated by Henry Ford as part of his anti-Semitic campaign. In the twentieth century it was popularized by Herbert Armstrong and, later, his son Garner Ted Armstrong, both well-known Christian evangelists. The story has some interesting effects. It allows people who are often anti-Semitic to claim they are no such thing because in reality *they* are the real Jews. It is *they* who will inherit the Promised Land and the blessings of God, not the so-called Jews.

In true Pseudo Empirical Story form, the Anglo-Israel Story appeals to "historical facts" to "prove" its claims. But before we look at some of these "facts," we ought to ask why the story in the New Testament, which says that Jesus made all people the *spiritual* inheritors of the promises God made to Abraham, is not enough. Many people believe, after all, that is really the whole point of the New Testament and why there is a "new" one at all. For people who are taken by the Anglo-Israel Story, being the spiritual heir to God's promise is too metaphorical. They must be the literal, genetic, actual heirs, the real Jews. And for that they need "facts," since these are historical and genealogical matters that can be investigated and tested empirically. On the other hand, Christ's claim that he will see to it that his father will take care of us all cannot be empirically falsified (or, at least, not in this life) and is not a Pseudo Empirical Story.

So what sorts of "facts" does the Anglo-Israel Story appeal to? Let's look at some. In the seventh and eighth centuries BC, the Babylonian and Assyrian occupations of Israel resulted in the deportation of the northern ten tribes from Israel. The Anglo-Israel Story claims that everyone was deported. No one was left behind. No one ever came back. They all moved west and eventually established a new homeland in the British Isles. This means that present-day British, British Canadians, and British Americans are the direct and actual descendants of the real Israelites. They are thus God's chosen people and the proper inheritors of God's covenant with Abraham—literally, not just spiritually and metaphorically.

The story claims that the daughter of the last king of Judah (King Zedekiah) went to Europe and there established the throne of David in Ireland (Jeremiah 43:4–7 is used as proof for this claim). In fact, the story claims that the prophet Jeremiah went with her to Ireland. The Stone of Scone (sometimes called the Stone of Destiny or the Coronation Stone) has been used as a coronation stone for the British monarchy for centuries. The Anglo-Israel Story claims that this is the stone used in the coronation of King David and that it is also the rock pillow that the Old Testament figure Jacob (Isaac's son and Abraham's grandson) used when he saw his visions as described in Genesis 28:10–12. The story says that this is why the stone is also sometimes called Jacob's Pillow. To give an example from one account:

The significance of the Stone of Destiny is deeply rooted in Bible prophecy, for the stone is thought to carry God's blessing upon those who possess it, and it was destined to follow God's people on their long journey through time. The story behind the stone is nearly 4000 years old, but the Stone of Destiny still plays an important role in modern history. This ancient stone, also called "Jacob's Pillow," was just another stone lying on the desert floor, until one night in 1950 BC when Jacob used it as his pillow while sleeping during a trip from Harab to Bethel. While sleeping on the stone, Jacob dreamed of a great ladder leading up to heaven with angels climbing up and down it. In the dream, God spoke to Jacob, telling him that his children would be a blessing unto the world.

When Jacob arose in the morning, he took this holy stone along with him on his trip, and thus the stone began it's *[sic]* long journey through time. According to Bible legend, the Stone of Destiny will witness the coronation of every ruler of God's blessed people until the Lord's return. The location of the stone remained a mystery for many centuries, until it was finally located in Britain. The story of how the stone ended up in Britain is a very interesting one, and is centered around the biblical prophet Jeremiah. It is said that around 580 BC, during the sacking of Jerusalem, the prophet Jeremiah removed the stone from the holy temple in Jerusalem and fled with it to Egypt accompanied by Tea Tephi, the daughter of King Zedekiah of Jerusalem. Jeremiah then sailed to Ireland, where Tea Tephi was wedded to the Irish king, Eochaide the Heremon, thus preserving the ancient bloodline of David upon a world throne.

From that time until the present, no British monarch could be seated on the British throne unless the Stone of Destiny was present at the coronation ceremony.

Proponents of the Anglo-Israel Story also use linguistic claims in support of it. For example, they claim that the name "Isaac" (Abraham's son) is related (via removing the letter *i*) to the word "Saxon," which they take to have been derived from "saacson" (meaning "Isaac's son"). And, of course, Isaac's son is Jacob, whose stone pillow supposedly lay beneath the British coronation throne. Another example: it is noted that *berith* is the Hebrew word for covenant and *ish* is the Hebrew word for man. By combining the two words, the word *Berith-ish* (Covenant Man) is derived, giving the basis for the word "British."

I could go on. The Anglo-Israel Story has been around so long, surfacing at times and going underground at other times, that it is replete with "facts" and "evidence" and "arguments," all of which sound good. But they are no such thing. They are all completely spurious and easily refuted by anyone who takes even a small amount of time to look them up in reputable sources.

For example, "Isaac" is the Latin form of the Hebrew name "Yitschak." Isaac is not a Hebrew name and could not be. While it is possible with word play to see the word "Saxon" in the word "Isaac," it is not so easy to do so with the name "Yitschak," Isaac's real name in the Bible. Actual historical scholarship, genetic research, and linguistics as an academic field do not support any of the claims of the Anglo-Israel Story. It is pseudo history, genetics, and linguistics. But that is its point: It is meant to sound good to people who know nothing and do not care to find out. It is meant for people who want to believe that their religious, ideological, and some-times racist beliefs are "literally" and factually true, not just metaphorical or spiritual claims.

The Anglo-Israel Story is just an example, though it is a story that has had a long and pernicious life. The world is full of Pseudo Empirical Stories. The recent story claiming that President Obama was not born in the United States is one example. This is a Pseudo Empirical Story promulgated by the so-called Birthers. It, too, is replete with empirical-like claims, none of which have any actual evidential support. To believe the story, we would have to believe that people faked evidence and documents from the time of Obama's birth in Hawaii, planning all along to make him president. This would have been an audacious plan, indeed, on the part of people who must have seen far into the future to know that a relatively poor black man raised initially by a single mother could become president. At least they were racially optimistic (but then Obama isn't black any more than he is white, since he is half of each, but that is another story).

It was—and is—not enough for the Birthers to claim Obama is "un-American" because he is black, liberal, urban, has visited Africa, once lived in Indonesia, or is an Ivy League "elite." All these things are not literal enough. Obama *has* to be really not an American; he *could not* be a *real* American.

Pseudo Empirical Stories appeal to people who have literal minds. They appeal to people who want literal truth as a total reassurance that their deeply held beliefs are actually true. And this can be any one of us if we are made desperate enough by actual or deeply felt dispossession, despair, fear, confusion, anger, or no real access to, or desire to have access to, actual facts. It is an irony that while the human mind is not really inspired by the grubby and often disappointing business of investigating actual facts and appealing to empirical data, it is deeply taken (and taken in) by arguments that sound empirical and "facts" that sound good and are too perfect for one's purposes actually to be true.

It should be said that Pseudo Empirical Stories flourish in the absence of genuine education. This does not mean that those who believe such stories have not been to school. Most of them have. And, of course, some people promulgate such stories out of self-interest and greed without actually believing them. We will have to take up later the issue of what would constitute a "genuine education." It is an important question, one of the most important we could ask today.

Pseudo-Empirical Stories are a very fascinating mental and social pathology. But there is a much more widespread mental and social pathology endemic to humans: our strong tendency not just to advantage our kin, but to invent kin and advantage them as well. This pathology has led to lots of stupidity, corruption, death, and destruction, and we turn to it in the next chapter.

12

Imagined Kin

IN THE LAST CHAPTER WE DISCUSSED AN IMPORtant pathology of the human mind, the need to tell and believe Pseudo Empirical Stories. Here we will discuss another pathology, the desire to bond with others who we believe are "like us" even to the detriment of other people. Bonding with others is, of course, a good thing. But it has forms that are pathological because they readily lead to greed, corruption, hatred, and disdain for others.

All humans feel a bond with kin. The basis of this feeling is undoubtedly biological. People who are biologically related share genes with each other. However, all societies have gone beyond biology in defining who constitutes kin. Marriage allows non-kin (an "outsider") to enter a family and become a legal or socially sanctioned kin. Humans often treat close friends as if they were kin. And some ethnic groups and even some countries have tried to tell their members that they are all kin, related in the long-ago past in terms of their origins. This creates wider fields of bonding and mutual help in a group. It allows humans to define insiders ("us") against outsiders ("them"), something that is helpful in times of war, but not necessarily at other times.

Just as our immune systems can tell "us" (our bodies' cells) from "not us" (molecular invaders of our bodies), so, too, we humans can and want to tell who is "one of us" or "like us" from those not "one of us," not "like us." However, this sense of who is and who is not "us" can be manipulated by social and cultural processes and systems to include or exclude more or fewer people.

It is in this way that "white people" become a group of "people like us" (fictional kin) and "black people" become another such group, even though there is more genetic variation within these groups than there is across them.

The reason, by the way, that groups that might seem biological (like white, black, or Jewish) are not is that they have interbred with "outsiders" so much over history, even though they may deny it in their stories. President Obama counts as "black" not because he shares any more genes with blacks than he does with whites (he does not), but because of a kin-like category ("black") made up by and enforced by society.

Any society faces a major problem: humans will, all things being equal, favor themselves and their kin (the people they view as "one of us"), but a society needs people to cooperate with others—and to have respect and regard for others—who are not their kin, not "one of us." This is why societies sometimes make up stories that everyone in them is "related," shares a common origin, and is, in some deep past, all biological kin. Of course, there are other ways to seek such cooperation, such as laws, force, or the creation of non-kin groups that seek to recruit people's loyalties in terms of shared goals (e.g., passionate environmentalists or free-market proponents).

Society is never fully successful at this. In all societies we know, greed and corruption are common. People at all levels of a society, if left to their own devices, will often favor themselves and their kin group, or the people they feel are "like them," over others. There are certainly individuals who are just simply greedy and corrupt. However, most humans are, when being greedy and corrupt, actually trying to advantage not just themselves but their families and others they consider "one of us." In fact, at some level, they will often tell themselves that what they are doing is not being greedy or engaging in corruption so much as fulfilling their obligations to themselves and their families.

Now it is certainly the case that humans can and often do "feel bad" when they hurt others, even others who are not related to them. It is also the case that few humans take pride in being seen as greedy, corrupt, and harmful to others. To alleviate such feelings, humans often define their actions, which others might see as greedy and corrupt, as, in reality, actions in support of "their people," a group they often define as superior to others.

The old Irish mayors of Boston, especially the immortal James Michael Curley, who once ran the city from jail, are excellent examples. They saw themselves as social service agencies and support systems for a group of people (Irish immigrants) who did not receive respect or help from the "elites" who looked down on them. In the name of such a higher goal of aiding (extended) kin, they could see what others saw as corruption in different terms. The deathbed scene in Edwin O'Connor's great novel *The Last Hurrah,* which is based on the life of James Michael Curley, says it all (there is a good movie adaptation as well, made in 1958, directed by John Ford and starring Spencer Tracy). I don't want to spoil the novel or the movie for you, but the old mayor makes it clear on his deathbed that he would have done nothing different and is dying with a clear conscience.

Humans have a great capacity to form and re-form in their minds who counts as "one of us," the people whose interests take precedence over others for them. Humans are also quite capable of changing sides and switching allegiances. They can move from seeing one group as "people like me" to seeing another group that way and even come to disdain the earlier group. In extreme cases that earlier group can even be one's biological family.

The human capacity to believe in groups of kin defined as "people like us" can even transcend biological relatedness altogether. Many a member of a religious group has come to see family as "false" and their fellow members as "true family." Consider this quote from the Gospel of Matthew 10:35–39 where Christ says the following (from the New Living Translation):

35   I have come to set a man against his father,

       a daughter against her mother,

       and a daughter-in-law against her mother-in-law.

36   Your enemies will be right in your own household!

37   If you love your father or mother more than you love me, you are
      not worthy of being mine; or if you love your son or daughter
      more than me, you are not worthy of being mine.

38   If you refuse to take up your cross and follow me, you are not
      worthy of being mine.

39   If you cling to your life, you will lose it; but if you give up your
      life for me, you will find it.

While it is unlikely that the historical Jesus said this, it is nonetheless in a canonical book of the New Testament and captures the common tendency for religions to define their members as "family" or "people like us" even against biological kin or others who are not believers.

Let's use the term "imagined kin group" for any group someone sees as people "like me" (people with whom they feel bonded and to whom they feel obligated in some sense) when the group goes beyond actual biological or legal kin. So, in the passage from Matthew above, Christ is speaking in the name of an imagined kin group: all of his followers. According to this passage, this imagined sense of relatedness and mutual obligation transcends biological and family relationships.

Political appeals to "real Americans," usually rural or small-town Americans, is an attempt to get people to accept and act on (at least in terms of voting) an imagined kin group. Hitler's claim about a Nordic super race was a blatant attempt to get people across different countries and languages to see themselves as imagined kin. So, too, appeals to "Western people," "Islamic people," "born-again Christians," or "Southerners" are sometimes attempts to create an imagined kin group. People will then die in the name of "Western culture," "Islam," "Christianity," or "the South," defending their "own," just as they would fight to defend their families.

Imagined kin groups need not be pathological. Indeed, lots of work in the world gets done via such groups. But such groups can readily turn pathological when people feel threatened, lack a sense of agency and control, or are manipulated by media and politicians to divide themselves from others. Humans have a strong tendency to define their humanity in terms of the groups to which they belong.

The human mind is made in such a way that it is heavily prone to thinking in terms of binary distinctions or dichotomies. People tend to define who is "like us" in opposition to those people who are not. They readily engage in "us" versus "them" thinking. Since they partially define their own humanity or sense of human worth in terms of the groups that are "us," they can easily slide into viewing those who are "them" as less human or, at least, less worthy.

None of this is news to anyone. We are all well aware that people like Hitler tried to divide Aryans as "us" from Jews as "them." Such dramatic examples, however, can hide from us less dramatic, but still damaging, appeals to imagined kin groups or groups with shared interests.

Imagined kin groups can become dangerous when the people in them isolate themselves from critique and different perspectives. It is, perhaps, all right for a group to fight for its shared interests and values or defend itself from perceived threats. But the situation becomes problematic when and if they cease to allow multiple opinions and perspectives. When a group contains too little diversity in opinions and perspectives and seals out the viewpoints of contrasting groups, they can polarize and come to share extreme and quite narrow views. This makes it all the easier for people in such a group to engage, without guilty consciences, in manipulation and underhanded tactics on their own behalf against the interests of others.

What polarizes a group and makes its members reject multiple perspectives and critique? One thing that can do it is a feeling of being oppressed or not appreciated, of being "cheated" of their rightful due. Another is when, for some reason, voices and viewpoints from outside the group are sealed off and go unheard. Little or no outside input comes into the group to refresh it and challenge it. And, of course, politicians, media, and various "special interest groups" can manipulate people to feel oppressed or cease to listen to others.

In the politics of the United States, so-called working-class people once bonded in unions in terms of their shared economic interests in fair wages and job benefits. Unions became, for some, kin-like groups. Thanks to the clout of unions, working-class people in the United States saw themselves as middle class and, indeed, for all practical purposes, were.

Today, unions have been greatly weakened by the global competition for jobs. Working people now often labor for poor wages with no benefits. Indeed, some people have argued that we are entering a new age of serfdom as companies bid down wages and benefits to the lowest possible level by moving jobs overseas and encouraging politicians to remove regulations and protections for workers. Workers today face a shortage of good jobs and little help from unions. One would have expected that, in the face of such shared economic woes and oppression, workers would bond together to demand better pay and a great share of the wealth of their country, a country that is progressively pooling wealth into an ever smaller share of the population. One would expect that workers would vote as a block against the interests of global corporations and the rich and for their own shared economic interests and even survival. But they actually do no such thing.

Just as global competition began to erode workers' wages and protections, they were addressed by politicians and the media as if it were their cultural and religious values, not their wages and benefits, that were under attack by "elites." They were told that they should see themselves as bonded around these cultural and religious issues—and vote accordingly—not around their economic interests connected to things like jobs going overseas and unions dying.

In turn, they were told that people who advised them to fight for their economic interests were "socialists" or anti-capitalists. They were encouraged to think and act as though cultural and religious conservatives, not their fellow low-wage workers, were their imagined kin group. In turn, they voted for conservative politicians who had sent their jobs overseas, destroyed their unions, and enriched corporate and financial industry elites. Whether you like unions or not, this would seem to be "stupid" from the point of view of people who have lost their jobs or are working at several and are still below the poverty line.

Workers and the diminished US middle class are told that giving more wealth and tax breaks to the very rich will make money and jobs "trickle down" from the top to their level and eventually enrich them. There is really no good reason to believe this. Little actual evidence supports this view. You would at least expect working-class and middle-class people to offer a trickle-up theory in the name of their own interests. But they do not.

It is often hard to tell whether members of a group see each other as "one of us" because they really share a common fate or because they have been manipulated by other groups to think so. Is the real common problem that working people share in the United States economic extinction or cultural extinction? Is the right to a living wage less important than the right to carry guns or to keep mosques out of their towns? I have shown how I feel about the claim that working-class people should bond more over cultural and religious issues than economic ones. But others will disagree with me. They will say this is not manipulation, but a discovery by working people themselves of their own "real interests." We will have to argue, appeal to evidence, and be willing to change our minds, but in a heavily polarized society like ours today, that is just what we won't do.

All people share a great many different interests with others over which they could bond. How they judge or are manipulated to judge which of these are predominant enough, at a certain time and place in history, to constitute an imagined kin group is a question for deep research. And, of course, the constitution of a group can represent, at one and the same time, people's sincere judgments and manipulation from others.

Having conceded all that, it is nonetheless clear that whom humans perceive as imagined kin is crucial for the health of society. When people come to see others in ways that harm their own very real interests or allow them to engage, with no moral qualms, in underhanded tactics and corruption in the name of group survival and solidarity, society loses its cohesion, and is in danger of disintegrating into tribal wars in which some tribes will be manipulated by others to fight on the wrong side. In the end, the "last man standing" may be, in the United States, a small group of very wealthy people, the winners in a winner-take-all society. This is a very privileged and elite imagined kin group indeed.

In the Gospel of St. Luke (10:25–37) Christ tells the famous parable of the Good Samaritan. I reprint it below (translation from the New International Version):

25   On one occasion an expert in the law stood up to test Jesus. "Teacher," he asked, "what must I do to inherit eternal life?"

26   "What is written in the Law?" he replied. "How do you read it?"

27   He answered, "'Love the Lord your God with all your heart and with all your soul and with all your strength and with all your mind'; and, 'Love your neighbor as yourself.'"

28   "You have answered correctly," Jesus replied. "Do this and you will live."

29   But he wanted to justify himself, so he asked Jesus, "And who is my neighbor?"

30   In reply Jesus said: "A man was going down from Jerusalem to Jericho, when he was attacked by robbers. They stripped him of his clothes, beat him and went away, leaving him half dead.

31   A priest happened to be going down the same road, and when he saw the man, he passed by on the other side.

32   So too, a Levite, when he came to the place and saw him, passed by on the other side.

33   But a Samaritan, as he traveled, came where the man was; and when he saw him, he took pity on him.

34   He went to him and bandaged his wounds, pouring on oil and wine. Then he put the man on his own donkey, brought him to an inn and took care of him.

35   The next day he took out two denarii and gave them to the innkeeper. 'Look after him,' he said, 'and when I return, I will reimburse you for any extra expense you may have.'"

36   "Which of these three do you think was a neighbor to the man who fell into the hands of robbers?"

37   The expert in the law replied, "The one who had mercy on him." Jesus told him, "Go and do likewise."

The Jews despised the Samaritans and looked down on them despite the fact that they were historically related to the Jews and practiced a very similar religion. The Samaritans claimed that their religion was the true religion of the ancient Israelites prior to the Babylonian exile, as opposed to Judaism, which they viewed as a related but somewhat changed religion brought back by those returning from exile. The Jewish people listening to Jesus would have been quite shocked to hear him speak of a Samaritan in a positive way.

Jesus was saying that the Samaritan saw correctly who was his "kin," and the Jewish people who passed by the man in need of help were misled when they saw no kinship with Samaritans or the needy man in the ditch, a man who may or may not have been Jewish. The Samaritan could cross the Samaritan-Jewish divide and see who was kin, who deserved help, in a more expansive way. Jesus leaves it vague whether the man in the ditch was Jewish or not. He thereby suggests that it does not matter and that, in the end and when we are in need, we are all kin.

In the next chapter we will see a new fad that tells us we are not all kin, but, rather, that each of us is a very special island. Modern digital technologies are leading to a proliferation of customization wherein we all get what we want, how we want it, when we want it, with the least hassle (if we can afford it). We can all be in "Schools for One." However, we have argued throughout this book that one can be a lonely and stupid number for us humans when we are left alone to "be me" and "do it my way."

Lonely Groups of One

HATING AND FIGHTING IN THE NAME OF IMAGINED kin groups is an old pathology for humans. In this chapter, we will discuss another old problem. This is a problem that has become much worse in the face of new technologies.

Over the last decade I have worked on research on how video games can be used to create good learning. I got into this because I played a game for children called Pajama Sam with my then six-year-old son Sam. I wondered what a video game for adults would be like. So I bought one and played it. I was simply amazed by how long and how hard it was. I was amazed, too, that people paid good money for this degree of difficulty in the name of entertainment.

I came, after much frustration and persistence, to love playing video games, games like Half-Life, Deus Ex, The Elder Scrolls, Rise of Nations, Halo, Grand Theft Auto, Chibi-Robo, and From Dust. I came to understand that such games are problem-solving spaces. As such, they must do a good job at teaching the player to master the problem-solving skills necessary to play and win the game. But, more importantly here, such video games are designed to challenge players and make them work hard to succeed.

One problem video game designers have, however, is a tendency seemingly inborn in human beings to optimize their chances of success. Gamers will often seek all possible advantages and use any tactics they can to win. They will, for example, engage in what gamers call "cheats." Cheats are pieces of code or hacks that can make the game easier or advantage the player in some way. The problem is this: gamers will often seek to optimize their chances of success up to the point where they undermine the game's design and even ruin the game by making it too easy.

Good game designers encourage optimization up to a point, as a creative and proactive activity of the gamer. However, they must forestall it from undermining the game and ruining the player's experience. It is a tricky balance and part of the art of good game design.

This human urge to optimize is, of course, old, and it applies much more widely than just to video games. Faced with significant challenges in the "state of nature," humans who survived were good optimizers. They did all they could to increase their chances of success (survival) and lower the level of difficulty they faced. Those who did not optimize in this way were selected out of the gene pool for good Darwinian reasons. In the state of nature, one could optimize only so far. The level of difficulty always remained high. One could not cheat death. Ultimately, every human "lost" the game.

Modern technologies allow the human urge to optimize and lower the level of challenge full rein and near endless application. In modern times, the human urge to optimize takes the form of customization. Modern technologies increasingly allow each of us, if we wish, to customize many things to fit with our skills, styles, desires, and beliefs in such a way as to leave us less challenged and feeling more "successful." This process goes ever forward with each new technological advance.

For example, today there are adaptive artificial (computer-based) tutors to teach algebra. Based on how the learner is faring, these tutors (which do quite well) customize presentation, problems, and the order of problems to each individual learner. They can also be equipped with sensors that tell the system when the learner is bored, confused, or frustrated, and adapt instruction accordingly. Each learner proceeds based on his or her favored style of learning in a way that lowers the level of frustration as far as possible. Artificial tutors do not care where you start, how long you take to finish, or how smart or stupid your initial answers are. They are far more tolerant than most humans.

There is nothing wrong with, and lots right about, such artificial tutors. They are just one device among many that seek to transform education into "a school of one." But they represent a perfecting of the human urge to optimize that can go too far and end with bad consequences. People who never confront challenge and frustration, who never acquire new styles of learning, and who never face failure squarely may in the end become impoverished humans. They may become forever stuck with who they are now, never growing and transforming, because they never face new experiences that have not been customized to their current needs and desires.

There is, in fact, an organization called School of One. Here is what they say about their approach:

School of One learns about the specific academic needs of every student and then accesses a large bank of carefully reviewed educational resources, using sophisticated technology to find the best matches among students, teachers, and resources.

School of One's learning algorithm helps to ensure each student is learning in his or her educational "sweet spot." As it collects data, it learns more about the students and becomes more effective at predicting the playlist that will be most effective for each.

I am sure (sort of) that all this is fine, though I wonder what happens when people with different "sweet spots" have to learn, solve problems, and collaborate with others who have different "sweet spots," as people so often have to do in modern workplaces. I wonder what would happen should, God forbid, children run into learning situations in the world that cannot be optimized for them individually. What if the world changes and the problems that arise just do not afford solutions that fit their sweet spot? What if their sweet spot is just no good for certain types of learning and problem solving?

In any case, we can use digital tools to create not just Schools of One, but, as odd as it may sound, "Groups of One." Let me hasten to explain. In the last chapter we discussed imagined kin groups. There is another, usually less intense, form of human bonding that is common, namely sharing interests with others. Humans can see themselves as members of groups not in terms of kin-like bonding, but in terms of common shared interests, values, and experiences. I will call these "shared interest groups."

For example, as a long-time academic, I see other academics, in some respects, as "like me," sharing with me certain interests and ways of being in the world. Academics are a shared interest group for me. The same is true for me of bird watchers, gamers, and lovers of nature, as well as other groups.

There is always a problem of level here. Is it just linguists who are "like me," share my interests and values, or is it even just discourse analysts, a subgroup of linguists? Is it social scientists? Or is it all academics? Is it academics as researchers or teachers whom I feel camaraderie with, or both? What about academic administrators like deans and provosts—do they count as academics?

People are often willing to die for both real and imagined kin groups, but they are rarely ready to sacrifice their lives for their shared interest groups. This does not mean, by the way, that they are not willing to favor such groups by behaviors that others might find greedy and corrupt. Furthermore, if circumstances force people in a shared interest group into an embattled common cause, and if they come to feel deeply challenged and oppressed, they can mutate into an imagined kin group for which they will fight and die.

For example, as the earth is increasingly destroyed, people who are "lovers of nature" will more and more fight alongside each other in the name of the earth and come to feel a sense of bonding, camaraderie, and kinship. Edward Abbey's novels capture this sense of shared interests carrying over into imagined kinship in the name of fighting for the environment quite well. Amy Waldman's wonderful novel *The Submission* captures perfectly how an

American Islamic architect comes to feel kinship with other Islamic people (heretofore, at best, a shared interest group for him) only after he is attacked for being Islamic by people who assume he must feel such kinship even when he does not.

Today, digital media allow an unbelievable proliferation of shared interest groups. If a small number of people across the world have a very rare disease, in the past they could never have found each other, and their common interest in finding a cure could never have been pooled. Today, they can find each other via the Internet. They can start a group, relate to each other in terms of their shared interests, and agitate for their cause.

It is close to impossible to name a group that has not formed an interest-driven shared space on the Internet, spaces that sometimes spill over into real life. For example, to test this point, I tried to think of something odd and Googled it. I came up with avocado carving. Well, I found sites devoted to decorative avocado carving and sites devoted to carving avocado pits for art. I found sites that expanded this interest to "vegetable carving" more generally. There was even, at least for a while, an avocado carving friends group on Facebook.

The Internet allows each person to join shared interest groups that fit their sweet spots. You can customize what you see and whom you interact with in as fine a way as you like. You can, if you want, ensure that you never see or hear viewpoints you do not like or face people who do not share your values, interests, and viewpoints. You can customize your politics, just as you can customize everything else, and always hear arguments you already agree with and news reports that never venture far from or challenge your worldview. You can also do this via television, thanks to cable news.

This phenomenon of carving out the groups that are "like us" and do not violate our sweet spots for politics, interests, and activities goes on in the world outside the Internet as well. People can, and more and more do, live, shop, and interact only in spaces filled with "people like them," people who share their views on politics, the environment, and how to behave and live.

Shared interest groups can get ever more specialized. I can leave the neo-conservative fundamentalist Christian political group, from which I have been getting most of my news of late, to join an even "better" neo-conservative fundamentalist Christian end-times-centered rapture-focused anti-environmental group (Who cares about the environment anyway, since the elect will all soon be gone to heaven?). If no such group exists (don't worry—it does), I can start one myself.

When people join groups or live in spaces in which everyone around them agrees with them and shares the same values, people start to polarize and develop extreme versions of their values and beliefs. Within groups, since everyone is alike, the only way to gain distinction, to stand out from the crowd, is to embrace extreme viewpoints. Groups splinter as interests, values, and beliefs become ever more extreme or customized. In the end we get Groups of One, not in the sense that they contain only one person, but in the sense that they contain only one kind of person.

Why is this a problem? Why isn't it a good thing that each person and group can "do their own thing"? The essential issue here is the health of the public sphere. The public sphere is composed of all those spaces in a society where all people are welcome and belong just because they are all parts of the "public"—members of the society at large—and not just because they are members of specific subgroups of that society. In any society there are restrictions on who counts as a member of the larger public. Perhaps, in one society, only Jews or Muslims count as members of the public, or perhaps only Orthodox Jews or Shiite Muslims. We can readily see that if the public sphere is restricted enough, it can become no more than a shared interest group.

In a healthy society diversity is honored because diverse people and viewpoints serve the same purpose as variation does in evolution. Such diversity expands the possibilities for new discoveries and survival in the face of change. A closed society, like a species with little genetic variation and too much inbreeding, is doomed.

In a society like the United States, the public sphere is meant not to be segregated by class, race, gender, sexual orientation, ability, or religion; since people of different classes, races, genders, sexual orientations, abilities, and religions all together constitute the "public" in the United States, the pool of variation gives us hope that we will always be able to adapt to change. When people seek to avoid such public sphere spaces, when they seek to segregate themselves with others "like them" and not see themselves as vital members of the "public" with others, then the public sphere is diminished and may, for all practical purposes, disappear.

Today, many Americans seek to avoid the public sphere. They send a "runner" to the Department of Motor Vehicles, or they use the Internet, so they do not have to stand in line with their fellow citizens. They avoid channels of communication where they would have to argue and debate, rather than just demonize, people who disagree with them and have very different life experiences. They drive through parts of town they don't like (meaning they don't like the people in them) to get quickly to those parts filled with people like themselves. This process has gone so far in the United States that words like "public park," "public bathroom," "public space," and "public meeting" have, for many people, a somewhat negative connotation.

A rich person in Concord, Massachusetts, feels more camaraderie with rich people in other such wealthy and beautiful suburbs across the country (maybe even the world) than he or she does with working-class or poor people in post-industrial Worcester, Massachusetts, and vice versa. Such working class people no longer seem to count as "fellow citizens," fellow members of a public sphere with whom the rich vote and argue to solve the state's or the nation's problems collaboratively.

Beyond the public sphere there is also the concept of global citizenship. This concept involves seeing oneself as a member of all humanity, regardless of where in the world that humanity resides. It involves seeing all humans as citizens with rights and responsibilities in a global, pan-human world. Today, ironically, it is easy to join global groups with quite specific interests and shared sweet spots. In terms of such groups, even people in one's own country can come to seem more foreign than "foreigners." This is, of course, not global citizenship—not a global public composed of humanity—but, rather, a global customization of life.

The public sphere sees the world in expansive terms. The proliferation of "Groups of One" sees the world in ever more specific niches, lifestyles, belief enclaves, and "values communities." We come to get inbred groups filled with people who share all the same ideas, interests, and values. Like inbred animals, they are in danger of "retardation" and stupidity of the sort that may leave all of us with no real future. Muscles hurt a bit when we exercise outside our sweet spot. Minds bend a bit when we think outside our comfort zone. These are the signs of growth. If people optimize such "pain" away, they become stunted.

If one is often a lonely and stupid number for us humans, we can often get smart when we partner with smart tools and other people in well-coordinated and well-resourced teams facing a meaningful and complex challenge. But today, in an age of highly interacting and high-risk complex systems, an old friend is a new enemy: "the expert."

14

When Not to Trust Experts

IT IS OFTEN SAID THAT ONE AREA IN WHICH MANY humans are intellectually challenged is mathematics. Consider the mental addition problem below:

> What is one thousand plus forty?
> Now add another thousand to that,
> And thirty more,
> Plus one thousand,
> Plus twenty
> Plus a thousand,
> And finally an additional ten.

When they try to do this problem in their heads, the majority of people arrive at the answer 5,000. The correct answer is 4,100. When I first saw this problem, I did it in my head over and over again and always came up with the answer 5,000. I just could not see how it added up to 4,100. Many humans, me included, are not good at mentally keeping track of decimal places. In frustration, I picked up a pencil and did the problem on a piece of paper. Then I readily saw that the answer was 4,100 and was amazed at how clearly it had appeared to be 5,000 when I did it in my head rather than on paper. Now it was obvious that the answer was 4,100.

This shows, however, that humans are not bad at math. Indeed, they are good at math if you let them use a pencil or a calculator and don't ask them to do it all in their heads. The genius of human beings was and is the invention and use of tools to make themselves smarter. It is misleading to talk about human intelligence and think only of unaided humans. Humans are tool users. The real unit of analysis for intelligence ought often to be human + tool. If you want to know how much a human can lift, pair them with a forklift. If you want to know how much information they can store, pair them with a computer. If you want to know how far they can see, pair them with a telescope.

There is a name for the ways in which knowledge and ability can be shared between a human mind and a tool. It is called "distributed cognition." The ability to see far is distributed (shared) between the eye and the telescope; each does part of the job and together they are powerful. The knowledge of mathematics is shared between the human and the calculator, and they can be powerful together, as well.

Human + tool is a winning combination. Part of what makes humans stupid is being left alone without tools or without collaborations with other people (people can be "tools" for each other). In many cases, we can transform human performance when we invent a new tool to share the job with the human mind and body. Humans certainly can plow a field a lot better with a plow than with their hands. Because this is so, it would not be correct to claim humans are not good "plowers." They are good at inventing and using plows and so, in reality, humans are good "plowers."

The human ability to build tools really took off when we learned to build tools to build tools. We have machines to build machines. We have tools to build bridges, which are tools to move people across obstacles. We now even have tools to build artificial minds, computers than can engage in some forms of intelligence (e.g., teach algebra).

For all their good, there is one big danger with tools. When a tool is first developed, it very often splits the labor with the human, but the human retains the upper hand, so to speak. Furthermore, the human understands the tool and how it works, but the tool does not understand the human. When biologists invented machines to splice genes, it took a great deal of knowledge to build the machine; the scientist understood intimately how the machine worked, and a good deal of the knowledge of how to splice genes was still inside the scientist's head and not just inside the machine's workings. Today using a machine to splice genes is a fairly routine task that can be carried out by technicians.

As tools get better over time, they can take on more and more of the work. Operating the machine can become a routine task that does not require much knowledge about what the machine does and how it does it. The operator pushes buttons and follows procedures. The operator, whether or not he or she has a PhD, is just a technician. The human is contributing less and less knowledge and oversight, the machine is doing more and more of the task. What was once fairly well distributed, a team effort between human and machine, becomes mainly the machine, with a human assisting it. The human loses the upper hand.

Even more dramatically, perhaps, we can now build machines that understand humans and manipulate them. We have lost the upper hand in who understands who. No longer do humans necessarily understand their machines better than the machines understand them. An artificial tutor learns how a learner behaves and what the learner likes and then adapts to the learner, which is a form of leading the learner to water and persuading him to drink (something they say you cannot do with a horse). Companies are building smart products that can learn what we do and what we like and make suggestions about when we should exercise, what we should eat, or how we should handle our daily schedule and inbox of e-mails and messages. Pandora—which I am listening to as I write—can learn my taste in music and make a better radio channel for me than I could make for myself. Amazon.com's book recommendations to me are uncannily correct, including their claim that I will like, but not all that much, my own books.

These two effects—that tools come to do more of the work, leaving humans as mere aids, and that they can learn to cater to us and come to understand us better than we do ourselves—are both outcomes of the human urge to optimize that we discussed in the last chapter. We make the machine better and better in order to make ourselves more and more successful right up to the point where the machine is doing most of the work and we are learning little and serving as a mere adjunct to the machine.

The guy running the blood test needs to know little about blood. He just needs to know how to get the machine to offer up information that someone else (e.g., the doctor) understands better. Pandora customizes my music so well that I never confront a song I do not already like, and am in danger of learning nothing new about music. Sailors navigate a ship by complex nautical equipment, never once looking outside, and run the boat aground when the equipment malfunctions. We learn to use a compass at sea, but then can never find our way home again when it drops into the ocean. We take pills, but have no real idea what they do in our bodies. We turn on the tap, but have no idea where the water comes from and where it goes.

In another book, written with my wife, Elisabeth Hayes, we studied people designing virtual clothes, buildings, furniture, and environments for a video game named The Sims. The Sims is a virtual world in which players design and sustain a family and a community. The player can buy clothes, furniture, and houses in virtual stores in the game, but if players want to do it themselves (DIY), they can use design tools to build their own clothes, furniture, and houses. They can then use what they created in their games and even share them with others. The Sims is the best-selling video game in history and has over the years come out in newer and newer versions.

In the early versions of the game, players who wanted to design had to learn a good deal. They had to learn how to use software like Adobe Photoshop and other equally complex pieces of software. There was a learning curve. Players were using tools like Photoshop, but these tools required that users still learned and retained a good deal of knowledge about images, vision, and design and a good deal of understanding of how Photoshop worked. Knowledge was really distributed pretty evenly between players and tools. However, as newer editions of the game came out, the game's designers made in-game building tools more and more user friendly. The tools became easier and easier for players to use without learning a good deal and without knowing how the tools really worked.

This had one good effect and one bad one. The good effect was that more people could design and unleash their own creativity. The bad effect was that people needed to learn less and work less hard. It was harder, too, to earn status, since more people could now design well without a lot of learning and hard work.

People who built things like houses, clothes, and furniture for The Sims in the earlier days worked harder but gained transferable skills. If you learn Adobe Photoshop, for instance, you can do a lot more than design for The Sims. You can manipulate all sorts of images. If you learn Photoshop, you gain some skills that transfer to learning other types of complex image-manipulating software, such as various 3D design tools. However, the design tools in the later versions of The Sims are so "good," so user friendly and so customized for the game, that fewer skills transfer, though, of course, aesthetic ideas and values may well still transfer to other settings.

There is gain (more people being creative) and loss (less hard work, status, deep learning, and transferable skills). This tradeoff is typical of how tools work in many areas of our lives. As tools get better, more people can do more things, but we get less learning and fewer transferable skills (less "value added," we might say). However, this trade-off—this form of the human urge to optimize—holds a genuine danger for society. It creates deeper and deeper divisions by creating different "classes" of people with different "classes" of knowledge.

For any machine that has been around long enough—and therefore optimized—there are people who know how it works, why it works, and how it was designed. They know just what sorts of knowledge the machine is using and producing. Such people understand the "science" that went into the machine. They are what we might call "tech insiders" or even "tech priests."

Many more people just operate the machine or use its products. They do not know what it really does or what sorts of knowledge it is manipulating and producing. Such people are results oriented. They want the machine to do the work and give them the answers they want so they can get on with life. We can call such people the "tech outsiders" or even "tech laity." They are the lay people who have to trust that the tech priests know about the workings of the machine.

I take cholesterol pills, and every six months I have blood tests done to see how well they are working. I do not myself understand what cholesterol does, how the pills control it, or how blood tests determine how much "good" and "bad" cholesterol I have. I do not know how much of all this the person who does the blood test knows. Quite frankly, though I know my doctor knows more than me about these matters, I am not really sure how much be actually knows, since he seems just to read numbers off a piece of paper and tell me they are good or bad based on numbers in medical texts.

It is certainly good that all of us do not have to know everything and that we can (sometimes) trust machines and the tech priests who really understand the theories and knowledge behind them. But it can be dangerous, as well. I discovered, by reading on the Internet, that one of the two cholesterol pills I was taking had been implicated in strokes. Furthermore, in another source, I discovered that there was skepticism concerning whether, in actuality, this particular pill did much good at all in the way of lowering "bad" cholesterol. It seemed a no-brainer to me to stop taking it. When I consulted with my doctor, he readily found such information and took me off the pill, though neither he nor earlier doctors had bothered with the matter until I did.

As we use our machines and trust our "tech priests"—many of whom are themselves on their way to becoming just higher-level technicians following procedures—we become awash in trust that has no real foundation that we ourselves could cite. The priests become all-powerful because we have to trust them, even if they have conflicts of interest we know nothing about (e.g., selling a medical test that does not work as well as it should).

Computers are now so user friendly (no more DOS, for instance) that most people know little about how and why they work. We are forced to trust the priests at Microsoft, who, in turn, can then design products to manipulate us in the name of being "user friendly" and optimizing. Students have no idea how a textbook is produced and how well it represents knowledge. In reality, textbooks cover everything in little depth, reproduce errors from other textbooks they have cribbed from, and are often produced by people who do little or no real research in the area to which the textbook is devoted. Nonetheless, the student and the teacher trust the book, assuming that the publishers and authors have their best interests at heart.

The issue of relegating knowledge to machines and trusting tech priests becomes most acute, perhaps, in our social and political lives. We have no idea how polls work, how media function behind the scenes, or how voting machines, especially digital ones, actually work or even how or whether they can fail or be manipulated. The vast majority of Americans have absolutely no idea how the electoral college works or why it was designed, yet it (not the majority) elects the president. As we face ads that tell us there are technologies that produce "clean coal" or that "fracking" is a safe technology for mining natural gas, we have no idea how these technologies operate and whether these claims are true or false (by the way, they are both false).

Wall Street financiers purposely invented complex new investment tools (e.g., mortgages rolled into bonds, derivatives, collateralized debt obligations, credit default swaps, and arcane rating procedures) in hopes that such complexity would confuse investors and regulators into trusting them as priests of esoteric new financial knowledge. They did gain such trust and brought the world economy down in 2008. We all need to beware of the "priest" who tells us the machine (tool or technology) knows what it is doing because HE knows what HE is doing.

There is a deeper problem than just misplaced trust in self-interested priests selling us pills, derivatives, polls, and user-friendly software. There are legitimate priests, experts who do know the medical, biological, technical, or economic knowledge (or some other type of knowledge) inside the tools, machines, and technologies we use. They actually helped build the knowledge before it was ever in the machine. At one level they certainly deserve trust. They worked hard to gain their expertise; that expertise was vetted by other experts; and they do not always have vested interests beyond discovering knowledge and getting adulation for doing so. Nonetheless, even these "good guys" can go bad.

Experts are people certified by other experts who know a great deal about one relatively narrow area. The disciplinary names we use, labels like "economics," "biology," and "law"—are actually too broad to characterize an expert. Experts specialize in sub-parts of these larger domains. In biology, for example, they concentrate in molecular biology, genetics, ecology, ethology, embryology, or any of a great number of other specialties. They often define their expertise in even narrower terms; for example, mycology, the study of fungi.

Economics falls into two major branches, macroeconomics (about the national or global economy in general) and microeconomics (about smaller things such as how people make decisions about what to buy). Within each area there are hundreds of subspecialties in terms of which real experts define their expertise.

The good thing about experts is that they are narrowly focused and know a lot in depth. The bad thing about experts is that they are narrowly focused and know too little about the "big picture." They tend to trust what they know but underestimate what they do not know. This is not necessarily a big problem when experts stay in their labs and deal with systems that are not too complex. When they venture out into the world and deal with truly complex systems, their expertise can become dangerous.

Let's take one telling example. In 2008, the United States and much of the rest of the world entered the largest recession since the Great Depression that started in 1929. The global economic downturn was caused by complex financial practices centered in the United States. These practices allowed mortgage brokers to give mortgages (loans on houses) to people who could not, in fact, afford them and then sell the mortgages to investment banks (thereby passing on the risk that the person who took out the mortgage loan would default on payments to the bank; the brokers made their money on fees, not on the mortgage payments). The bank then took lots of these mortgages and rolled them into bonds that they sold to investors, who collected the mortgage payments (the bank, too, passed on the risk to others and made its money primarily from fees for its services).

An investor in Iceland might end up owning a mortgage on a house in California as part of many mortgages or pieces of them rolled into a bond. The relationship between the homeowner and the person who owned his or her mortgage was not local, but spread across a distance and a global world. In order to get investors to buy the rolled-up mortgages, banks encouraged rating agencies to give their bonds a high rating, which meant the investment was considered safe (when often they were not). When everyday people defaulted on their home payments, all at much the same time, the whole system collapsed. The last people or institutions holding the bonds lost and lost big. Many of them were countries, cities, and pension funds that had been "suckered" into being the last to hold the "hot potato" in the naïve (but cultivated) belief that the house of cards would not collapse.

The institutions that carried out these practices (brokerage firms, investment banks, rating agencies, regulators that did not properly regulate) claimed that they were all too complex and technical for everyday people, and even government regulators, to understand. We all had to trust their expertise as they got rich, and eventually most "everyday people" got poorer as the economy collapsed. The last institutions holding the "hot potato" (now called "toxic assets") at the end lost as well, but many of them were powerful enough to get bailed out by the government's taxpayer money.

We see here a complex set of relationships among institutions. It is a complex system with many interacting variables, unpredictable consequences, unintended consequences, and high risk for damage and harm. The world today is filled with risky complex systems and their results, like the environment and global warming, the global economy, global population growth, global cultural and religious conflicts, and outcomes of the interrelationships between man-made and natural systems (like the heat island effect in cities). Experts tell us they understand these things much better than we do, but things often get worse and the experts can't explain why they went wrong.

When the economy collapsed, Alan Greenspan, a man long considered the leading economic expert in the world, a long-time head of the Federal Reserve Bank in the United States, and the man who for many years set a good deal of US economic policy, said he had no idea why the collapse had happened, had never seen it coming, and could not explain it. His expertise had run dry. Greenspan told Congress that "Those of us who have looked to the self-interest of lending institutions to protect shareholders' equity, myself included, are in a state of shocked disbelief." Asked by Congress, "Do you feel that your ideology pushed you to make decisions that you wish you had not made?" Greenspan said, "Yes, I've found a flaw. I don't know how significant or permanent it is. But I've been very distressed by that fact."

If there was ever a vetted and adulated expert in economics, it was Alan Greenspan. A book about him by the famed reporter Bob Woodward was titled *Maestro*. Yet he led the world to economic disaster with great confidence. Today, in the face of complex systems, individual expertise is dangerous. Such experts undervalue what they do not know and overvalue what they do. They fail to integrate their knowledge well with the vast amount of other sources of knowledge that are necessary to deal with complex systems. Like Greenspan, they often have trouble telling apart what they know and what follows only from their ideology.

Understanding and dealing with the consequences of complex sys-tems requires pooling different types of expertise from different domains in a highly collaborative way. Going it alone is out of date and dangerous. Greenspan needed to collaborate with people who thought about history, human psychology (and greed), cultural changes (including in business), in-stitutional relationships, global economies and politics, and the sociology of human interactions within institutions. Economic theory by itself, especially as it resided just in the head of Alan Greenspan, was dangerous because it allowed Greenspan to account for too little of the big picture and to trust too much in his own expertise (and to ask everyday people for this same trust as well). Alan Greenspan, a very smart man, was stupid.

If tools can make us smart and experts can make us stupid, then we hu-mans, if we are to bear the burden of being smart (with others) must carry the heavy weight of knowledge with us as we go. We have to be willing to learn now what may not be useful until tomorrow. But we humans don't like to carry heavy things, whether they are physical or mental.

15

Evading Knowledge

EVERY CHAPTER IN THIS BOOK HAS DISCUSSED SITU-
ations in which human intelligence can easily run off the rails. We humans
can be made stupid in many different ways, ways that often combine to lead
to super stupidity. Why should this be so?

I believe there are two major reasons for this, two basic foundations for
why the human mind can so easily go awry in the modern world. One is
that humans are not oriented toward truth but to meaning. The second is
that humans do not like to carry heavy things around in their minds. Let's
take these in order. First, we will discuss the human tropism toward meaning
rather than truth.

Living organisms tend to move and grow toward positive stimuli and
away from negative ones (this is called "tropism"). For example, the stems
of plants move and grow toward the light. Light is a positive stimulus for
plant stems; it is necessary for their development. Stems growing toward the
light will expose their leaves to the sun so that photosynthesis can take place.
However, plant roots move and grow away from the light. Light is, for plant
roots, a negative stimulus. Roots growing down and away from light are more
likely to find the soil, minerals, and water they need for growth and survival.

Humans, all things being equal, move and grow toward meaning. Meaning is what nourishes their minds and souls. Even meaning without truth is a
positive stimulus for humans. Humans tend to orient away from truth when it
has no meaning for them. Truth without meaning does not nourish humans.

But in what sense am I using "meaning" here? This is a word with a great many different interpretations. What I intend when I say humans orient toward meaning and not truth is not some technical philosophical or linguistic concept of meaning. It is closer to an everyday sense of the word. By "meaning" I refer to the sort of thing we have in mind when we say things like: "This picture of my mother holds great meaning for me"; "Your gift was very meaningful to me"; "Life has lost its meaning for me"; "My wife means a great deal to me"; "My own daughter no long means anything to me."

Humans orient toward meaning in the sense that a person, thing, or event has significance and value within a story that gives their life and actions, and the world they live in, a purpose. For humans, meaning in this sense answers questions like "Who am I?," "Why am I here?," and "How am I part of something larger than myself?" This is why things like family, ethnic groups, and religions are so important to people. They give ready answers to these questions.

A picture of my mother is meaningful to me because it connects me to my past and to a story of my life that gives it some coherence and, at least partially, enables it to make sense in terms of a bigger picture. A gift may have special meaning to me because it tells me who someone else thinks I am in ways that I appreciate as part of, or adding to, my story of self. Religions allow people to see themselves as actors in a larger story with a long past and a bright future.

For humans, suffering and death are problems because they are very difficult to fit into a story of who I am, why I am here, and how I am part of something bigger than myself. Why was I born if I am just going to die? Why should I suffer when this suffering is nothing I would have chosen and in which I see no point or purpose? How can it be a meaningful part of my story if it is a matter of chance or fate, and not part of what I have chosen to do and be?

We humans try, in any way we can, to recoup suffering and death in ways that make them meaningful, that fill them with purpose, and make them parts of our stories that we can own and integrate with the other parts and not just see as matters of chance. If we cannot do this, we can become depressed or sick. Life can become "meaningless." We can feel small and insignificant.

It is true we are going to die. But being true does not make it meaningful in the sense in which I am using the term here. Humans will seek to make death meaningful right up to the point of denying it and believing they will live forever, though not, in the end, in this world. It is true we will all suffer loss and disappointment. But we will try with all our might to render them meaningful, happening "for a reason," part of a coherent story about ourselves and "people like us."

The human urge to find meaning is lifesaving and sometimes soul satisfying. But it can have all sorts of down sides. In a simple world, like the world of hunters and gatherers in which our minds evolved, this urge led to few problems and lots of good things. In a complex world, full of interconnected systems we humans have built (e.g., cities) or changed (e.g., the global climate), the urge can lead to disaster for us personally and for all of us together.

The human urge to find and create meaning is closely related to what we called in an earlier chapter mental comfort stories. In the search for meaning we humans will settle for cold comfort if it is all the meaning we can find, rather than live without meaning altogether. In the face of a tragic accident to which we cannot assign any really satisfying meaning or purpose, we still want to believe that it "happened for some reason" even if we cannot grasp what it is. If we lose in love, we can always say it was "better to have loved and lost than not to have loved at all." If we fail in our career, we can, at least, take (cold) comfort in the fact that "I did it my way" or "I gave it the old college try," so in a sense, I am still a "winner" after all.

When events happen that humans find unacceptably meaningless, their minds are built to seek out local causes, not global ones. If the economy turns bad and you lose your job, you need to make sense of this bad event that has befallen you. You do not immediately turn to global economics, financial risk taking, corporate fraud and corporate lobbying from which to spin a meaningful story. These are too abstract, complex, and distant. Rather, you look for more concrete and local causes.

Your boss has always had it in for you because you are smarter than he is. Other workers kissed up to the boss when you were too moral to do so. Your talents are so special they have never been properly recognized by mediocre minds. You should never have taken that last drink at the office party given how you behaved in front of the boss afterward; losing your job was a sign for you to finally seek help for your drinking.

There are many ways to give the event of losing your job meaning that are up-front and personal and can right your ego. Whether these "causes" are true or not, believing in them can still lead to some good, if only giving you the power to go on or the will to attend AA meetings.

Even if humans do turn to more abstract, complex, and global causes, they tend to personify them in terms of stories about good guys and bad guys. In such fertile ground conspiracy theories flourish. The traitorous liberals wrecked the economy by selling out to the minorities and the poor who just want a handout. A Jewish global cabal controls the world economy, or perhaps it is the Illuminati, the Masons, the Knights Templar, the Catholic Church, the Trilateral Commission, or the Koch brothers (if you don't know who the Koch brothers are, Google them). I myself find a Jewish Cabal or the Illuminati ridiculous, but I am not so sure about the Koch brothers.

We want our meaning local or at least filled with bad and good people doing bad and good things. Now, the world probably is filled with bad and good people doing bad and good things, but very often, in a complex world, solutions lie in understanding complex relations in interconnected systems, for example, how government regulation, lobbying, the legislative process, and markets interact and can be changed to give better and fairer outcomes.

Though we like to think of such complex systems in terms of colorful actors within them, such as the Koch brothers, these colorful actors are often just playing roles that would be readily filled by others if they disappeared, thanks to the way the system works. Furthermore, people often change their behaviors when systems, and thus incentive structures, change. Yet to change systems we have to convince people to change or, at least, to act. To do this, we sometimes have to get them to face "reality" and not just immerse themselves in stories that explain away problems they do not want to face squarely.

Those who like the Koch brothers much more than I do are going to say: "You yourself are not facing reality. You are, again, just showing your politics. You would advocate system changes (probably government regulations) that fit your ideology and liberal animosity toward the poor Koch brothers." Indeed, I would. But that is not what I am advocating here.

I am not claiming I have any better access to "reality" than anyone else. What I am advocating is that we all, at times, give up our stories and our search for meaning and purpose in terms of local causes and action-filled stories of bad and good human actors, and offer arguments and evidence for the changes we want, with an open mind that could conceivably be changed. This need is as great for liberals as it is for conservatives. It is the foundation of democracy. So, let's talk, Koch brothers. But while I will have to put my well-earned "class hatred" aside for a moment, you will have to put your money and power aside for a moment, and we will have to fight with evidence and argument, not just rhetoric, deception, and comforting stories that support our self-interest.

Unfortunately, humans do not find arguments and evidence very satisfying. They seem too cold and abstract and too frail in the face of power, hatred, and corruption. They just don't seem to be able to send people to the barricades. And they hold out the real possibility that we might discover that we are wrong about something that is closely related to our interests or things that give meaning to our lives, something humans have a very hard time with, indeed.

Argument and evidence are a game—a game we will discuss in a later chapter—that most of us, liberal or conservative, do not want to play. We often think we play it—no one likes to be heard saying "damn the evidence"—but we don't. We rarely seek actively to falsify our views, but that is the key move in the game of argument and evidence. This is as true of me as of you. It is true of the Koch brothers as well. And, to make matters worse, we have few forums today in which the argument and evidence game is or can be played in public.

So that is the first basic impetus of the human mind's ability to jump the rails and go off the cliff to stupidity: the urge to find meaning at all costs, even if the cost is truth. The second basic impetus is the human aversion to carrying heavy objects when they are mental objects. Humans have what I will call "mental bush consciousness."

In the "old days" Native Americans who had to go into the "bush" (the wilderness) to hunt and bring back food for the group had what Ron Scollon once referred to as "bush consciousness" as opposed to "modern consciousness." When you live off the bush, you have to travel light. You cannot take anything with you that will slow you down or restrict your movements. You do not carry stuff you are not going to use and use soon. Even if you had a TV or a refrigerator—you didn't of course—you would not have taken them with you on the hunt, since you had no RV in which to carry them.

Scollon argued that this principle applied not just to physical stuff, but to mental stuff as well. Such people did not value learning things that they were not going to use. They did not value storing knowledge that would not help out in the bush or in the other activities necessary to their survival. That is to say, they did not value storing knowledge just because it was knowledge. Why burden your mind with useless information any more than you would burden your back with useless supplies? The bush required that you packed just the right stuff physically and mentally.

We moderns no longer have any trouble with packing the heavy stuff physically. We can take the whole house out in a massive RV and hunt from the comfort of a full hook-up. We can buy stuff and store it in our houses until they are stuffed to the gills. We can fill our lives with useless objects and knickknacks to our heart's content. In regard to "things" we are modern. We are weighed down in a way that would never let us be agile hunters and warriors.

Perhaps ironically, we humans have never become modern mentally. Most of us still do not like to carry in our heads knowledge that does not seem applicable or useful in the near future. We are still caught up with the struggle for survival in a tough world, and we want to learn and store in our minds only what we need now and in the near future to make it through. We do not have the time or inclination to read Hume or Kant just in case, in some possible future, they might come in handy. If we are going to read "worthless" stuff, it might as well be entertaining and stress relieving.

We still want to pack light for the bush when it comes to our minds. We need all our wits and mental storage facility for the hard tasks at hand, such as keeping our jobs and managing our families in hard times. We cannot spare room for classical philosophy or the details of macro-economic theories. These things feel "heavy" just because we cannot see where we would use them out there in the bush of real life and its struggles. Indeed, our mental comfort stories and the stories we tell in our search for meaning and purpose can replace a library full of books and esoteric knowledge. They allow us to be agile hunters and warriors, as far as our minds go, at work in the world surviving.

So, almost all humans have bush consciousness when it comes to the mind, though no longer the physical world. Indeed, those poor humans who seek to carry along heavy and "useless" knowledge are "geeks" or "effete snobs" or live in "ivory towers." Even more so today than in the past, perhaps, it seems to many people almost laughable that a college student would major in some area that did not lead to a "good job." They are "wasting" their parents' money. Knowing for knowing's sake is a fool's errand, we believe.

Now there is this problem: to play what I called the argument and evidence game above, people have to be willing to learn things that are potentially not useful right now and maybe never will be. They have to consider possibilities and alternatives, some of which, maybe many of which, are not or will not turn out to be true or useful. To get ready for a fruitful discussion of why the economy failed in 2008 and why, in reality, I lost my job, I have to learn and store more knowledge than the actual solution may require. This is a hunt on which you have to bring a wide variety of weapons since you do not know what creatures you will actually face in the battle for understanding. Sometimes the "foe" turns out to be quite unexpected; what we sought is not what we find.

Humans are mental lightweights seeking meaning and purpose in a world they do not understand or, in the end, care to understand. When all that mattered was getting food for the table on a successful hunt, this was just fine. But when what matters now is understanding how the benefits of industrial farming could ultimately destroy the environment (think massive pig farms) and the human body (think obesity) and yet leave half the world starving amidst plenty, it matters. When people make fuel for their Hummers out of food (e.g., corn) and drive up the price of food in a starving world, we have reached an iconic moment of human stupidity, like Midas with his gold. We can comfort ourselves with the story that it is all in the name of "growth" and "economic progress" and wealth that will "trickle down" to the poor and starving wherever they are. But this story will not pass the test of the evidence game because it is a game that cannot be played with a light mind.

Nothing weighs heavier on the human mind than complexity. We humans are very poor at dealing with it. Too bad, then, that the modern world is replete with high-risk complex systems and a myriad of unintended consequences from bone-headed human interventions into them.

Flight from Complexity

COMPLEXITY BEDEVILS THE HUMAN MIND AND HU-
man institutions, today more so than ever. We find it very difficult to understand and manage complex systems such as the interactions between humans
and their environments, the clash of cultures and civilizations in a globally
interconnected world, and the workings of global markets filled with computers that can move money at the speed of electrons.

Complex systems are systems in which a great many variables of all different sorts interact with each other in complicated ways. In such systems it
is hard or impossible to predict outcomes. This is so because even very small
changes in the initial conditions of the systems can lead to vastly different
results. In complex systems there are too many variables and too many interactions among them to control them all. Thus, they are not directly open to
being studied through "controlled studies" of the sort normal in less complex
areas of science.

Complex systems defy human control, but not always some, albeit limited, degree of human understanding. We must seek to understand complex
systems not via controlled studies or testing predictions, but by building
models or simulations of the systems. These models or simulations are
scaled-down versions of the system—sometimes in a computer—versions
around which we can seek to build theories, try out explanations, and engage
in interventions. Our understanding of such systems is never complete and

always vulnerable. We are always subject to possible harmful unintended consequences when we seek to intervene in such systems.

Ecological systems are complex systems. Humans have regularly introduced animals or plants into such systems in an attempt to control things they do not like, such as insects that eat crops. Sometimes these introduced animals or plants wreak havoc on the system without actually controlling the pests they were meant to control.

The cane toad *(Bufo marinus)* is a good example. The cane toad is a very large toad that has poison glands. It and its tadpoles are highly toxic to most animals if eaten. The cane toad gets its name from the fact that it has been used in a number of countries to control beetles that eat sugarcane plants. Following the apparent success of the cane toad in eating the beetles threatening the sugarcane plantations of Puerto Rico, Hawaii, and the Philippines, the cane toad was released in Australia to control two species of cane beetles that were ravaging Queensland cane fields. Ironically, both these species of beetles had themselves been introduced and were not native to Australia. The toads became established in Queensland and then extended their range into the Northern Territory and New South Wales. They now exist in massive numbers, perhaps over a billion, in Australia.

Unfortunately, the toads turned out to be failures at controlling beetles in Australia. The beetles are still common, though the toads are yet more common since they are masters at reproduction. Since its original introduction, the cane toad has become a threat to Australian biodiversity. The main threat posed by cane toads occurs when other animals attempt to prey upon them. When the toads are threatened, they release a toxin (bufotoxin) from the glands behind the eyes and across their back. Now Australia is seeking something that can control the toads.

The cane toad is the subject of two movies by Mark Lewis: *Cane Toads: An Unnatural History* (1988) and *Cane Toads: The Conquest* (2010). The movies are simultaneously funny and sad, as Australians seek to cope with the toad invasion they brought on themselves.

Stories like the cane toad story are, unfortunately, a dime a dozen in human history. We humans have repeatedly sought to intervene in complex systems in arrogant ways that try to deny complexity in the name of profit and greed. The trouble is that how an organism behaves in an ecological system is not solely dependent on its properties as an individual species. It is dependent on its interactions within a complex web of processes and events. It is part of a tapestry that it can tear apart or help weave together. It is very hard to predict ahead of time what will happen when a thing like the cane toad is moved from one place (system) to another.

Today across the world forests are being destroyed. Huge swaths of forests are now dead across Alaska, Canada, and the United States, for instance, due to the action of bark beetles. These beetles are indigenous to these areas and have evolved with the trees for millions of years. They destroy old trees and thereby allow the forest to renew itself through new growth and a more diverse set of tree species. They are gardeners of forests—as is fire.

However, human policies like not allowing forests to burn, clear-cutting forests, and dumping carbon in the air (thereby causing global warming) have led these beetles not just to renew forests, but to eradicate them and, with them, some species of trees. Logging practices ensure little diversity in the species and age of the trees in the forest and then the beetles eat them all. Global warming stresses younger trees that can no longer protect themselves from the beetles. Global warming also causes the beetles to mature earlier, have more broods per year, and avoid dying off in the now warmer winters.

Human attempts to defeat the beetles with poison, bombs, and clear-cutting have totally failed. The beetles are the size of a grain of rice, and smart and tough enough to win every time. Human intervention disrupted a system millions of years old, one that relied on diversity, fire, and beetles for renewal. The consequences have been dire for people's livelihoods and environments.

In every sphere of our lives we humans are confronted by what I call "big questions." I mean by this questions that can only be answered by considering and at least partially figuring out the workings of a complex system or a system complex enough to count as a complex system to our human understanding (even if not complex in the fully technical sense). Such questions cause humans a lot of grief since we keep trying to answer them in simple terms that are satisfying to us ideologically but not likely to be correct or useful.

Why are our school systems so immune to real reform? Why does one business plan succeed and another similar one fail? Why does one technology spread and another seemingly better one does not? Is the Internet making us smarter or dumber? Why does history turn out the way it has and how could it have been different? Why do people believe in seemingly stupid things such as the earth being less than 10,000 years old or that humans did not evolve along with other animals, even in the face of massive counterevidence? Why does one change in language or fashion "catch on" and spread and another does not? Is government good or bad? When is big better and when is it not? Is free trade in a global world good or bad? How could we make it better? How much regulation do "free markets" need to be effective and fair? How should we deal with overpopulation and worldwide poverty? Why do humans go to war so often and how could we stop them? What should we do about global warming and why didn't we do it earlier? Will the coming hurricane wreak havoc or weaken and pass me by safely? Why do good people do bad things?

There are endless questions that are too complex for simple answers, answers based on only one area of expertise, or answers based on ideology or old books. Such questions require pooling lots of different sources of knowledge, building models, trying and re-trying different interventions, testing various explanations, and returning again and again to the drawing board. They require looking at things from different perspectives and seeking alternative viewpoints and new sources of ideas. They require humility and questioning of our own values and ideologies. They require the search for new tools and new uses of old ones. And they require knowing when to stop asking one question and start asking a better one. They require both critiques (something academics are good at) and positive proposals for better ways to do things that go beyond criticism of what is, to ideas about what realistically could be (something academics are bad at).

It is essential in dealing with a big question that we pool different and competing perspectives, even ones that do not fit our ideology. Such pooling is hard in a politically polarized world and with universities that value narrow specialties and departmental silos. It is hard, too, in a world where credentials are crucial but often do not really align with intelligence or ethics. It is hard also in an Internet-connected world where each person can so readily customize information and communication so as to live within their own bubble and rarely confront different viewpoints or challenges to their ideologies and mental comfort stories.

When we consider complexity and big questions, we arrive at the very root of what constitutes true liberals and true conservatives in politics (though few who call themselves liberals or conservatives in the United States are actually true to the root difference between the two). I should caution that I am using the term "liberal" in the American sense, not the European one. In Europe and much of the rest of the world "liberal" means a believer in free and unrestricted markets. In the United States it means people who believe government should ameliorate social ills in a society.

At root, a conservative believes that, faced with complexity, we should change things in small ways. Intervening in complex systems (like markets, health care, schools, regulation, policies, etc.) in large and wholesale ways can have dire unintended consequences. We do not fully understand complex systems and we should have the humility to be cautious and careful in our interventions. However imperfect current systems might be, they might have historically become the way they are because that is about the best we humans can do. It is easy to do worse, hard to do better in many cases.

At root, a liberal believes that when systems have bad consequences or significant imperfections, we need interventions that make big and systemic changes. Small changes, tinkering at the edges, usually just keep the system as it is because complex systems are good at reorganizing in ways that co-opt change and "right" the system back to its normal workings (this is called "adaptation"). Systems often need to be "shocked" so that they reorganize into truly new and better forms. Human-made systems are often not the outcome of any rational process in history; rather, they are usually the product of human self-interest and power seeking that can be mitigated in the name of equity and social justice.

Neither of these viewpoints can be proven. History is too complex to show either one right or wrong as a whole. Conservatives can point to major social interventions ("social engineering") that went badly awry. Liberals can point to tinkering and small changes that simply left the same people suffering over long periods of time. Both can point to examples where neither small nor large changes worked out as planned. History—like the Bible—is replete with examples that can be cherry-picked to support one's favored view.

We know this though: complexity and our inability as societies to deal with it is killing us. Global warming, environmental degradation, global flows of economic speculation and risk taking, overpopulation, global debt, new viruses, terrorism and warfare, and political polarization are killing us. Dealing with big questions takes a long-term view, cooperation, delayed gratification, and deep learning that crosses traditional silos of knowledge production. All of these are in short supply today. In the United States and much of the developed world, decisions are based on short-term interests and gain (e.g., stock prices or election cycles), as well as pandering to ignorance. Such decisions make the world worse, not better, and bring Armageddon ever closer.

Our universities could have served as the driving force for long-term, deep, cooperative, boundary-crossing thought, innovation, and action in the world to deal with complexity. But our universities are now just short-term-focused entrepreneurial centers largely devoted to "job training" (worthless though it usually is) and credentialing students who do not much care about "academics." God forbid that someone majors in something "worthless" (for getting a job) like history or philosophy or anything that involves ethics. God forbid that university experts in linguistics, sociology, or physics cooperate to educate the public and solve worldwide problems that engage and challenge many academic disciplines at once, rather than publish in "gold standard" journals. God forbid that people without PhDs and other "real" credentials contribute to teaching and knowledge building. Actually, God does not forbid any of these things. Only inertia and stupidity do.

So where in our society is there a genuine forum for discussing big questions? Where is there a forum for answering them over the long haul? Where is there a forum for freely sharing what is discovered and letting people around the world test it? Where is there a forum that demands evidence, models, and well-thought-out theories rather than ideology and self-serving? Where is there a forum that can allow the "worthless" and the "not relevant" and the not "immediate" to germinate like a mutation that may go nowhere or may yet in the end save us? Where is the DNA of human innovation stored, recombined, mutated, and set loose to give rise to new birth, new ideas, new worlds, and new sorts of human beings?

Nowhere. The forum—what used to be called the "public sphere"—is closed. But the market is open, though more now for short-term gain and speculative gambling (of the sort that has repeatedly led to bubbles and collapses that impoverish those of us who were not the speculators) than for the actual buying and selling of any worthwhile goods.

Our public sphere is in tatters. We are divided by ideology and harmed by greed. More and more in our highly competitive societies, it is each of us for ourselves or our families alone. And we often fail alone when we could have succeeded together. We have reached the limits of the human mind left alone or only with like-minded friends and family. We can't be stupid any more. It is just too dangerous in a global world. Can we humans get smarter? Can we save ourselves from our own stupidity? Is it too late? The next part of this book is about how we can get smarter, save our world, and make ourselves better people (and God knows we all need it).

PART II

How to Get Smart
Before It's Too Late

17

Inclusive We: How We Can All Get Smarter Together

I HAVE OFFERED A NUMBER OF REASONS WHY HU-mans can be stupid. There are more, but hopefully the point is made. There is no need to wallow in it.

Human stupidity is actually worse than I have portrayed it to be. The rational arguments in this book fail to capture the grief, damage, and violence humans have unleashed on each other, on animals, and on the environment across history and today. They fail to capture human gullibility and duplicity. They fail to capture the way humans, under the banners of religion and state, have maimed, tortured, and killed those who disagreed with them.

So why are we such sorry creatures? Without any doubt, fear of suffering and death plays a large role. We humans will believe and sometimes do anything to forestall suffering and death.

Without a doubt, too, the way in which we humans value kin (and ourselves) over others plays a great role. Modern humans have to live in society with a bunch of strangers. Yet they are biologically, socially, and culturally programmed to help and advantage people like themselves, whether this is defined in terms of genes, ethnic groups, or fictional national "families."

Without a doubt, as well, the struggle for survival—not just physically, but emotionally and economically as well—plays a great role. In a complex, competitive world filled with poverty and risk, it is hard enough for most people just to cope and survive, let alone find a little dignity, or spend time reflecting on the sorry state of humanity, or lend a hand to causes that help strangers.

And without a doubt, simple greed—abetted by things like rabid individualism in places like the United States—plays a major role. What human won't take and keep taking if he or she believes that is the way things are or should be, that everybody does it, that it's for the good of their family, or that it will make society better as their wealth "trickles down" to others less fortunate than themselves?

Religions are often designed to get people to think in more expansive terms. They are often designed to get people to see strangers as "one of us" and as a part of a wider human family. They are often designed to make people feel they have social and moral obligations to others less fortunate than themselves. However, religion's track record in reducing human violence and greed is a mixed bag.

But fear, overvaluing kin, the struggle for survival, and greed do not get to the heart of the matter. They just tell us that humans, whether they like to hear it or not, are animals. However, humans do have "higher intelligence." So the question arises why we do not use it better to act more intelligently. Why don't we use it to compensate for our animal weaknesses? Why don't we use it to compensate for our propensity to lie, deceive ourselves, and revel in mental comfort stories rather than face "reality" and, perhaps, lift people out of poverty and heal our shared environment?

What is WRONG with us?

Here is an idea: what if human beings are not meant to be individuals, but rather, are meant to be parts of a bigger whole? After all, looked at as an isolated individual, an ant is a pretty pitiful thing. But looked at as part of an ant colony, the ant is very impressive indeed. What if humans are missing their colony? What would their colony be?

Here is another idea: what if human minds are not meant to think for themselves by themselves, but, rather, to integrate with tools and other people's minds to make a mind of minds? After all a computer operates only when all its circuit boards are integrated together and communicate with each other. What if our minds are actually well made to be "plug-and-play" entities, meant to be plugged into other such entities to make an actual "smart device," but not well made to operate all alone? What if we are meant to be parts of a networked mind and not a mind alone?

What if WE are not stupid, but only I alone am stupid? Now surely this stress on "we" seems un-American. We are, are we not, individuals whose self-interest within free markets creates the best of all possible worlds? And, indeed, groups who see themselves as "we" in the exclusive sense—the sense in which some of us are "we" and others of us are "they"—cause great and endless havoc in the world. But is there an inclusive "we" that is human, humane, smart, and all of us?

That inclusive "we" would be a true public forum. People would enter the forum as members of the public, citizens with equal rights and worth. They would bring their beliefs, diversity, passion, values, and even prejudices to the forum along with those of everyone else. In the forum all would vie with each other in a game where everyone wants "the best man" to win, for their own good, as well as for the good of others. But the "best man" in the forum is not a human, it is an idea. And it will often be an idea that no one brought originally into the forum, but was discovered in the push and pull of ideas that jostle together in the public forum like molecules in a rich sea to give rise to the birth of new and better ideas.

The leading questions are: Is there a sense of "we" that does not diminish but enhances the dignity and creativity of each and every human being? Is there a sense of "we" that does not pit us against our own environment as "non-human," but rather incorporates our environment as part of the "we"? When and if we become "we," what must each of us bring to the forum for democracy to work? These are not just questions. They are agendas for action and they are questions whose answers will come only in action. They require discovery through trial and error focused on a moral vision and not just an intellectual theory.

In the forum of ancient Athens only free men could participate. Most people in this "birthplace of democracy" were not free; only about 10 percent of the population was free. Women, slaves, and the poor were not free. There has been a longstanding belief in Western culture, shared by the Greeks and the founders of America, that only people with a stake in a society (often defined as people who owned land) should be able to participate in a democratic forum (e.g., vote). The idea was that people who owned little in a society would have nothing to lose and thereby might vote irresponsibly. Those with some wealth would vote more carefully so as not to endanger the society that engendered and protected their wealth.

While it is most certainly true that the rich and powerful have most often acted in their own best interests and not those of their societies, there is nonetheless something to this idea of participants in a democratic forum being "free" and having something at stake. In fact, the health of a democracy crucially depends on everyone being free and having something at stake. Otherwise, a democracy degenerates into an oligarchy.

But what does it mean, really, to be free and have something at stake? An answer to this question can come from a surprising place: public health. As I mentioned in an earlier chapter, there is an interesting phenomenon, long known in public health, sometimes called the "status syndrome." If you line up people in any society in terms of status, from lowest to highest, on average anyone lower in the hierarchy is less healthy than a person higher in the hierarchy. And it really does not matter how you define status. You can define it in terms of income, education, job, or even the size of one's house.

The status syndrome is true of all societies unless they are undeveloped and poor. But the effect is larger for some than for others. For example, the effect is relatively small in Japan and quite large in the United States. Note that the status syndrome does not mean just that the poor are less healthy than the rich; it means that status affects everyone's health all the way along the line of the status hierarchy. Lower status = less health; higher status = more health all the way along the line as a matter of statistical probability.

The status syndrome is actually part of a bigger picture. Hierarchy affects more than health; it affects a good number of social factors such as crime, success in school, and teenage pregnancy. As with health, the effect on these other factors is worse the more unequal a society is. If we compare developed countries, the countries with the most inequality have more social problems in regard to things like health problems, crime, education, and other social ills than do the more equal societies. And, here too, it does not really matter how you define inequality, whether in terms of how much wealth the top 1 percent has, or the top 10 percent, or the top 20 percent, or the average wealth of each person.

High status makes a person likely to be better off in terms of health and well-being in a given society. But more equality in a society as a whole makes more people (including richer people) likely to be better off in health and well-being compared to other less equal societies, and it makes whole societies better off in terms of health and well-being than other societies.

Why is all this so? Human beings are social beings. They judge their own "worth" in terms of how they compare to others on factors that their society deems important and indicative of a worthy human being. They also feel a sense of agency and control when they feel that their actions count and contribute to society, when they feel like participants and not spectators. We have seen in an earlier chapter that these needs are integral to human beings. When they are not met, humans feel anxious and stressed, even if they are not poor and starving. Anxiety and stress can readily lead to health problems in mind and body and to social problems like alcoholism, obesity, and a lack of attachment to society that can lead to crime.

In more equal societies more people feel they are worthwhile participants in the society. They do not feel less human because they are less wealthy. In highly unequal societies—where wealth is distributed very unevenly, as in the United States—people can feel that only wealth makes them a fully worthy person. They can feel that there is something wrong with them, that they are failures, because they are not wealthy. This does not mean they do not sometimes project false esteem based on bravado and intolerance for others, but such false esteem is based on the need to feel important when one really does not feel that way.

Ironically, high inequality is bad for the rich, the poor, and everyone in between. It engenders social problems that make everyone's lives less good than they otherwise could be. It exacts massive social costs from a society in regard to health care and other social problems. Remember that even in a rich society like the United States, the rich are less well off in terms of health and other factors connected to well-being than are the better-off people in more equal societies. Increasing inequality is no good for individuals or for societies as a whole. Past a certain point, for people and for society, more wealth does not translate into anything particularly good as far as happiness and well-being are concerned.

In a real sense, more people in a society are "free" and have something at stake in the society when there is greater equality. More people are "free" when they feel they are contributing, worthwhile members of that society. A democratic forum for a healthy society requires that everyone in that society feel that inequality has not gone so far as to render them non-participants. It requires healthy people who are not anxious and stressed about their status as worthy human beings. Otherwise, we don't just get an oligarchy; we get a sick, greedy, rapacious, overstressed, and hostile society. Many rich countries today have just such a society, even as they see their wealth dissipating amidst financial crises brought on by the greed of rich people who feel less attachment to their society than they do to more accumulation of wealth, accumulation that in the end harms them and everyone else.

None of this is to say that a society should have total equality in terms of wealth or status. None of it says people should not benefit from their hard work or achievements. What it does say is that there should be more significant routes to status in a society than money. It says, as well, that if only a small number of wealthy people truly participate in the forum of democracy, then there really is no democracy, but only lots of sick people, rich and poor.

It is commonplace to believe that social ills are caused by the fact that poor people often live in bad housing, have poor diets, and lack education. We expect that rich societies, at least in the developed world, would have fewer problems with such social ills, the ones we readily associate with poverty. We expect that people in rich societies at all levels would be healthier and happier and would suffer fewer social ills. But this is not true. Some of the richest societies on earth suffer more social ills than do less rich (but still developed) societies. Some of these ills, such as ill health and less success in education, are suffered by people who are not poor, but simply members of highly unequal societies.

Like many people interested in education, I have spent a good deal of my time worrying about what sorts of educational reforms in our schools could improve the performance of poor and minority students. Is it small class sizes, higher standards, teacher accountability, more crosscultural understanding, better teaching, or something else? We have tried all of these over the years, and the educational gaps between rich and poor remain, as do many of our other problems with schools.

However, it is high inequality in a society that creates deep divides in educational success. It is not poverty per se. If we do not address such inequality—and the stress and feelings of not really counting in the society that often come with it—then specific reforms will probably not matter all that much over the long haul. Our problems in education are not rooted primarily in our schools, no matter how bad or how good some of them are, but in our society.

The stress and anxiety prevalent in modern developed societies did not originally stem from high inequality. They came from the breakdown of stable communities where people knew each other and gained respect and worth in networks of reciprocity and support. For the last fifty years, however, people in developed societies have become much more mobile. Most of us now live among and interact with many strangers or near strangers in person and via digital media. We often feel little solidarity with these strangers and, in a highly competitive world, do not get respect and esteem from them for much beyond wealth and success. Our basic needs for solidarity and respect are not met as well as they were in more cohesive communities. However, inequality makes these effects worse. It creates more social distance between people in a society. It makes strangers even "stranger." It greatly exacerbates people's feelings of being "left out" or "left behind," of being judged in terms of how high their status is in terms of wealth, consumer goods, or jobs. It makes us all anxious about our worth as humans and our meaningfulness to others in our society.

Christ said "the poor you will always have with you" (Matthew 26:11, New International Version). He did not say that being less well off than others should mean you do not count as a worthy human being. And, too, he said that the kingdom of heaven belonged to the poor in spirit and that the meek would inherit the earth (Matthew 5:3–10). As I mentioned in an earlier chapter, Christ had no regard for status. So, at least, we can conclude that it is not Christ or true Christianity that licenses high levels of inequality in rich societies. It is hard to say what moral or even merely practical force does.

18

Big Minds, Not Little Minds

WE ARE AT THE POINT NOW WHERE WE CAN OFFER an answer to Orwell's problem: why are humans so stupid when it seems they should be smarter?

We have seen that humans are not primarily oriented toward evidence or even truth. They are oriented toward meaning. They want to know that their lives and efforts are significant. They want assurance that they are not the victims of chance in a universe that is indifferent to them, their hopes, and their dreams. They want to find patterns and to believe that things happen "for a reason."

We have seen that humans can be smart for practical ends when they use the circuit of reflective action. But this requires lots of experiences in and interactions with the world. One such necessary experience is supportive mentoring from others. This mentoring guides what can be called one's appreciative system. It is our appreciative system in different domains that tells us whether the results of our actions—our probes into the world—are good or bad for accomplishing our goals. We often cannot discover what constitutes a good result and a fruitful path of action all by ourselves. We need help from the accumulated experiences of those who mentor us into different valued activities in the world, whether gardening, tinkering, physics, or civic participation.

Faced with fear of suffering and death—and feelings of worthlessness in a market-driven, status-oriented world—people seek comfort from mental comfort stories. They are prone to believe almost anything and often seek to impose their beliefs on others. They easily become "true believers" who despise "heretics." They live in an "us" versus "them" world.

So how can humans get smarter? Well, we would need to learn to orient toward evidence and truth when a question is empirical. "Why are we here on earth?" is not an empirical question. No evidence we can imagine in our current state of knowledge could answer this question. "Is the world warming because of human actions?" is an empirical question. It is dangerous in a complex world when people seek to answer empirical questions on any basis other than evidence and theories that guide the collection and analysis of that evidence.

This does not mean that only credentialed scientists can seek to answer empirical questions. We have seen that in a world full of complex systems we need to recruit multiple sources of information and evidence. "Everyday people" can engage in thinking and acting empirically. Crowd sourcing has helped to solve real scientific problems. For example, gamers playing a protein-folding game called Foldit discovered the correct fold for a protein that is a factor in causing AIDS. Maybe someday their discovery will help lead to a cure for AIDS.

We all face significant empirical questions in our everyday lives and we need to know how to deal with them empirically rather than ideologically. Was President Obama born in the United States? Why are all the trees in my backyard dying? Is the school my children attend a bad school? Is buying a home a good investment? Are video games harming my child? Is there such a thing as clean coal? Are large degrees of inequality in a society bad for people's well-being and health? These are all empirical questions.

Answering an empirical question does not ever lead to absolute truth. The "game" of answering empirical questions is a "pragmatic" game. We seek the best answers we can, act on them as our "best bets," and stay open to revising them and learning more. Ideology can give false certainty, and acting on ideology to answer empirical questions is one good way to get bitten hard by the world.

The empirical game (what we called the truth-seeking game earlier) is really just the circuit of reflective action on steroids. In the empirical game we probe the world based on a theory. A theory is a set of ideas (often encapsulated in a "model") about how things connect and interact in the world in a particular domain. Our probe is set up to test a specific hypothesis (educated guess) connected to our theory. It works best to seek to falsify our hypothesis, no matter how attached to it we are. If the results of our probe appear to support our hypothesis, we open our results to others to see if they can either knock them down or replicate them. If the results of our probe appear to falsify our claim, we ask whether our probe was really the right one or whether we need to revise aspects of our theory or get a new theory altogether.

When we or others have accumulated enough evidence for our hypothesis and none of us have been able to falsify it, we tentatively accept the hypothesis as "true." In addition, we gain some degree of greater trust in our theory, the theory that suggested the hypothesis and that helps explain why the hypothesis might be true. We keep our theory and act on it until we lose trust in it from further rounds of the empirical game.

The empirical game is through and through a multiplayer game. It is social and collaborative. We share theories with others. We seek their help in how we should analyze our results. We build on what others have already accomplished and take off from there. We want others to try to falsify our claims because their different desires, interests, and even prejudices will counteract our own, as ours will theirs.

This is science at its heart. Science is the empirical game and we have seen that the empirical game is just the normal circuit of reflective action on steroids. It is a more formalized version of the circuit of reflective action, one based on seeking to falsify claims even if we cherish them and they give us mental comfort. The empirical game deals with more formal (explicit) and widely shared and vetted theories. But, in the end, the empirical game and the circuit of reflective action are the same. Science is a fully human activity.

Today, thanks to the Internet and vast sources of readily available information, people can join with others to engage in the empirical game. They do not need formal credentials to do this. They need only follow the rules of the game. They can readily learn the opinions of formal experts, but we have seen that such experts cannot always be trusted. In our complex world, the empirical game requires everyone to play together. It is crucial to the empirical game to pool as many diverse sources of information and viewpoints as we can. A rare piece of information or a rare viewpoint may be crazy and, if so, it will wash out as we pool all our sources. But it may be wise, in which case it could change the course of our reasoning and actions. Indeed, one problem with narrow experts is that, faced with complexity, they often pool sources of information and viewpoints that are not wide or diverse enough.

In the modern world—a complex, risky, and fast-changing place—it is crucial that people know when and how to play the empirical game. It is crucial to their role as citizens and crucial to a healthy society faced with a world that can bite and bite hard. The empirical game can widen people's experience of the world and their interactions with it. In the act, it can improve their everyday uses of the circuit of reflective action. There is certainly no reason not to continue gardening based on your family's accumulated knowledge and traditions. This will probably work quite well. But today you can also join a passion-filled, interest-driven Internet site devoted to gardening, a site that pools everyone's knowledge and vets everyone's claims. In this case, you can help produce new knowledge about gardening, maybe get a better garden, or even make the world itself a better garden.

Where do people learn to play the empirical game? Well, school is one place where we would expect them to learn when and how to play this game. But today, alas, many schools teach no such thing. In fact, many people today only learn to play the empirical game, if they learn it at all, when they join interest-driven groups on the Internet to explore important topics with a diverse set of other people.

Getting people good at the empirical game will not really work if they live in fear of suffering and chance and if they feel worthless in a market-based, status-driven, highly unequal world. In this case, people will seek comfort. The empirical game is not a comfort game. It is a game in which we risk being wrong. It is a game that means living beyond our comfort zone, which is, in my view, really living and not just "existing" in stasis (a form of death).

What this means is that the empirical game, whether played by credentialed scientists or by all of us, must always and everywhere be coupled with social activism with the goal of making a better world where more people count and contribute. A society in which everyone feels that they count and that their actions can have a meaningful impact on others for the good is more likely to be a society that does not ignore Mother Nature to its own detriment. It is more likely to be a society that will respect and properly vet science and experts. It is more likely to be an innovative, creative, healthy, and happy society.

Where would people learn how to engage with this social activist project? Again, we might expect that people would learn it in school. But, again, they rarely learn any such thing in school. Some people—not enough—learn how to engage in this social activist project when they join interest-driven groups on the Internet or in "real life" to explore civic engagement and social transformation with a diverse set of other people.

As a society we cannot trust the Internet alone to be our primary educator in the empirical game and in the social activist project for greater equality. While it is true that the Internet is full of groups engaged in the empirical game, it is also full of ideologically driven sites where people echo each other's views and values endlessly and mindlessly. While it is true that the Internet is full of groups engaged in social activism, it is also full of ideologically driven groups engaged in prejudice and demonizing others.

There is no substitute for an education, though what I would call a real education is hard to come by in the world today. Schools often socialize students into the status quo, a status quo that often supports large degrees of inequality and offers patriotic comfort stories in place of empirical realities. To begin to think about what a school might be, we need first to return to the limitations of the human mind.

The human mind is unique in nature in that it works most powerfully when it plugs into a tool. We saw earlier that while many humans are poor at mathematics, they can be good at mathematics when they have a calculator. In general, we humans evolved, in mind and body, to be tool users. While there are other animals that use tools, they are not true tool designers and users in the way humans are.

For humans, tools are not just artifacts like calculators, hammers, and drafting tables designed to make thinking and work easier. For humans, other humans are tools as well. Now, of course, this sounds bad. Who wants to be a "tool"? But what it means is that we humans think and act better when we do so by getting the help of others and giving help to them. We are powerful team players when we want or have to be. We are reciprocal and mutual tools for each other, networked together as a more powerful thinking unit. The real unit of human intelligence at work in the world is this: humans as reciprocal tools for each other + nonhuman tools (artifacts and technologies) all networked and integrated together. We are "plug-and-play entities," not stand-alone entities, when we are at our best. That is the only way we humans have built bridges and cities and cured diseases.

Of course, just giving people tools and getting them together does not make an effective thinking/acting team. They have to learn to dance together, to coordinate with each other—and by "together" I mean humans and nonhuman tools both. A tool like a hammer only works when you know how to use it. And knowing how to use it means understanding the way in which it is designed to get good work done. This is true of all tools, including humans as reciprocal tools for each other.

Let's call an effective, well-integrated "humans as reciprocal tools for each other + non-human tools" network a "Mind" with a capital "M." A Mind is what you get when you plug minds and tools together in the right way. Of course, there are many different right ways to plug them together and we can discover new ways as we face new problems. Just as there are machines that build machines, it is Minds that discover new Minds.

So where do people learn to be effective Minds? We might have thought school would be a main place. But it is not. School is all about little minds, not big Minds. There are institutions in the world where it is so important to have Minds and not just minds at work—some businesses, the military, and activist groups, for example—that people sometimes learn to be good Minds in them. But, as we saw earlier, institutions are vexed and within them Minds can often break apart into mere minds.

When I as an individual person (a mind) choose to plug and play with certain tools and certain other people as a Mind, there is a crucial problem. I must choose to support the work and outcomes of this Mind. Just as I am morally responsible for my own thoughts and deeds, so, too, I am responsible for the thoughts and deeds of the Minds I join. I do not want to be a promiscuous plug-and-play unit and play with the wrong tools and people. In the end there is a values choice here, a moral one. This choice is one I ultimately make as an individual (a mind), but one influenced by the Minds I have chosen to join or have been socialized by early in life.

The moral choice about what Minds to plug and play with is, at its foundation, about what we see as the purpose of life and of our lives. Which people and what tools I plug into and play with are those I hope and believe will make my life and my world meaningful and valuable. And this question—what is the purpose of life and of my life?—is not an empirical question. We do not play it by playing the empirical game. Since we play our most powerful empirical games as Minds and not minds, this moral question (what Minds we will be part of, based on our values) is at the heart of the empirical enterprise. Our answer to this question is at the origin of the empirical games we choose to play and hope to win. This may seem odd, a moral question being at the heart and origin of our empirical games. But good scientists have always known that since the world is full of billions of facts to discover and questions to ask, it takes "taste" (a good nose for what is important, timely, and pregnant with possibilities) to know which questions to ask and when to ask them. I am simply pointing out that such "taste" has or should have a moral dimension in all our dealings with the world, a "nose" for what will make a better world for all of us.

So how do we answer questions like: What is the purpose of life or my life? How ought we to choose what Minds to plug into and play as part of? The question of what we should plug our minds into is not unlike the question of whom we should have sex with. If we see having sex as making love (in a literal sense) then the choice of a sexual partner is itself based on what we see as the purpose of life and of our life and whom we want to share that purpose with. In the end, both science and love are about how we want to change the world we live in together.

19

Mind Visions and New, Better Worlds

AS WE SAID IN THE LAST CHAPTER, IN MANY CON-
texts, humans are not smart alone. They are plug-and-play devices that are
meant to link to good tools and good collaborators who serve as tools for
each other. Such teams of tools and people—or what we called "Minds" in
the last chapter—can do great good or great harm. Minds linked to other
Minds to form a large interacting network of Minds can wage vast war or
save vast numbers of lives in public health interventions. What Minds do
(whether in small groups or in vast networks) is determined by some vision
of what is good, right, or necessary. Where do such visions that underpin
large projects—we can call them Mind Visions—come from?

Mind Visions are ideas about what groups and whole societies, coupled
with their tools, ought to do. They can be visions of the good life, of morality, or of power and destiny. They can lead to great good or great ill. Mind
Visions do not really come from any one person. They have to be ideas that
are contagious and that spread. They must be shared by a sufficiently large
group of people in order to be implemented. They are, even if started by one
person, inherently social by the time they can energize action.

Let's say that I asked you, "What Mind Visions would (or do) YOU
support and want to see spread and engage action and change in the world?"
This question asks for your "world view" not as a social isolate, but as a

person who needs and wants to plug into powerful tools and other people to sustain or remake the world or parts of it. If you can answer this question, then I would ask you, "Do you know where these Mind Visions came from and how they arose and spread, if they have?" and "Have you thought critically about these Mind Visions or have you accepted them passively without much critical thought?" It is hard to engage in critical thinking about Mind Visions if you do not really know where they came from and how and why they have spread.

Mind Visions are not about just your private values and morality. They are ideas about what is good, right, or necessary not only for individuals to do (and we have seen that as individuals we can be pretty stupid and ineffective), but about what is good, right, or necessary for Minds to do. Mind Visions are about what is good, right, or necessary for our most powerful selves—ourselves as parts of Minds—to do. Such visions are our theories of society and of life as members of a social species, as beings who, whether we like it or not, are integrally connected to others and the world in all sorts of ways, large and small, local, national, and global.

One good way to get at your Mind Visions is to pretend that the world turned to you and said "What do YOU think WE should do?" You are the coach, the leader. Can you state any clear vision of what is good, moral, or necessary? Can you argue convincingly for your visions in a public forum where you cannot coerce people, but where people are willing to listen and are open minded? Can you pick the tools and the sorts of people (in terms of attitudes, skills, and values) that ought to form Minds to sustain or change the world? Can you listen to others and learn and transform your vision to make it better or potentially more effective? Can you form a good Mind (work with good tools and good people) to debate how networks of Minds should make and remake the world in large and small ways?

Forming and revising Mind Visions involves empirical evidence, but it goes well beyond empirical evidence. This process requires us to continually reassess our values and guiding principles in light of the outcomes of our actions, in how they contribute to making the world a better place as we come to define it with others who share our Mind Visions.

If you are not equipped to engage in this enterprise—the "What do YOU think WE should do?" game—then you are not equipped to be a real citizen in a real democracy. You are equipped only to be a follower and, perhaps, a dupe and victim of others. Societies that see to it that only a small sample of people can engage with the "What do YOU think We should do?" game are not democracies. People in such societies suffer in terms of well-being and health. Some may claim that not all people can be equipped to think like leaders and not just followers, but in a democracy we certainly must try. We may be surprised to discover more in others than we thought possible.

It is impossible to imagine a society in which everyone could and did engage with the "What do YOU think WE should do?" game unless people in that society had the opportunity to get the right sort of education and to engage in learning throughout their lifetimes. In most societies in history this has not been possible, since only the wealthy have had enough "leisure time" to engage in such an enterprise, if they chose to do so. Most people have been too busy with backbreaking work and struggle to have such leisure time. Indeed, in many countries around the globe today, this is still true. In such cases, it is not surprising, I suppose, that the people with lots of leisure time often choose not to engage in the "What do YOU think WE should do?" game in the public forum, but simply use their power and wealth to coerce people to act in the ways they want them to.

In developed countries today there are a great many people with a "cognitive surplus." Work and struggle do not take up all their time. They spend lots of time engaged in media like television, video games, and social media. The time, thought, and energy they devote to media can be passive and unchallenging, a form of rest or leisure or even escape. Or it can be used for learning, development, and social transformation. It can be used for engaging in the "What do YOU think WE should do?" game, for thinking about how things are, how they got that way, and how they should be. Even if our jobs do not allow a full expression of our capacity as Mind Visionaries (and few jobs do), our lives outside of work can allow for this if we choose and get the help we need. It should not be only the rich, or credentialed, or powerful who play the "What do YOU think WE should do?" game.

I am well aware that a great many people in developed countries—most certainly in the United States—live lives of such struggle that they have no time or energy, inside or outside of work, to be Mind Visionaries. So, for me, part of my Mind Vision is that we all need to see to it that in lands of plenty, such lives of struggle cease, so that everyone can get on with our Mind Visions for making a better world. And we need, further, to see to it that all lands become lands of plenty in material necessities, mind, and spirit. Some will say this is only a vision, not a real possibility. I say we can only know if and when we seriously commit ourselves to pursue the vision (which we have yet to do). And, indeed, pursuing such a vision will make a better world for all of us even if we cannot save everyone. There is ample empirical evidence that such a world will be one in which everyone, whether richer or poorer, will be healthier and happier. We do not even need to appeal to values or morality to make this point, though, indeed, we still should.

The empirical game (the truth-seeking game) is, at heart, science. The Mind Vision game ("The what do YOU think WE should do?" game) is, at heart, the humanities and the liberal arts. The liberal arts are fundamentally about envisioning better worlds and selves. The empirical game is dangerous without the Mind Vision game because it can underwrite evil as well as good. In fact, it is undirected in any deep way without it. It is our visions and values that tell us what is worth studying empirically and why. The Mind Vision game is the guide for the empirical game, and each game is equally dangerous and undirected in any deep way without the other. Visions and values that evade facts are unsustainable and can lead to disaster. A real education would have no wall between the two games.

20

Synchronized Intelligence: Getting Our Minds and Tools in Synch

IF THERE IS ONE BASIC MESSAGE IN THIS BOOK, IT IS this: Humans are the sort of creatures who seek meaning rather than truth. They are the sort of creatures who get sick and stupid when they lack a genuine sense of worth, participation, control, and counting to others in terms of a bigger picture than themselves. People can often only face and deal with the truth when they feel a genuine sense of worth, participation, control, counting. We can only solve our problems and save ourselves from stupidity if we can find a way for our societies to make more people count. At the same time, in an age in which knowledge is too big for any one mind, no matter how smart, we desperately need more people to count and to contribute.

Our world is now so complex, our technology and science so powerful, and our problems so global and interconnected that we have come to the limits of individual human intelligence and individual expertise. We are entering an age in which we will need what I will call "synchronized intelligence." Synchronized intelligence is a well-coordinated dance among humans and tools in the service of a better world. It is the intelligence of people linked to each other and to good tools, not left on their own. Synchronized intelligence is the product of Minds working well.

By no means does synchronized intelligence mean individuals do not count. In a dance, each dancer counts and there is no dance without the dancers. By no means does synchronized intelligence mean that tools are more important than humans—but try to play basketball without a ball and without coordinating with the ball.

Let me tell you a little story that captures some of what I am talking about. Tabby Lou was a woman in her late sixties who became too sick to work. She retired and become a shut-in, unable to leave her home. When Tabby Lou's six-year-old granddaughter came to visit, the little girl often played a video game called "The Sims," the bestselling video game in history. As noted earlier, the Sims is a game in which players simulate a life by building families, careers, and neighborhoods. The game has virtual stores in which players can purchase (for virtual, fictional currency) things like land, clothes, furniture, and houses. Or they can go DIY and use 3D building tools outside the game to design and build their own. At the time Tabby Lou's granddaughter was playing the game, these 3D tools were things like Adobe Photoshop and other complex pieces of software. Today the game has much more user-friendly building tools built into it.

One day, Tabby Lou's granddaughter told her there were no "purple potties" in the game's stores and she wanted a purple potty for her Sims family's children. Could Tabby Lou make her one? Tabby Lou started to play the game (and loved it) and looked into how, for heaven's sake, someone could build a virtual purple potty. She discovered it could be done only through mastering some pretty complex software and thinking about how such software manipulates visual objects at a deep design level. It seemed a daunting task, and all for just a purple potty. But what grandmother does not want to make her little granddaughter happy?

Tabby Lou discovered something else as well. She discovered on the Internet an interest-driven, passion-fueled site (one of many) where people design and build things for The Sims. On the site people of all ages share their creations with other players, who can upload them into their games (and thereby have unique clothes, furniture, houses, and landscapes for their "Sims," their "little people," as some players call them). Sometimes people sell their creations, though most often they give them away.

Elsewhere I have called such sites "affinity spaces," for reasons I will tell you below. On this site, people mentored Tabby Lou. They did not tell her how to make a purple potty, and they certainly did not do it for her, but they taught her how to learn to do it. After a good deal of time and effort, Tabby Lou mastered 3D design tools and made a purple potty. She gave it to her granddaughter, who was thrilled—the only kid with a purple potty in The Sims—and wonderfully proud of her grandmother. But that is not the end of the story. Tabby Lou got hooked on the interest-driven, passion-fueled affinity space itself. She didn't want to leave. She wanted to learn more and help others.

Tabby Lou eventually became an award-winning and adulated designer on the site, designing clothes, furniture, houses, and landscapes. Millions of people from all around the world have uploaded her designs and over a million have written "thank you" notes in her guest book on the site. She is now a tech wiz, a designer, an artist, and a mentor. She is still a shut-in, but she is definitely not shut out of the global world. The other people on the site have given her a new lease on life and renewed her sense of worth, belonging, and contributing.

But that's not the end of the story either. There are lots of sites like the one Tabby Lou joined. These sites have different value systems and incorporate different norms for interaction. One such site we studied, also devoted to designing for The Sims, had a "tough love" form of interaction, treating newcomers roughly until they knew the rules and became more expert. This site stressed being an individual tech expert. At one point a discussion on this site raised the question whether Tabby Lou, known to be adulated on the other site, was "really" an expert. She did not fit their image of a hard-core, self-contained tech expert, though they sometimes asked her for advice or help. We decided to ask Tabby Lou whether she was an "expert." She said "No." She said that the expertise was in the community she belonged to and the tools they mutually used, developed, and taught each other about. She knew how to leverage expertise, extend it, and sustain it in the community. But it was not in her. Tabby Lou's response was a twenty-first-century response to the question of expertise. She was smart because other people and good tools were smart with her.

Tabby Lou's story is a very modern story. It is the story of our future and not our past. In that future, people of all ages, not just young people, will have to learn, change, and adapt continuously. And people of all ages will do so through synchronized intelligence, a dance with good people and good tools.

The interest-driven, passion-fueled site Tabby Lou joined is what I call an affinity space. Such spaces can be, when they operate at their best—and they often don't, of course—the learning spaces and the democratic forums of the future. They can be the basis of a new and reinvigorated public sphere, nationally and globally.

Why do I call them spaces and not, say, groups or communities? Because people can enter such spaces (which are often sites on the Internet) and contribute in many different ways, large or small, with different people for different reasons. They are places where people can go to share resources and values and flexibly form and re-form in different groups. The place or space can be an Internet site, a real place, or a combination of the two.

Affinity spaces, at their best, are key examples of synchronized intelligence. Multiple tools, different types of people, and diverse skill sets are networked in ways that make everyone smarter and make the space itself a form of emergent intelligence. The sum is more than its parts; the collective is smarter than the smartest person in it. At their best, then—and in terms of not just how they are now, but how they could be even better in the future—affinity spaces should have the following features.

1. People are in them by choice. They are in the space because of a shared interest in a common endeavor, not because of their race, class, or gender. Their affinity for each other is based on a shared endeavor. In fact, on the Internet people can hide their race, class, and gender (and other aspects of their identity) and use these as assets strategically if, when, and where they want to. In an affinity space people choose who they will be and which parts of themselves they will invest and share.

2. People of diverse ages and backgrounds are in the affinity space. They are not age-graded.

3. People with different skills and different levels of expertise are in the affinity space. People range from "newbies" to "old hands." In some affinity spaces credentialed experts comport with amateurs. Sometimes amateurs get to be as expert as credentialed experts, becoming "pro-ams" (professional amateurs).

4. Some people in the space have an interest in the common endeavor and some have a real passion for it. The space is built to fan interest into passion. However, one need not go all the way to passion—people can satisfy their interest and move on—but they must respect the passion as an attractor to the space.

5. Those with passion set high standards that others acknowledge and seek to emulate. There is no "grade inflation" or "dumbing down," only multiple routes to mastery for those who seek it. This does not mean standards are not negotiated and contestable, but it does mean that people in the site have allegiance to discussing and pursuing excellence.

6. The space is focused on knowing and doing (production, solving problems), not just on knowing.

7. Some people make massive numbers of contributions to the space, others make many less, but every contribution, large or small, has the chance to matter, change things, and contribute.

8. The space recruits a diverse array of talents. Even someone with limited skills or quite rare or special skills can find a place where their contribution counts. The space is designed to allow for multiple contributions, to leverage diversity so that no piece of knowledge or skill goes untapped, and, yet, too, to focus people's attention on the places, problems, and parts of problems to which they can make their best contributions. Yet people are still allowed to roam free if they want to and try new things.

9. In an affinity space, leadership and status are flexible. People sometimes lead and mentor; sometimes they follow and are mentored. There are no fixed bosses and teachers, though people acknowledge different paths to mastery and know where people are on them.

10. There are different routes to status. People can achieve status at different levels within their group of similarly skilled peers in the affinity space, a group that changes as they move up in skills. Status is based on what you do and how you do it—and on how well you help others—in the space, not on who you are outside the space or what you have done in unrelated spaces.

11. An affinity space has lots of powerful tools to help with the work of the space, but these tools are modified by their users and uses. People in the space create diverse ways to learn the tools, suitable for different styles of learning.

12. An affinity space allows people to specialize but demands that they share general knowledge and skills with people in the space as a whole, so that they can work and coordinate on larger projects with others who have different specialties.

13. Affinity spaces link to other related spaces so that knowledge from the outside can transform the space and so that the space does not become an echo chamber of agreement. At the same time, each space retains a distinct culture, vision, and set of norms, negotiated within the space over time.

14. Affinity spaces take a proactive stance on learning. It is always good to ask for help, never all right not to be a proactive agent managing one's own learning. Everyone has an obligation to facilitate the learning of others and should have the attitude that there is always something new to learn and someone else who can help.

15. People enter the space for different reasons. Some use it as a stepping-stone to other affinity spaces, a form of transfer. Others stay put for a longer term to become guardians, but not bosses, of the space.

16. In an affinity space, there is no tight distinction between work and play, since people have committed to do something in which they have an interest, an interest potentially on the way to becoming a passion, or already a full-blown passion.

17. In an affinity space, there is lots of socialization of all different sorts, but it is always subordinated to the endeavor that defines the space, in the sense that socialization is not allowed to undermine the real work/play of the space.

18. Affinity spaces are based on "truth" and "evidence" in the simple sense that they contain people with lots of different backgrounds and, thus, people must argue for their claims, based on examples and evidence, not on the basis of power, ideology, or status. Affinity spaces are based, too, on "truth" and "evidence" in the simple sense that they contain tools and produce things that must actually work. There is no way in The Sims to argue that the house you built is good even though it fell down.

Affinity spaces have flourished on the Internet with some successes and many failures, as is always the case with us humans. But they point a way forward. They need not be solely on the Internet. They can be in a real physical space or in a blend of real and virtual space. At their highest point of imagination, in my view, schools and colleges could have been and should be in the future a network of well-designed interacting affinity spaces devoted to synchronized intelligence.

Affinity spaces can be devoted to any human passion, whether this is designing for The Sims, recruiting civic participation, studying women's health, recreating life in the Middle Ages, or solving hard problems in politics, mathematics, or the environment. People are in them not to get jobs or to be "practical." They are in them to fuel passion, play, learning, and synchronized human intelligence. They are in them because there they can count and contribute, grow and not be judged by their wealth or status in our winner-take-all societies.

Nonetheless, affinity spaces have been, and will be ever more in the future, the source of new ideas, new solutions to hard problems, and skills for jobs not yet in existence. People are in them not to make money, but to matter to others and to themselves. And yet, there is evidence that what people do in affinity spaces eventually spills over more and more into our economies, as people gain new skills and some become entrepreneurial.

Since they recruit diversity and the intelligence of people both with and without formal credentials, affinity spaces are a type of "wisdom of the crowd" and "crowdsourcing," two topics much written about these days. But they are more than this. They are a new type of synchronized intelligence for an age where the cost of stupidity and individual go-it-alone expertise is too high to countenance much longer.

Collective intelligence, where people contribute to a problem as a group, is but one type of synchronized intelligence. In its full form synchronized intelligence is not just about solving hard problems. It is about, as well, new forms of living and socially interacting to discover new ways to move forward to make a better world for more people. It is about finding multiple spaces where we can share lots even if we don't share everything and where different people can share different things in different spaces. They allow people to be creative even when working on problems that—unlike in mathematics and some areas of the hard sciences—do not always have clear-cut or rigorously testable answers.

Affinity spaces take work to sustain. They can fall apart or degenerate for many different reasons. One reason is that new tools are introduced that are much more user friendly and easier to learn. This often means that the inside workings of the tools are hidden from everyone but technical experts. This can extend how many people can be creative, but it can ruin the distinction earned by hard work. It can make the tools harder to modify by the users and, thus, less owned by them. Therefore, it is important that tools develop but remain open and modifiable.

Affinity spaces can also degenerate when they cease to demand new and ongoing learning from everyone, no matter how expert. Real experts always try to find new hard problems that challenge and eventually extend their expertise. Pseudo-experts are people who rest on their laurels and let their expertise become stale and routine.

It is interesting and exciting that we are now talking about people being real experts in spaces where everyone is invited to be an expert if they wish and if they are given the chance to do so. We are talking about spaces where people are judged as experts based on their work and contributions, not on their credentials or outside status. And yet, we are also talking about spaces where people can still count and contribute even if they do not wish to go all the way to expertise.

Imagine a college that was nothing but hundreds of linked affinity spaces built around many different important problems or endeavors. People graduate when they have found a passion through a trajectory of different interests they have pursued in the search for that passion. Their "major" is constituted by the significant contributions they have made to the affinity space or spaces devoted to their passion. Typically, to find that passion a student will explore a wide range of different problems and potential interests, along the way acquiring a broad understanding of different knowledge domains. To make significant contributions in any of these interest-driven, problem-focused spaces, a student will need to collaborate and consult with others who have different kinds of knowledge and expertise, further enhancing their appreciation for different disciplinary perspectives. In addition, to participate successfully in these affinity spaces, students will need to develop skills in communication, teamwork, problem-solving, and so forth.

When they "graduate," they can stay on in an affinity space, helping others, still affiliated with the college, even as a type of mentor, "graduate student," or "faculty member." The college is a set of blended physical spaces and virtual ones, virtual ones linking people not just via the Internet, but via virtual worlds and social media. There are no Carnegie units and there are no letter grades, but, rather achievements honored by people with whom they have, at least for a time and in a place, walked the same path and shared an important endeavor. People start and finish at different times, go and come back, and their achievements, contributions, and even legacy remain in the space, a record of growth, rather than a "transcript."

So Tabby Lou—old and shut-in—plus good people, plus good tools, plus an affinity space that owns the tools and coordinates the people for learning, mastery, and innovation: that is one good example of synchronized intelligence.

One thing we badly need today are affinity spaces in which we tell what I will call "storied truths." In storied truths, evidence is storied. I have argued in this book that people like stories because they are good, not because they are true. Good stories can motivate, comfort, and inspire. But they can be dangerous when they are not true in areas that matter.

It is important that we learn and cultivate the skill of creating good stories around important true things. To sell a society on health care for all, statistics and facts are not enough. A good story that displays the meaning and moral value of those statistics and facts is crucial to move us humans. If we want to change the world, or now even survive in it, we need to stop separating facts and figures as science from stories as the humanities. There is an art to telling the truth. It is a harder and better art than telling lies.

Individual artists can, of course, tell such stories. Many a good film or novel does. But I am suggesting something more. Imagine a political party, a think tank, an institution, an advocacy group devoted to storied truths, to motivating people to face evidence and truth rather than just seek mental comfort. Such an endeavor would not make up lies to manipulate people. Rather, such an endeavor would be as devoted to evidence as a good scientist and as devoted to storytelling as a good artist. Such an endeavor would contextualize evidence. It would show us what the evidence means to the heart and the mind.

The telling of storied truths would be a blend of good science and good art. The goal would be to motivate action, engage understanding and imagination, and compete with mental comfort stories and with ideology untied to evidence and truth. Yes, the goal would also be to make evidence and truth "sexy."

Storied truths are really about getting people to engage with perspectives based on evidence. They are not really about "converting" them. And, indeed, different storied truths can clash, since evidence is always partial. But that is a clash of minds and truth that is all to the good. You show me your story and I will show you mine, but let's both of us seek not just comfort, but truth, solutions, and progress as well.

In addition to storied truths, there are also storied possibilities. Storied possibilities would tell stories about what might happen, what might be in the future, based on ways of looking at our partial evidence. Such stories would set visions in terms of which we can interpret current evidence but move beyond it to make new things happen. Because, after all, we humans are not victims of the way things are, we are makers of worlds. Affinity spaces are good places to imagine new possibilities and even to help make them come true. They can recruit different perspectives, diversity, and multiple talents to tell stories no one person could have made up on his or her own.

So we could imagine an "assignment" like this: if you believe in universal public health care, tell me a storied truth or storied possibility that would make me really engage with the idea, want to find out more about it and about the evidence for its viability and morality. If you believe in market-driven, profit-based health care, you do the same. Don't tell me lies, don't make up facts, but don't just give me figures, facts, and statistics. At the very least, your story should force me to make mine better and vice versa. I am not arguing that all public debate should be storied, only that some of it should be, because good stories motivate humans to think and act, and untrue good stories motivate them, too often, to act badly or, at least, to invite the world to bite back long and hard.

But my talk here about storied truths and storied possibilities is getting too abstract. Let's look at an actual affinity space producing storied truths. We turn again to The Sims. A German woman who calls herself Yamx on the Internet read the bestselling nonfiction book *Nickel and Dimed: On (Not) Getting By in America* by Barbara Ehrenreich (2001). Reading the book inspired her to make up a game, actually a new way to play The Sims, in a sense to engage in a "translation" of the book into game play in The Sims.

In *Nickel and Dimed,* Ehrenreich tells of going undercover as a low-wage worker in Florida, Maine, and Minnesota. She wanted to find out how nonskilled workers make ends meet. She spent one month in each location, where she worked full-time and attempted to live only on the money earned in the low-wage jobs she could find.

Ehrenreich's book details the mental and physical rigors of low-wage jobs and makes it clear that such jobs deserve a living wage. Her book makes it clear, too, that so-called low-skilled jobs require a great deal of skill in coping with time pressures, multiple jobs, physically demanding work, and demeaning customers and managers. Being poor is hard work since managing life with little free time and even less money is a massively demanding task and survival is always in the balance. In many respects, Ehrenreich herself just didn't have the skills required.

From Germany, writing in English on the Community Forum on Electronic Art's The Sims2 website (http://thesims2.ea.com), Yamx offers Sims players the following challenge:

SIMS 2: NICKEL AND DIMED CHALLENGE

This challenge was inspired by, and is named for, the book *Nickel and Dimed* by Barbara Ehrenreich (which has nothing whatsoever to do with Sims, but is nevertheless highly recommended). The idea is to mimic, as closely as possible, the life of an unskilled single mother trying to make ends meet for herself and her kids.

THE GOAL:

Raising your kids successfully until they're old enough to take care of themselves. If you can get all children to adult age without anyone dying or being taken away by the social worker, you've made it. If you want a kid to go to college, they can, but ONLY if they manage to raise at least $2500 in scholarships, since you won't be able to help them. Also, they have to live with you until their late teens (after all, 13 year olds don't go to college). Once the age indicator reads "becomes an adult in 5 days" (or less), you can have them move to college, but not before that.

The Sims lends itself to this sort of challenge very well in some respects. It is, after all, a life simulator. It is well suited to translating real-world actions into game choices and actions. There are, however, two problems. First, acting out the actions people have done in the real world can be a bore in a game. While shooting in a military game might be engaging for some, shopping for clothes when you have very little money is much less so. That certainly does not sound like a good game mechanic.

Second, while The Sims is a life simulator, it is not a very good simulator of poverty. It is a commercial game and because being poor is neither fun nor entertaining, The Sims tends to best represent virtual lives that are considerably more pleasurable. The game certainly does not include much of the aggravations of real-world poverty. For example, if you call the fire department, they come quickly and put out your fire, regardless of what neighborhood you live in.

Because The Sims is not a great tool kit for building the sort of simulation Yamx's challenge demands, she creates many rules to render it a better tool. In fact, she builds a veritable rule book. She uses The Sims not just as a game in itself, but as a tool with which she can make up elaborate rules of play. She is making up her own game.

Yamx has players download a residential lot and house she created herself to greatly restrict their resources. She stipulates many conditions that limit what parts of the game can and cannot be used. Let's look at just a few of these rules, such as this one:

> No cheats (except move_objects to remove bugged items)—in particular no kaching, motherload, maxmotives, or anything that aids survival. (If you want to use a hack to make the phone ring only five times instead of twenty, that's fine with me.) Custom content is okay if its things like recolors or hairstyles. No special objects that will make your sims life easier, like a bottomless fridge or items priced $0.

Lots of Sims players use "cheats" to give themselves infinite money or other advantages so that they do not have to go through the drudgery of starting at the bottom and slowly working themselves up in the world. These cheats are not necessarily a bad thing. They allow players to play the game in the way they want, for example, to concentrate on building houses and designing clothes without worrying about low-end jobs and tight schedules or money running out. But, obviously, for Yamx's challenge, such cheats would ruin its "realism," its fidelity to the life of a poor and struggling single parent.

We can note something that is quite apparent in many of Yamx's rules: She is thoroughly knowledgeable about the technical details of The Sims as a game, as a simulation, and as a piece of software. She has considerable technical knowledge, but she is using it to build social engagement with both the game and issues of poverty.

Here is another one of Yamx's rules:

No quitting without saving after bad events.

The last rule above is a tough one for gamers. Gamers, young and old, often just turn off a game without saving what they have done when things have gone badly wrong and they do not want to live with the consequences. Obviously, poor people cannot do this in real life, and players taking Yamx's challenge cannot do it either.

While Yamx is designing a rule kit, she is not a "boss." Players regularly write to her in the thread and dispute her rules. In turn, Yamx defends her rules or changes them. For instance, some players write back to Yamx telling her that her restrictions are not realistic in terms of how poor people actually live in the real world, as in the post below:

> Hi, I am about to start this challenge. I just have one thing to say before I do. Being a poor person, I am very well qualified to say that no smoke detector is completely unreasonable. They are required by law in all low-income housing and given away freely by fire depts to poor residents for the asking, at least in the USA.

Yamx's response to this post suggests what counts as "realism" in her challenge and here we begin to get at the heart of what she is doing. Her response, in this and other such cases, shows us that she is focused not on a set of rules that are fully realistic in terms of the real world, since this cannot be achieved in The Sims or, for that matter, in any simulation. Any simulation is a simplification of reality made to help us understand issues that are often too complex to be dealt with all at once. Yamx is focused on modifying how people play the game so that their game play captures the degree of challenge in a poor's person's life and "the feel" of being a poor single parent:

Oh, I realize that in real life, there are fire alarms in poor neighborhoods. Just as in real life, poor people can be terribly creative, and charismatic, and great cooks, and . . .

The point is that within the game, many real-world difficulties simply don't happen. There is no rent—everyone owns their house, no medical bills, no vandalism (except maybe someone kicking over your trash can), you can get away with having only one outfit, which never needs to be washed or mended, your children automatically get a full set of new clothes when they outgrow the old ones . . .

In a nutshell, the life of a poor sim is still MUCH easier than the life of a poor person (as you know). So therefore some of the rules are there simply to make sim life harder, and thereby bring it a little closer to real life.

Also, the fire alarms in the game work unreasonably well. Where on earth do you find one in real life that has the fire brigade on your doorstep in ten seconds?

There are many queries and responses like this on the thread. Yamx makes it clear that she knows "the challenge can only mimic the real thing to a small extent" and that she is trying to generate a feeling of "barely scraping by" and "of having very few options and just having to put up with a lot of stuff that was so apparent in the book." Yamx is using The Sims as a tool kit to design a simulation that creates the "feel" of being a poor single parent, not to engage in a realistic depiction like a documentary or realistic novel. Her simulation is a game with consequential decisions and problems to be solved by the players and a clear win state that is delineated in her rules.

The Sims allows players to make an "album" that works something like a storyboard for a movie. The player can annotate pictures, creating an illustrated story. Yamx makes writing such an illustrated story after one has finished the challenge part of the challenge. She offers her own illustrated story as an example. Throughout the thread, Yamx reads and comments encouragingly on people's stories (and they avidly seek her feedback). For players who do not know how to create such illustrated stories and upload them, she provides a link to a tutorial and offers them guidance, encouragement, and support. She is a teacher in the sense not of telling people what to do, but in the sense of encouraging and resourcing their own creativity and productivity. This is very much a role we want for twenty-first-century teachers in our schools.

Finally, consider the two posts below in which players clearly bridge the game (both The Sims and Yamx's challenge) with their real lives.

This is pretty true to life! And I love it. When my son is older, I'll show him this as a story, he's only 11 months right now . . . So yeah! But I love that there are people out there who truly understand and have empathy for single parents, moms or dads.

. . .

So, even though this is . . . wow . . . so much like history repeating itself (I had a child and a toddler when I became a single mom; then I had a baby and had to go back to work in 7 weeks—and had to pay $125 a week for a sitter back when I was making only 10 bucks an hour. It was . . . interesting. We made it though. My daughter's going for her master's, my son is a musician writing his own stuff and my youngest son just got high marks and is about to enter college. So, the single mom gig is tough—but it's doable.

This might be a nice way to tell my kids a bit about their history in a Sim-ish kind of way. :) Very very well done challenge Yamx. Kudos!

Note here how the trafficking between the virtual world and the real world goes in both directions, and neither side is privileged. Yamx's game reflects real life and, in turn, the play sessions and illustrated stories her game has generated can be used to inform people in real life. The players' own play sessions and illustrated stories are treated as legitimate representations of reality, right along with novels, movies, and real-life storytelling, each with their own "truth" to tell.

Yamx's challenge as a whole—the play, the discussions on the thread, the illustrated stories done and discussed after play—is one example of an affinity space being used to story truth, to render true things intellectually and emotionally meaningful by means of design, play, and art. We do not have a "true story," which is just a narrative of facts, but, rather, we have facts and realities storied in ways that make them "real" to those of us who have not experienced them or thought deeply about them.

Yamx's challenge is a good example of synchronized intelligence. The people engaging with each other in various countries share a passion for the Sims and leverage their own individual intelligence in coordination with Yamx, with all the others on the thread who are engaged with the challenge, and with powerful tools. These tools are the Sims software, its album function, the various design tools people can use for illustrating their albums, and the social media built around the game, in this case, the thread in which the challenge was conducted. It is clear that Yamx and others really own these tools. They readily open the hood and modify them and recruit them powerfully for their own purposes.

In school, Yamx's challenge would have crossed the borders between social science, technology learning, and design and art. All the better. Schools should readily do the same in the name of real understanding and problem solving.

Affinity spaces based around a game like the aforementioned Foldit, in which players fold pieces of proteins to see if they can discover the optimal fold for the protein as a whole (a daunting task even for a super computer), have led to important scientific discoveries. Players in this game, as a group, have published in prestigious scientific journals and have discovered, for example, the correct fold for a protein that helps cause AIDS, a discovery that had eluded scientists for years. They also readily discuss protein chemistry and ways that the game could be improved, though they are not professional chemists or game designers. Affinity spaces can be used to crowdsource knowledge building, even on the part of "amateurs." But I have suggested here that they can be used for gaining skills and understanding, producing things, and illuminating real-world political and social issues as well.

Synchronized intelligence in an affinity space is a dance of people and their tools with low barriers to entry and high standards. People become not just minds, but Minds. They become plug-and-play minds ready to accomplish things in the world. They do not need formal institutions, great wealth, professional credentials, or high status to underwrite their efforts. They have, in many ways, short-circuited some of the key sources of human stupidity.

21

Interlude to Forestall Possible Misunderstandings

IN THIS BOOK WE HAVE MOVED FROM STUPIDITY TO smartness. But as we now try to identify twenty-first-century solutions to human stupidity, several possible misunderstandings need to be forestalled before we finish.

In the last chapter I was not trying to romanticize affinity spaces and other groups on the Internet. I well know that they can be bad and go bad as easily as they can be good. Furthermore, even in the good ones, a fairly small number of people tend to make the most contributions and gain higher-order skills, though it is all to the good that everyone else's contributions can count as well. The Internet will not save us.

Digital tools and social media of any sort will not save us either. They are as easy—perhaps easier—to use badly as they are to use well. They can do harm and they can do good, just as books have done: remember the death and destruction caused by people reading sacred texts in violent ways. Tools are dangerous when they control us and we don't control them. The smarter and the more user friendly tools get, the more dangerous they can become if we handle them without reflection and without occasionally opening them up to see what is inside.

Despite being the topic of many books that claim otherwise, collective intelligence alone won't save us. It is true that modern science is no longer an individual enterprise, but ever more an enterprise of collective intelligence. Over the last fifty years, levels of teamwork in science have increased greatly. While the most highly cited papers in a field used to be the product of individuals like Einstein or lesser bright lights, today papers by multiple authors receive more than twice as many citations as do those by individuals.

Both scientists and amateurs are more and more linked to virtual spaces where they collectively contribute to hard problems. In the Polymath Project, professional mathematicians put up unsolved problems on the Internet and let other mathematicians have a try at them while everyone considers and builds on each other's contributions. However, professional scientists and mathematicians still spend a great deal of time talking and working with each other. Face-to-face talk and physical space have not become less important, despite New Age hype about the matter.

Amateurs have been networked in Foldit to play with different ways proteins can fold and in Galaxy Zoo to classify different types of galaxies. While this means that such amateurs have made important contributions to science, it does not mean that they are learning a lot of science unless they join with others to engage in proactive learning beyond Foldit and Galaxy Zoo—and some do and some don't.

Collective intelligence, whether on the part of professionals or amateurs, works best with problems, as in science and mathematics, in which questions have definitive answers, however hard they are to discover. It does not work as well for addressing social concerns and policy issues, where there are no definitive empirical solutions. However, we saw in the last chapter that we can and must connect people and good tools to solve problems in areas where there are no definitive answers, yet there are still better and worse ways to proceed in relation to specific purposes, values, and goals.

I have argued that individual intelligence on its own is today insufficient and even dangerous, given the complexity and high risk of the modern world. But groups, as we all know, can easily be dumber than the dumbest person in them. Many liberal educators have championed group discussion and brainstorming as a panacea for modern learning. In such discussions and brainstorming, liberal educators often downplay criticism and debate in favor of uncritical acceptance.

Research has shown that brainstorming, in which students throw out as many ideas as they can with no critique—supposedly to free them up from fear of criticism—can easily make students less creative than they would have been if left on their own. Teams, whether students or not, actually perform better when the free flow of ideas is coupled with critique and debate.

Furthermore, the constitution of a group is crucial to its creativity. The presence of perspectives unfamiliar to others in the group—even of creative wrong answers—can increase creativity. Furthermore, groups in which everyone is a stranger or is new to the project and groups in which everyone knows everyone else or has worked together a good deal are both less creative than groups in which there is a balance of the two.

At least in the case of scientists, face-to-face interaction is still crucial. In research that assessed the quality of the scientific research conducted by groups by counting the number of subsequent citations—the gold coin in academic research—it was found that the best research was consistently produced when scientists were working close to each other, often sharing the same physical space and could interact with each other face-to-face. I see no reason why the same is not true for many types of group endeavors that seek to enhance intelligence and creativity.

It turns out, as well, that the sorts of physical spaces that lead to creativity tend to be ones where chance encounters can take place, often among people from different and unexpected backgrounds. This trend has been found both for science and for business (in fact, Steve Jobs championed it).

I started my career in theoretical linguistics engaged in syntactic theory. At the time, linguistics had been revolutionized by Noam Chomsky. The linguistics department at the Massachusetts Institute of Technology was for decades the premier linguistics department in the world, not just because of Chomsky but because of a bevy of great linguists and graduate students. The linguistics department was in a ramshackle building called Building 20, built quickly and cheaply during World War II for defense work and kept alive after the war by the need to accommodate the growth of the university due to the GI Bill. The building housed groups of academics and technicians that had been placed there by chance and in some cases by low status at MIT (e.g., linguistics prior to Chomsky).

By the time it was demolished in 1998, Building 20 had become a legend as a creative space, "a building with soul." Scientists working there made a significant number of important discoveries in areas like high-speed photography and the physics of microwaves. The Bose Corporation had its origins in Building 20. In 1956, Amar Bose, a graduate student working on a dissertation on non-linear systems in electrical engineering, was unhappy with the quality of the speakers on a new high-end hi-fi system he had bought. Bose dropped into the Acoustics Lab near his office in Building 20, and began to tinker. The Bose Corporation was founded in 1964 and made Bose a billionaire. In 2011, Amar Bose donated a majority of his company, in non-voting shares, to MIT. His success, with its origins in the haphazard collection of scientists and students in Building 20, suggests that fancy buildings or sequestering scientists by discipline do not always lead to the best results.

Building 20 gave rise to the first video game (a field I now work in) and to Chomskyan linguistics (the field I started in). Building 20 housed people in linguistics, biology, psychology, computer science, and other fields—fields which had less to do with each other before Building 20 than after it—in a haphazard way. Chomsky has said:

> Building 20 was a fantastic environment. It looked like it was going to fall apart. But it was extremely interactive. There was a mixture of people who later became separate departments interacting informally all the time. You would walk down the corridor and meet people and have a discussion.

Building 20 was not fancy. Stewart Brand, in his paper "How Buildings Learn," uses Building 20 as an example of a space where creativity seemed to flourish precisely because the space was designed in such a low-level way and was so unwanted by others who were more focused on institutional rules and status. Rooms could be remade, walls torn down, places decorated without anyone caring. The building's "temporary nature"—it was constructed hastily during the war and meant to be torn done afterwards—meant its occupants could abuse it in ways no administrator would have tolerated in a "better" building. As a website devoted to Building 20 says: "If you wanted to run a wire from one lab to another, you didn't ask anybody's permission—you just got out a screwdriver and poked a hole through the wall."

Jonah Lehrer in a *New Yorker* article called "Groupthink: The Brainstorming Myth" points to this lesson that Building 20 has to teach us:

> The lesson of Building 20 is that when the composition of the group is right—enough people with different perspectives running into one another in unpredictable ways—the group dynamic will take care of itself. All these errant discussions add up. In fact, they may even be the most essential part of the creative process. Although such conversations will occasionally be unpleasant—not everyone is always in the mood for small talk or criticism—that doesn't mean that they can be avoided. The most creative spaces are those which hurl us together. It is the human friction that makes the sparks.

Human intelligence is not tied primarily to individuals operating alone, nor is it tied primarily to groups discussing in a critique-free space. It is not tied primarily to digital tools, virtual spaces, or fancy buildings, even ones where the room is smarter than the people in it thanks to "smart tools." It does not seem to be tied to anything much like what our current schools and colleges have become, though many a public school today certainly qualifies in terms of underfunded ramshackle buildings. Rather, human intelligence and creativity, today more than ever, are tied to connecting—synchronizing—people, tools, texts, digital and social media, virtual spaces, and real spaces in the right ways, in ways that make us Minds and not just minds, but also better people in a better world. Of course, we don't know yet how best to do this and there will surely be more than one way. But it is where we need to head as educators, policy makers, parents, and citizens.

22

Getting Smarter
Before It's Too Late

WE NOW HAVE A WEALTH OF DIGITAL TOOLS. FOL-
lowing is a list of just some of them:

- Adaptive artificial computer tutors that can teach and be taught
- Multimedia that can represent information in many different modalities
- Simulations
- Virtual worlds
- Video games
- Animated pedagogical agents that can teach and mentor
- Digital tools for collaboration and collective intelligence
- Digital design and production tools that allow for professional level quality
- Interest-driven and passionate affinity spaces devoted to almost anything you can name
- Social media for both real-time and asynchronous interaction
- Collaborative writing and research sites (e.g., Wikipedia)
- Search tools
- Augmented reality (real-world environments augmented by computer-generated images)

Though many of these tools have been around for some years, they are not used or are poorly used in schools and even in colleges. Too often, they are separated from, rather than blended with, face-to-face interactions, physical spaces, and deep educational uses that go beyond entertainment. All these tools are like crayons: they are just tools that can make and do good things (e.g., art) or make a mess (e.g., crayon all over the walls).

Let's say I asked you to consider all the tools above and tell me how they could best help poor children, in their early years, prepare for school and success in mainstream society after school, thereby closing the "literacy gap" between poor and rich children. The answer might be (a) to engage children (and help parents engage with their children) in extended conversations about the world and (b) to show them, through rich images, goal-based actions, and extended experiences, what oral and written words mean and do in the world. This could best be done by using a suite of these tools in combination with non-digital tools and real-world interactions. It would have the best chance of success if it started early and was extended through the first eight years of a child's education at school and in libraries, community centers, and after-school programs. All these programs would share data (something that digital media can help with) in order to support children's learning in a coordinated way. In this scenario, digital media are a suite of tools and servants in a larger mission, not shiny toys of any real interest in their own right.

Digital media can make us smarter. They can make our schools and society smarter. But only if we realize they are tools that need to be put to good use. Digital media—games, the Internet, social media, and various production tools—are ways to make and take meaning. We use them to produce meaning (not just information, but emotion as well). We use them to receive meaning. In this sense, digital tools are just like books. In fact, books and digital media are both technologies for making and taking meaning, forms of "writing" (producing meaning) and "reading" (consuming meaning), as are television and film. They are all, in that sense, "literacies."

We know a good deal about books, about becoming literate in the sense of both learning to read and learning to write. Books do not make you smart all by themselves. In fact, they can make you stupid if you believe everything they say or if you only read books that contain viewpoints you already believe in.

For most people (though not for all) success in school is necessary (but no longer sufficient) for success in mainstream society. We have known for a long time that there are two early home-based factors that correlate most strongly with success in learning to read and success in school more generally: how much talk a child before five has heard from adults and the child's *oral* vocabulary at five (especially in terms of more formal language that is also found in books). These two factors are obviously related.

By "talk" here I don't mean mere talking, I mean lots of talk that is not just about the here and now or directions (do this, don't do that), but sustained talk on topics that involve experience and how to think about it. More privileged parents tend to talk a good deal in this way to their kids. Poorer parents often do not, either because they are too busy with work or because they accept cultural forms that stress giving directions to children rather than having elaborate conversations. Sustained, elaborated talk and interaction with adults is the foundation for learning to read. In turn, learning to read and to talk in "academic language" when appropriate is the foundation of learning content throughout later schooling.

The most effective forms of talk and reading with children are interactive. The child is not told to sit silently and listen, but is actively recruited as a participant, led to ask questions and make comments. Parents engaged in such interactive talk and book reading with their children support them in interactions around the book. They attribute meaning to their children's talk even when the child can only respond in fairly minimal ways.

The most effective forms of talk and reading with children also involve the adults' stressing links between talk, books, other media, and the world. For example, a parent might point to a chipmunk in a picture book and say,

"The chipmunk in the forest is just like the one in 'Henry's forest' in *Thomas the Tank Engine*." The child plays with *Thomas the Tank Engine* toys, but also watches videos about real trains and goes to a train museum. Furthermore, parents who engage in this sort of talk and interaction encourage their children to develop, as young as two or three, "islands of expertise" around things like dinosaurs, trains, or anything else. When the child becomes a "little expert," he or she develops knowledge and vocabulary in terms of which the adult can carry on yet more complex interactive talk and reading.

Interactive, elaborated, sustained talk about experience; connecting books, media, talk, and the world; and cultivating islands of expertise—all before the age of five—these are the foundations of school success and often of later success in college and society, at least as they now exist. Let's call this essential early foundation "talk, text, and knowledge mentoring," or "TTK mentoring" (where "talk" means interactive, sustained, elaborated talk).

It is extremely difficult to overcome the advantage that TTK mentoring gives a child when it begins early in the home well before the child starts school. Furthermore, such early mentoring gives the child a deep social and emotional connection to literacy, to school-based knowledge, and to elaborated (book-like) talk. It gives literacy a social and emotional charge because literacy is connected to children's early socialization into their families and family-based identities.

A child who comes to school without a great many hours of such mentoring—and the differences here between richer and poorer kids are astounding—and without such a social and emotional affiliation with literacy and academic language is at a very high risk for school failure, especially if what the child gets in school is only instruction about literacy without any TTK mentoring. The problem can be remedied with great effort over a long period of time—actually over the course of the first eight years of schooling at the least—but it is not easy and it gets ever harder the longer one waits to remedy it in a deep way via TTK mentoring and good teaching. Furthermore, something has to give the child a social and emotional connection to school-based literacy, a connection that often does not happen in today's urban schools.

We know much less about digital media than we know about books. But what we know about digital media all indicates that digital media, if they are to be tied to success in school and society, work just like books. Digital literacy, too, depends on early TTK mentoring of just the sort that print literacy does, and it requires such mentoring later for kids who do not get it at home early. The parent or mentor needs to involve children in interactive talk around video games. For knowledge and vocabulary building, they need to help children develop early "islands of expertise." Parents need to make connections among digital media, talk, texts, and the world. And they need to help the child develop an affective affiliation with ("feel for") digital media as a crucial form of meaning making in the modern world.

Some parents want to keep their children away from digital media in the first few years of life. This is as silly as keeping them away from books or crayons. Furthermore, texts, complex forms of talk, and digital media constantly intermingle with and reinforce each other in the modern world. Take a look at Pokémon or Yu-Gi-Oh (typical forms of convergent media involving card games, books, video games, television shows, and movies). Even though quite young kids now engage with Pokémon and Yu-Gi-Oh, the cards, books, and games involve complicated, complex, and specialist forms of oral and written language, surely as complex as any seen in school for most children at this age (see example in the References).

Later forms of digital media use involve yet more complex forms of narrative language and technical language. Children today will have to "read" (consume) and "write" (produce) with a whole suite of technologies, including texts, digital tools, and social media of different forms often used in complex combinations with each other. The point is not to keep digital and social media away from kids early, but to build on experiences with these media to create a pathway toward higher-order and complex thinking, skills, talk, and texts, just as we want to do with books.

TTK mentoring is important not just before age five, but throughout the trajectory of a child's acquisition of print literacy and digital literacy. As time goes on, the successful child has other mentors, today often ones found in the sorts of affinity spaces I discussed in the last chapter or in various other sorts of interest-driven groups on the Internet or in real spaces in community centers, after-school programs, libraries, museums, camps, and other centers of focused interest and possible expertise.

Apart from TTK mentoring, a necessary ingredient for success—more so today than ever before—is learning to sustain interest for the long haul, and this requires "grit." "Grit" is an invented term that means perseverance and passion of the sort necessary for "persistence past failure" through long hours of practice. In the United States, even many privileged children who have received a great deal of TTK mentoring do not go on to learn grit. Parents and mentors indulge them in switching interests before they have achieved mastery and learned true grit.

Above I said that school today is, for many young people, still a necessary, but no longer a sufficient, condition for success in society. For some young people, lack of meaningful learning in school can be ameliorated via learning out of school. For all children there are twenty-first-century skills that are, at least today, more often developed out of school than in it. These are skills like the following: ability to master new forms of complex and often technical language and thinking; ability to engage in collaborative work and collective intelligence where the group is smarter than the smartest person in it; creativity and innovation; ability to deal with complexity and to think about and solve problems with respect to complex systems; ability to find and marshal evidence and to revise arguments in the face of evidence; the ability to produce with digital media and other technologies and not just consume their content; and the ability to avoid being a victim of social forces and institutions that are creating a more competitive, stressful, and unequal world. If one cares about one's own child, or about equity and everyone's children, these are essential matters.

It is crucial that young people, as they move past early childhood, engage with books and digital media in what I will call a "higher-end, value-added" way. Just reading books does not make you smarter or more successful. You have to read them and interact with them in certain ways. You have to push yourself to read things at or just above your current level of understanding; you have to use your reading to think about and solve problems; you have to persist past failure and sustain effort over many hours and years for areas you want to master; and you have to relate what you read to new but related skills, to ways of intervening in the world, and to other forms of meaning making, digital or otherwise.

Finally, you have to be able to read like a writer (asking how the book is written, why it is written that way, and how it might have been written otherwise), read with critical questions in mind that make you suspend belief in what the book says until you have thought deeply and widely about the matter, and you need to engage in your own writing. Since digital media and social media are (like books) ways of making and taking meaning, the same thing is true for them.

The higher-order value-added way to deal with digital and social media is the same as it is for books. Every feature I have listed above for traditional literacy is true of any digital literacy, whether this be video game playing, using the Internet, engaging in an affinity space on the Internet, or using social media to make connections.

This does not mean that we cannot and should not use books or digital media for fun and entertainment. What it means is that unless we take some books or some digital media further in terms of persistence, problem solving, connection making, skill building, production, and critique, they will not, in the end, really make us smarter. For many people, taking books or digital media beyond entertainment or mere interest requires developing a passion, a passion that will carry them past challenges and failure through thousands of hours of engagement and practice. It takes thousands of hours of practice and persistence past failure to become expert in

anything deep. Helping young people find a passion or a trajectory of related passions is often a crucial requirement for a twenty-first-century education in or out of school. In today's world, if your child's books, games,
or media don't have "legs" in this sense, in my view the child is at risk for
failure—even for victimhood—in the modern world, whether they are rich
or poor, good in school or not.

THERE IS A PROFOUND PARADOX in all that I have said thus far
in this chapter. I have been talking about the essentials for success in school
and society. But school and society are both in crisis today. I have argued
throughout this book that lots of things about today's schools, institutions,
and society make us all stupider, not smarter, and this in a world where stupidity is more dangerous than it has ever been.

Let's consider college and inequality. For the first decades after World
War II colleges served as a powerful force for social mobility. They do so
no longer. Today a college education serves as a powerful force for class
stratification. The vast majority of young Americans who currently hold a
bachelor's degree are from families above the median income level. Nearly
75 percent of students attending the most competitive (high-status) colleges
come from families in the top quartile of income. College has become a
powerful force for "the intergenerational reproduction of privilege" and the
growth of inequality. Furthermore, scores on tests like the SAT and the ACT
do not fully account for this class-based disparity in college education. Even
less-well-off students with good scores have a significantly smaller chance of
going to college.

Higher education today has become highly polarized. At the top, competitive colleges enroll 46 percent of all post-secondary students. At the bottom, community colleges enroll 49 percent of all post-secondary students.
The middle is disappearing. Less-competitive four-year colleges enroll only 6
percent of all post-secondary students (and face the stiffest competition from
e-learning and for-profit colleges). We are moving toward a system where

there are "good" degrees and "poor" ones and few in-between (sounds a bit like the "disappearing middle class," doesn't it?).

We have seen throughout this book that growing inequality is bad for everyone's health and well-being. It is bad for a participatory society in which people must feel that they count, matter, and can contribute. Worse yet, we are in danger of becoming a society in which the highest point of our education system (college) gives degrees worth more in terms of status than in terms of knowledge, innovation, problem solving, and twenty-first-century intelligence.

I have pointed out that our education system, from beginning to end, should not be defined in terms of job skills and employment, though that is, alas, the direction in which we are moving fast. A focus on jobs means we are using our education system primarily to train people for service work (the biggest source of jobs in a developed economy) or for higher-status jobs that, in the fast-changing modern world, often do not even exist at the time a young person is in school or, if they do, will not last anywhere nearly as long as the student's career after school.

Education must focus on giving every member of society a valued life and the ability to contribute, to learn how to learn, and to adapt to changing times. It has to create a sense of equality at the level not of status or jobs per se, but at the level of participation in knowledge, innovation, and national and global citizenship for a smarter, safer, and better world.

The digital age, coupled with the complexity and risk of the modern world, has caused a massive change in how we humans deal with knowledge. Unfortunately, this change has not yet moved to most schools or colleges. Schools and colleges are focused on content. Content is the body of facts, information, and formulas to which the activities of science and other knowledge-building enterprises have given rise. Schools and colleges often stress this content rather than the activities that gave rise to it. However, digital media now allow us to store, search, access, and represent this content in many different ways. Anyone can find the content any time.

This content, though we have often assumed that storing it in heads and writing it down on tests is the goal of education, was never really worth much when separated from the activities and thinking and problem-solving skills that gave rise to it. It is worth even less now when it is so readily available. Today, thanks to technology and the massive growth of complexity, science and other knowledge-building enterprises focus on what we can call "hard problems."

Hard problems are deep problems that are often not centered in only one academic discipline or in any academic discipline at all. To attack, solve, or even offer plausible answers to hard problems requires persistence, smart tools, good means of representation, and effective forms of collaboration. Hard problems have "legs" in the sense that attacking them leads to a wealth of connected knowledge and skills. Hard problems require us to learn lots of "content" (facts, information, and formulas), not just to memorize, but to use to think with, solve problems with, and offer explanations with.

Finding the correct fold for a protein in Foldit (or in chemistry itself, for that matter) is a hard problem. It requires good tools (e.g., the game itself) and good visual representations of the 3D structure of proteins. Finding good ways to collaborate with others is important if one wants to perform at the higher levels. Thinking about the problem leads to a wealth of connections to chemistry and other aspects of science and the human body, connections that can be explored in affinity spaces connected to the game.

Designing a house in The Sims or in Second Life can be a hard problem. It requires good tools for designing and building and good representations of the geometry of built structures. If one wants to meet high standards for design, it is important to collaborate with others in affinity spaces that mentor people, set standards, and offer critique. The problem has a wealth of connections to 3D design, graphic arts, architecture, and environments. Another example: taking the "Nickel and Dimed Challenge" and trying to live the life of a poor single parent in an entertainment simulation like The

Sims is a hard problem indeed. It has a wealth of connections to simulations, social science, and the problems of society.

How to balance economic growth and environmental protection; how to lessen inequality without lessening motivation for hard effort; how to story facts and truths so that they motivate people to make better worlds; how to reform our schools; how to leverage diversity and still create a "commonwealth"; how to move past ideology toward pragmatic solutions to problems; how to solve the drug problem without putting people in prison; how to enable small-town stores to compete with big chains; how to make knowledge and discovery open source without killing incentives for creativity; how to deal with global warming when it is getting too late for some of the sanest solutions; what to do about a society where most of the jobs are poorly paid and don't generate a deep sense of human worth—these are all hard questions.

Here is one of my favorite hard questions: Recent evidence from studies of the brain has shown that violent action video games like Call of Duty lead to some quite positive cognitive effects. People who play games like this or even those who are trained on them in a laboratory are better than others at managing their attention to solve problems and at learning and transferring what they learn. Surprisingly, players of such games even have a better basic "math sense" than non-players, and their ability to estimate quantities and categorize is better. The hard question is how we can extract the features of such games from their violent contexts and use them in different contexts to the same good effect. This problem connects to a wealth of knowledge about learning and the human mind.

In the digital age, we need to stop defining "courses" in terms of bodies of facts called "content." We need to define them in terms of hard problems that recruit facts as tools for problem solving. Even young children can engage hard problems. Asking why things float is a hard problem. Forming a good deck of the required forty Yu-Gi-Oh cards out of the thousands of cards available is a hard problem, one most young people solve collaboratively over time (and Yu-Gi-Oh has great legs to literacy, numeracy, and strategic thinking). We know that negotiating with young children is often better than simply ordering them around. Negotiating with an adult is a hard but fascinating problem for a child, one with connections to cognitive and language growth and school success.

I STARTED THIS BOOK DISCUSSING the many things that make us humans stupid: brain bugs and social bugs. But these things—if reversed— are just the factors that can build a deeper and better education for all. Then they become the basis for a new learning paradigm for schools, colleges, and society. To be smarter today we need Minds not just minds. We need synchronized intelligence; we need to be able to dance the dance of collective intelligence with others and our best digital tools. What I have called "talk, text, and knowledge (TTK) mentoring" and digital tools can be deployed in ways that reverse our brain bugs and social bugs to make us smarter. Looking back at the chapters in this book, let me sketch out the beginnings of such a paradigm change for smarter schools, people, and society:

The Circuit of Human Reflective Action: Real learning requires new experiences connected to goal-directed actions and to ways of properly assessing the results of our actions in terms of our goals. This requires mentorship from people who know how to assess such actions for such goals.

Digital media should extend, supplement, complement, or augment deep real-world experiences and interactions. We cannot be an electron in the real world, but we can be one in a video game for learning physics. Social media can connect us to people whose experiences we could never have imagined. Digital media are not ends in themselves. They are best when they extend us.

Human memory: Humans are not computers and computers are not humans. Humans and computers work best together when each supplements the weaknesses of the other. Human memory is really not memory in the sense that computers have memory. Human memory is about giving accounts and achieving accountability to ourselves and others. Computers should give us well-organized and well-represented facts and information to make this accounting process better suited for reaching shared goals and achieving collective intelligence in shared projects. For example, today computers can collect copious moment-by-moment data ("data mining") on a multitude of different variables (for example, when a student is using an artificial algebra tutor) and represent it in many useful ways that allow teachers, learners, and policy makers to assess learning and growth across time. There is less need then for our "drop out of the sky" standardized tests with their single scores generated out of the contexts of teaching and learning.

Mental comfort stories: We humans need stories that sustain and encourage us in the face of the difficulties and challenges of life. A real education should give us the resources to design and share better comfort stories, ones that are "storied truths" creating an evidentially based sense of possibility and hope, even as the story goes beyond facts to incorporate dreams and desired new worlds. I have cited the New Testament in this book several times because, whether one is a Christian or not, Christ told storied truths. Great literature is often storied truth. So, too, is the wisdom generated from lives lived well, like the sermons and speeches of Dr. Martin Luther King. The comfort such storied truths give us is often not the soft comfort of wishful thinking, but the hard comfort of possibility and hope in the face of despair.

Contexts: People need to learn in contexts where something is at stake for them, where what they are going to learn matters to them, and where they understand why it is important, worthwhile, and a valuable use of their time. I once met a young woman who failed geometry in school when it was called "Geometry," but came to love it when she designed virtual houses in a virtual world called "Second Life" (if you do not respect geometry, houses collapse).

Experience: Humans can communicate across social and cultural differences when they form shared associations for words and concepts based on shared experiences. The diverse experiences and backgrounds each person brings to the group offer rich opportunities for sharing experience and building new associations for others. At the same time, diversity must not destroy the possibility of a shared "common wealth" that is the basis of solidarity that goes beyond narrow niches. People who join passionate affinity spaces (see Chapter 20) on the Internet to discuss cats, health, video games, or almost anything else you can name, pool a great wealth of fruitful differences in age, class, backgrounds, skills, and experience. But they all share a common passion and language about that passion. And they often discover things that even experts did not know.

Status and solidarity: Every human being needs to feel a sense of worth and respect (status) and a sense of belonging and acceptance (solidarity). These are basic mental health needs. A deep learning space needs to create multiple routes to status, mitigate the effects of outside status that are not central to the goals of the learning space, and create solidarity (bonding) around shared passion, goals, and values in a group diverse enough not to become an isolated self-replicating echo chamber. People who join a good passionate affinity space to design virtual clothes, houses, and landscapes for the Sims (a life and community simulation and the bestselling video game in history) can contribute to the design community in many different ways, large and small. They come in all ages and sizes and races. Some days on the site a person leads and mentors, sometimes the person follows and learns. There is ample status and bonding for everyone. Like a candle flame, no one loses their status because someone else gains theirs.

Words: Meaning is based on associations rooted in our experiences. But when people come together across different identities and backgrounds, the "truth-seeking game" becomes an important way to make progress toward problem solving and shared goals. The truth-seeking game (based on public evidence and making claims that can be falsified) gives us a shared language referenced to a common world whose properties we are seeking jointly to discover. In a truth-seeking game we agree to engage in problem solving and discovery collaboratively with others with a goal of reaching truth and not just persuasion or the fulfillment of our desires and interests alone. To play this game requires that we formulate our claims in ways that are "falsifiable," that is, open to disconfirmation by ourselves or others (others who need not have our interests and desires at heart). Learning to play this game should be central to schooling, since it is the very foundation of a democratic civil society where problems can be effectively solved.

Agency: Humans need to feel like agents whose actions count and who have a chance of success or impact. They cannot feel as if what they do does not matter, does not count, or will never really work. This, too, is a basic mental health need. Digital tools are opening up many ways to focus, leverage, and empower the actions of all sorts of people, to resource their creativity, and to engage their active participation. The passionate affinity spaces we discussed earlier are one example, too often seen out of school rather than in it. So, too, are the tools (if used wisely) that allow people to produce their own media, news, video games, and ads and counter-ads.

Institutions: Formal institutions often freeze thought and solutions in the name of efficiency, something that can be dangerous in fast-changing times. Digital media and social media can allow us to organize outside of formal institutions in more emergent, flexible, and evolving ways. They can allow some institutions to become a home base for multiple, more flexible and adaptable affinity spaces, thereby mitigating the inertia of formal institutions. At the same time, any young person today will need to know not just how to navigate formal institutions, but also how to navigate and participate in the many more collaborative and adaptable forms of organization and collective problem solving to which digital technologies are giving rise. Knowing how to follow rules will become less important than knowing how to make them and change them.

Groups of One: Individual minds and isolated experts are dangerous in our complex, high-risk global world. Students will need to learn to face challenges and adapt to new ways of learning. While customization is good, students cannot and should not expect everything to be customized to their own styles. They should not be in new digitally enabled "Schools of One," but in "Schools of Five" in the sense that they can be members of teams in which each member not only has deep expertise but also can share and integrate this expertise with other people's skill-sets to solve problems that no single skillset can solve. Businesses call these teams "cross-functional teams." World of Warcraft calls them "hunting parties" (which is where I got "five" from, since this is the basic hunting party, which can, in turn, integrate as a team with other teams to make bigger parties).

Experts and Tools: In an age of collective intelligence rather than individual expertise, it is crucial to resource collective intelligence through smart tools that allow groups to learn, design, produce, and solve problems. These tools must be "owned" by the group in the sense that they can adapt the tools, transform them, mentor others in their use, and integrate them into their social organization.

This means user friendly is not always good. Today 3D printers hooked to computers allow everyday people to manufacture things for themselves. 3D design tools allow everyday people to make their own media. But such tools do not tell people what to make. They do not tell them what is good and what is bad. When they are used, owned, and modified as part and parcel of collectively intelligent groups with a good mission they can greatly enhance the world. When they are just used to fill up the world with more plastic (3D printers) or mindless media, then they are tools for stupidity.

Evading Knowledge: Humans do not like—and have a hard time—carrying "heavy" stuff in their heads. This is one more way in which human memory is not like computer storage. Digital tools can, in many different ways, serve as external storage devices for humans. But they should go much further and help humans to search, powerfully represent in multiple ways, and negotiate the meaning of information and facts. The Internet and other digital tools store information for us. This information only becomes knowledge when we have the good taste to know what to pick up and how to put it to good use. We need not only browse the web, but mine it. Developing "good taste" and "mining skills" should be central to school in the twenty-first century.

Complexity: The world is now so complex and so much at risk from the interactions of complex systems and from the unintended consequences of human interventions in them that learning to deal with complexity and think about complex systems is the most important twenty-first-century skill. This is a place where digital tools and digitally produced representations are essential. Humans cannot really deal with complexity and complex systems without digital tools like simulations and interactive models. Understanding and being able to use these tools collaboratively for problem solving (just as they are in science) should be basic to any modern schooling. Models (graphs, diagrams, prototypes, small-scale model objects, and representations of all sorts) are the basis of much modern thinking, knowledge, discovery, and problem solving (in science and in art).

Inclusive "We": High levels of inequality are lowering the health and well being of everyone and endangering our society as a democracy and civic/civil space. Inequality can make us unhealthy, untrusting in our society and its institutions, and it can cut society off from important sources of new insight and innovation. In short, it can make us all stupid. We must make more people—everyone—count. We cannot do this right now right away by giving everyone a "good job." But we can do it by helping everyone explore different interests and helping them find one or more interests to fan into a passion, a passion which can fuel lots of active participation and practice in the service of developing deep skills.

A key purpose of school and college must be to allow students to find passions for a good life and not just a good job. But this will require a paradigm shift in schools and colleges. They will have to stress not only that different people find different passions, but also be able to teach others and learn new things from others as they will need to combine their passions with others' for larger projects. Colleges today could be composed of a great multiple of passionate affinity spaces, blended in digital worlds and the real world. For example, students could live in, study, build, and problem solve in a digital version of the Italian Renaissance with others who are passionate about the Renaissance (see the video game *Assassin's Creed* for a realistic and modifiable Italian Renaissance world where you can enter and interact in authentic buildings and public spaces). This Renaissance space could live long past any one course and could allow students to stay long enough to become "teachers" or "faculty."

Big Minds, Not Little Minds: In an age of collective intelligence and passionate affinity spaces, where we cannot simply trust "experts," we all have to learn to be part of big Minds with big ideas. A Mind is a synchronized, well-choreographed integration of smart tools and individual minds to form a collective intelligence that can learn and adapt. Neither the tools nor the minds in a Mind lose their identities or distinctiveness. They just gain new powers as do dancers in a dance. The game *Foldit* is a great example. Everyday people are organized with each other via the game and its associated web site to compete with protein scientists and have fun in the process.

Mind Visions: What do YOU think WE should do? If you cannot help answer this question and motivate people to action for a vision, or if you trust "experts" or politicians to answer it alone, you have not been educated. You cannot really be a citizen in a democratic society in a high-risk world that will be driven by collective, synchronized intelligence or will be "out of business." How can school encourage Mind Visions? This is what the Liberal Arts at their best were always about: multiple visions, from art and science, of a better, fairer, sustainable world. What we have to add to this is the demand that each student become a maker of visions, a visionary, and not just a spectator of visions. Today's digital media, used well, can facilitate students to be visionaries.

For any learning, in or out of school, ask if that learning has any or all of the features we have just listed. For any use of digital tools or technology, ask if it is contributing to, truly enhancing or enabling, any or all of these features. I suggest that we use these features as our test for what a true education should be in the twenty-first century and what we should expect from digital media and technology when we are not entertaining ourselves to death. I am optimistic that we now have—or soon will have—the tools to save ourselves and make a better world where more and more people count, though we have just begun to put digital media to its best uses, especially globally.

But the key question is this: Do we have the will to save ourselves? Will we each sink in our own boat, however large or small it is, or will we bail water together in a journey to a better future? Will we let stupidity swamp us or will we gain the smarts to save ourselves and our children?

We need transformed schools and colleges to make us smarter, but even transformed schools and colleges cannot do it alone. And we certainly can't do it with the schools and colleges we have now. Getting smart is now a 24/7 enterprise because intelligence comes from cultivating our lives and all our experiences in the service of learning and growth. Digital media today can make learning in and out of school, for children and adults, engaging (not just "fun"), social, and life enhancing. Digital tools can make better minds and a better society, but they cannot do this by themselves.

References

PREFACE:

On more education not leading to more respect for evidence or science, see:

Brockman, J. (Ed.) (2012). *This will make you smarter: New scientific concepts to improve your thinking.* New York: Harper Collins.

Gee, J. P. (2004). *Situated language and learning: A critique of traditional schooling.* London: Routledge.

Haidt, J. (2012). *The righteous mind: Why good people are divided by politics and religion.* New York: Pantheon.

Malka, A., Krosnick, J. A., & Langer, G. (2009). The association of knowledge with concern about global warming: Trusted information sources shape public thinking. *Risk Analysis,* 29.5: 633-647.

Pierce, C. P. (2010). *Idiot America: How stupidity became a virtue in the land of the free.* New York: Anchor.

On the class gap becoming wider than the black-white gap:

Duncan, G. J., & Murnane, R. J. (2011). Introduction: The American dream: Then and now. In G. J. Ducan & R. J. Murnane (Eds.). *Whither opportunity? Rising inequality, schools, and children's life chances* (pp. 3-23). New York: Russell Sage Foundation.

CHAPTER 1

On Orwell's question:

Chomsky, N. (1986). *Knowledge and language: Its nature, origin, and use.* New York: Praeger.

Orwell, G. (1949). *Nineteen eighty-four.* London: Martin Secker & Warburg Ltd.

On the confirmation bias and other built-in biases in the mind, as well as why people often believe silly things:

Ariely, D. (2008). *Predictably irrational: The hidden forces that shape our decisions.* New York: HarperCollins.

Buonomano, D. (2011). *Brain bugs: How the brain's flaws shape our lives.* New York: W. W. Norton.

Chabris, C. F., & Simons, D. J. (2009). *The invisible gorilla: How our intuitions deceive us.* New York: Crown.

Gazzaniga, M. S. (2011). *Who's in charge: Free will and the science of the brain.* New York: HarperCollins.

Kahneman, D. (2011). *Thinking fast and slow.* New York: Farrar, Straus and Giroux.

On folk beliefs about memory:

Simons D. J., & Chabris, C. F. (2011) *What people believe about how memory works: A representative survey of the U.S. population.* PLoS ONE 6(8): e22757. doi:10.1371/journal.pone.0022757

For figures on poverty and inequality given in this chapter, see:

Shah, A. (2010). *Global issues: Social, political, and economic issues that affect us all: Poverty facts and stats.* http://www.globalissues.org/article/26/poverty-facts-and-stats#src24.

On the treatment of women in the world:

Kristof, N. D., & WuDun, S. (2009). *Half the sky: Turning oppression into opportunity for women worldwide.* New York: Vintage.

On everyday ("amateur") people using digital media to produce expert-level things on their own (including ads) and the response of credentialed experts:

Gee, J. P., & Hayes, E. R. (2011). *Language and learning in the digital age.* London: Routledge.
Rose, F. (2011). *The art of immersion: How the digital generation is remaking Hollywood, Madison Avenue, and the way we tell stories.* New York: W. W. Norton.
Shirky, C. (2008). *Here comes everybody: The power of organizing without organizations.* New York: Penguin.
Shirky, C. (2010). *Cognitive surplus: Creativity and generosity in a connected age.* New York: Penguin.

On the problems with and crises in our colleges and universities today:

Arum, R., & Roksa, J. (2011). *Academically adrift: Limited learning on college campuses.* Chicago: University of Chicago Press.
Brandon, C. (2010). *The five-year party: How colleges have given up on educating your child and what you can do about it.* Dallas: BenBella Books.
Cole, J. R. (2009). *The great American university: Its rise to preeminence, its indispensible national role, why it must be protected.* New York: Public Affairs.
Hacker, A., & Dreifus, C. (2010). *Higher education? How colleges are wasting our money and failing our kids—and what we can do about it.* New York: St. Martin's Press.
Kamenetz, A. (2010). *DIY U: Edupreneurs, and the coming transformation of higher education.* West River Junction, VT: Chelsea Green.
Menand, L. (2010). *The marketplace of ideas: Reform and resistance in the American university.* New York: W. W. Norton.
Schrecker, E (2010). *The lost soul of higher education: Corporatization, the assault on academic freedom, and the end of the American university.* New York: The New Press.
Taylor, M. C. (2010). *Crisis on campus: A bold plan for reforming our colleges and universities.* New York: Knopf.
Tuchman, G. (2009). *Wannabe U: Inside the corporate university.* Chicago: University of Chicago Press.

I discuss rising inequality in the United States and in the rest of the developed world, as well as the crisis in our institutions of higher learning, in later chapters. Additional references can be found in corresponding chapter reference lists.

CHAPTER 2

On the evolution of the human mind:

Marcus, G. (2008). *Kluge: The haphazard evolution of the human mind.* New York: Houghton Mifflin.

Renfrew, C. (2009). *Prehistory: The making of the human mind.* New York: Random House.

On experience and simulations in the mind:

Barsalou, L.W. (1999a). Language comprehension: archival memory or preparation for situated action. *Discourse Processes, 28:* 61-80.

Barsalou, L.W. (1999b). Perceptual symbol systems. *Behavioral and Brain Sciences, 22:* 577-660.

Barsalou, L.W. (2005). Continuity of the conceptual system across species. *Trends in Cognitive Sciences, 9:* 309-311.

Bransford, J., Brown, A. L., & Cocking, R. R. (2000). *How people learn: Brain, mind, experience, and school* (Expanded ed.) Washington, DC: National Academy Press.

Gee, J. P. (2004). *Situated language and learning: A critique of traditional schooling.* London: Routledge.

Gee, J. P. (2007). *Good video games and good learning: Collected essays on video games, learning, and literacy.* New York: Peter Lang.

On the circuit of reflective action and assessing the outcomes of actions:

Bereiter, C., & Scardamalia, M. (1993) *Surpassing ourselves: An inquiry into the nature and implications of expertise.* Chicago: Open Court.

Schön, D. A. (1983). *The reflective practitioner: How professionals think in action.* New York: Basic Books.

That a focus on facts and information does not lead to problem-solving abilities:

Bransford, J., Brown, A. L., & Cocking, R. R. (2000). *How people learn: Brain, mind, experience, and school* (Expanded ed.). Washington, DC: National Academy Press.

Chi, M., Feltovich, P., & Glaser, R. (1981). Categorization and representation of physics problems by experts and novices. *Cognitive Science, 5:* 121-152.

diSessa, A. A. (2000). *Changing minds: Computers, learning, and literacy.* Cambridge, MA: MIT Press.

Gardner, H. (1991). *The unschooled mind: How children think and how schools should teach.* New York: Basic Books.

Pellegrino, J., Chudowsky, N., & Glaser, R. (Eds.) (2001). *Knowing what students know: The science and design of educational assessment.* Washington, DC: National Academy Press.

Shaffer, D. W. (2007). *How computer games help children learn.* New York: Palgrave Macmillan.

On the importance of caring and emotion in thinking:

Damasio, A. R. (1995). *Descartes' error: Emotion, reason, and the human brain.* New York: Quill.

Damasio, A. (1999). *The feeling of what happens: Body and emotion in the making of consciousness.* Orlando, FL: Harvest Books.

Damasio, A. (2003). *Looking for Spinoza: Joy, sorrow, and the feeling brain*. Orlando, FL: Harvest Books.

For the text on weathering and abrasion, see p. 93 of:

Martin, J. R. (1990). Literacy in science: Learning to handle text as technology. In F. Christie (Ed.), *Literacy for a changing world* (pp. 79-117). Melbourne: Australian Council for Educational Research.

CHAPTER 3

On human memory:

Gazzaniga, M. S. (2011). *Who's in charge: Free will and the science of the brain*. New York: HarperCollins.
Glenberg, A. M. (1997). What is memory for? *Behavioral and Brain Sciences, 20*: 1-55.
Loftus, E. F. (1976). *Memory: Surprising new insights into how we remember and how we forget*. Lanham, MD: Rowman & Littlefield.
Loftus, E., & Ketcham, K. (1991). *Witness for the defense: The accused, the eyewitness and the expert who puts memory on trial*. New York: St. Martin's Press.
Schacter, D. L. (2002). *The seven sins of memory: How the mind forgets and remembers*. New York: Houghton Mifflin.

On memory practices in earlier ages:

Carruthers, M., & Ziolkowski, J. (2002). *The medieval craft of memory: An anthology of texts and pictures*. Philadelphia: University of Pennsylvania Press.
Yates, F. A. (1966). *The art of memory*. Chicago: University of Chicago Press.

On the *Santa Clara County v. Southern Pacific Railroad* case and corporations as persons:

Hartmann, T. (2010). *Unequal protection: How corporations became "people"—and how you can fight back* (2nd ed.). San Francisco: Berrett-Koehler.

CHAPTER 4

On narratives and stories and their role in human life:

Bruner, J. (1987). *Actual minds, possible worlds*. Cambridge, MA: Harvard University Press.
Labov, W., & Waletsky, J. (1967). Narrative analysis: Oral versions of personal experience. In J. Helm (Ed.), *Essays on the verbal and visual arts* (pp. 12-44). Seattle: University of Washington Press.
Lévi-Strauss, C. (1979). *Myth and meaning*. New York: Schocken Books.
MacIntyre, A. (1981). *After virtue: A study in moral theory* (3rd ed.). Notre Dame, IN: University of Notre Dame Press.
Mishler, E. (2000). *Storylines: Craftartists' narratives of identity*. Cambridge, MA: Harvard University Press.
Pattison, R. (1982). *On literacy: The politics of the word from Homer to the age of rock*. Oxford: Oxford University Press.
Ong, W. J. (1982). *Orality and literacy: The technologizing of the word*. London & New York: Methuen.

On humans becoming sick in mind or body by feelings of a lack of control:

Pickett, K., & Wilkinson, R. (2011). *The spirit level: Why greater equality makes societies stronger.* New York: Bloomsbury Press.

For the "whatever's gonna happen is gonna happen" text:

Schiffrin, D. (1987). *Discourse markers.* Cambridge: Cambridge University Press, pp. 49-50.

On the interpreter:

Gazzaniga, M. S. (1985). *The social brain: Discovering the networks of the mind.* New York: Basic Books.
Gazzaniga, M. S. (1988). *Mind matters: How mind and brain interact to create our conscious lives.* Boston: Houghton Mifflin.
Gazzaniga, M. S. (2011). *Who's in charge: Free will and the science of the brain.* New York: HarperCollins.

On the historical Jesus:

Beilby, J. K., & Eddy, P. R. (Eds.) (2009). *The historical Jesus: Five views.* Downers Grove, IL: InterVarsity Press.
Crossan, J. D. (1994). *Jesus: A revolutionary biography.* New York: HarperCollins.

CHAPTER 5

On literacy and the hammer-log problem:

Gee, J. P. (2011). *Social linguistics and literacies: Ideology in Discourses* (4th ed.). London: Taylor & Francis.
Olson, D. R. (1996). *The world on paper: The conceptual and cognitive implications of writing and reading.* Cambridge: Cambridge University Press.
Scribner, S., & Cole, M. (1981). *The psychology of literacy.* Cambridge, MA: Harvard University Press.

On human thinking and the sorts of problems in Case 1 and Case 2:

Barkow, J. H., Cosmides, L., & Tooby, J. (1995). *The adapted mind: Evolutionary psychology and the generation of culture.* New York: Oxford University Press.
Cosmides, L. (1989). The logic of social exchange: Has natural selection shaped how humans reason? Studies with the Wasson Selection task. *Cognition,* 31.3: 187-276.
Wason, P. (1966). Reasoning. In B. M. Foss (Ed.), *New horizons in psychology* (pp. 135-151). Harmondsworth: Penguin.
Wason, P. (1968). Reasoning about a rule. *Quarterly Journal of Experimental Psychology,* 20: 273-281.
Wason, P.C. and Johnson-Laird, P.N. (1972). *Psychology of reasoning: Structure and content.* London: Batsford.

The cases on pages 40–41 and more discussion of problems in human thinking can be found in Wendy Steiner & Mark Liberman's Humanities 101 (University of Pennsylvania) course materials:

Case 1: http://www.ling.upenn.edu/courses/hum100/evolutionary_psychology.html
Case 2: http://www.psych.ucsb.edu/research/cep/socox/wason.htm#Social%20Contract

On learning abstractions bottom-up from experience:

Brown, A. L., Collins, A., & Dugid, P. (1989). Situated cognition and the culture of learning. *Educational Researcher,* 18: 32-42.

Clark, A. (2008). *Supersizing the mind: Embodiment, action, and cognitive extension.* Oxford: Oxford University Press.

diSessa, A. A. (2000). *Changing minds: Computers, learning, and literacy.* Cambridge, MA: MIT Press.

Lave, J., & Wenger, E. (1991). *Situated learning: Legitimate peripheral participation.* Cambridge: Cambridge University Press.

Shaffer, D. W. (2007). *How computer games help children learn.* New York: Palgrave Macmillan.

On language and context:

Duranti, A. (1997). *Linguistic anthropology.* Cambridge: Cambridge University Press.

Duranti, A. & Goodwin, C. (Eds.). (1992). *Rethinking context: Language as an interactive phenomenon.* Cambridge: Cambridge University Press.

Eisenkraft, A., Heltzel, C., Johnson, D., & Radcliffe, B. (2006). Artist as chemist. *Science Teacher,* 73(8), 33–37.

Gee, J. P. (2004). *Situated language and learning: A critique of traditional schooling.* London: Routledge.

CHAPTER 6

On meaning and associations:

Gee, J. P. (2010). *An introduction to discourse analysis: Theory and method* (3rd ed.). New York: Routledge.

Gee, J. P. (2011). *How to do discourse analysis: A toolkit.* New York: Routledge.

Hanks, W. F. (1996). *Language and communicative practices.* Boulder, CO: Westview Press.

Hofstadter, D. & the Fluid Analogies Research Group (1995). *Fluid concepts and creative analogies: Computer models of the fundamental mechanisms of thought.* New York: Basic Books.

Holland, D., Lachicotte, W., Skinner, D., & Cain, C. (1998). *Identity and agency in cultural worlds.* Cambridge, MA: Harvard University Press.

Kahneman, D. (2011). *Thinking fast and slow.* New York: Farrar, Straus and Giroux.

Williams, P. J. (1991). *The alchemy of race and rights: Diary of a law professor.* Cambridge, MA: Harvard University Press.

On media:

Jenkins, H. (2006). *Convergence culture: Where old and new media collide.* New York: New York University Press.

Reeves, B., and Nass, C. (1999) *The media equation: How people treat computers, television, and new media like real people and places.* New York: Cambridge University Press.

Wasik, B. (2009). *And then there's this: How stories live and die in viral culture.* New York: Viking.

On the wisdom of crowds:

Howe, J. (2008). *Crowdsourcing: Why the power of the crowd is driving the future of business.* New York: Crown Business.

Shirky, C. (2008). *Here comes everybody: The power of organizing without organizations.* New York: Penguin.

Surowiecki, J. (2004). *The wisdom of crowds.* New York: Doubleday.

On deception and lying:

Byrne, R. W., & Whiten, A. (1988). *Machiavellian intelligence: Social expertise and the evolution of intellect in monkeys, apes, and humans.* Oxford: Oxford University Press.

Hare, B., Call, J., & Tomasello, M. (2006). Chimpanzees deceive a human competitor by hiding. *Cognition,* 101: 495-514.

Smith, D. L. (2004). *Why we lie: The evolutionary roots of deception and the unconscious mind.* New York: St. Martin's Press.

CHAPTER 7

On status and solidarity in human interactions:

Bishop, B. (2008). *The Big Sort: Why the clustering of like-minded America is tearing us apart.* New York: Houghton Mifflin.

Brown, P., & Levinson, S. C. (1987). *Politeness: Some universals in language usage.* Cambridge: Cambridge University Press.

Gumperz, J. J. (Ed.). (1982). *Language and social identity.* Cambridge: Cambridge University Press.

Labov, W. (1972). *Sociolinguistic patterns.* Philadelphia: University of Pennsylvania Press.

Lareau, A. (2003). *Unequal childhoods: Class, race, and family life.* Berkeley: University of California Press.

Milroy, L. (1987). *Language and social networks* (2nd ed.). Oxford: Blackwell.

CHAPTER 8

The quote from President Bush:

"On September the eleventh, enemies of freedom committed an act of war against our country": http://articles.cnn.com/2001-09-20/us/gen.bush.transcript_1_joint -session-national-anthem-citizens/2?_s=PM:US

The quotes on "democracy":

" . . . thoroughgoing restrictions on economic freedom" is from: http://www .becker-posner-blog.com/archives/2006/11/on_milton_fried.html

" . . . high quality public pedestrian space": Brown, L. R. (2008). *Plan B 3.0: Mobilizing to save civilization* (Rev. ed.). Washington, DC: Earth Policy Institute, p. 193.

"That is the fate of democracy":

> Weisberg, J. (2008). *The Bush tragedy.* New York: Random House, pp. 181-182.

On how words get meaning:

> Hanks, W. F. (1996). *Language and communicative practices.* Boulder, CO: Westview Press.
>
> Holland, D., Lachicotte, W., Skinner, D., & Cain, C. (1998). *Identity and agency in cultural worlds.* Cambridge, MA: Harvard University Press.
>
> Holland, D., & Quinn, N. (Eds.) (1987). *Cultural models in language and thought.* Cambridge: Cambridge University Press.
>
> Lakoff, G. (1987). *Women, fire, and dangerous things: What categories reveal about the mind.* Chicago: University of Chicago Press.
>
> Lakoff, G., & Johnson, M. (2003). *Metaphors we live by* (2nd ed.). Chicago: University of Chicago Press.
>
> Williams, R. (1985). *Keywords: A vocabulary of culture and society* (Rev. ed.). New York: Oxford University Press.
>
> Wittgenstein, L. (1958). *Philosophical investigations* (G. E. M. Anscombe, Trans.). Oxford: Basil Blackwell.

CHAPTER 9

On the human need for agency and a sense of control:

> Maslow, A. (1954). *Motivation and personality.* New York: Harper and Row.
>
> Rigby, S., & Ayan, R. M. (2011). *Glued to games: How video games draw us in and hold us spellbound.* Santa Barbara, CA: Praeger.

On the "winner-take-all" nature of modern capitalism:

> Frank, R. H., & Cook, P. J. (1995). *The winner-take-all society: How more and more Americans compete for ever fewer and bigger prizes, encouraging economic waste, income inequality, and an impoverished cultural life.* New York: The Free Press.

On the Pareto principle:

> Gee, J. P., & Hayes, E. R. (2010). *Women and gaming: The Sims and 21st century learning.* New York: Palgrave Macmillan.
>
> Gee, J. P., & Hayes, E. R. (2011). *Language and learning in the digital age.* New York: Routledge.
>
> Shirky, C. (2008). *Here comes everybody: The power of organizing without organizations.* New York: Penguin.

On inequality in the United States (statistics on wealth distribution in this chapter are from the second source below):

> Pickett, K., & Wilkinson, R. (2011). *The spirit level: Why greater equality makes societies stronger.* New York: Bloomsbury Press.
>
> Wolff, E. N. (2010). *Recent trends in household wealth in the United States: Rising debt and the middle-class squeeze—an update to 2007. Working Paper No. 589.* Annandale-on-Hudson, NY: The Levy Economics Institute of Bard College.

On the kick theory:

> Zuckerman, H. (1977). *Scientific elite: Nobel laureates in the United States.* New York: The Free Press.

On "luck" as a part of success:

> Gladwell, M. (2008). *Outliers: The story of success.* New York: Little Brown.

On the status syndrome:

> Marmot, M. (2004). *The status syndrome: How social standing affects our health and longevity.* New York: Holt.

On the distribution of work in developed countries:

> Drucker, P. F. (1993). *Post-capitalist society.* New York: Harder.
> Reich, R. B. (1992). *The work of nations.* New York: Vintage Books.
> Reich, R. B. (2007). *Supercapitalism: The transformation of business, democracy, and everyday life.* New York: Vintage Books.

Sense of worth off market:

> Anderson, C. (2006). *The long tail: Why the future of business is selling less of more.* New York: Hyperion.
> Gee, J. P., & Hayes, E. R. (2010). *Women and gaming: The Sims and 21st century learning.* New York: Palgrave Macmillan.
> Leadbeater, C., & Miller, P. (2004). *The Pro-Am revolution: How enthusiasts are changing our society and economy.* London: Demos.
> Shirky, C. (2010). *Cognitive surplus: Creativity and generosity in a connected age.* New York: Penguin.
> Toffler, A., & Toffler, H. (2006). *Revolutionary wealth: How it will be created and how it will change our lives.* New York: Knopf.

CHAPTER 10

On institutions in our changing world:

> Douglas, M. (1986). *How institutions think.* Syracuse, NY: Syracuse University Press.
> Drucker, P. F. (1993). *Post-capitalist society.* New York: Harder.
> Friedman, T. (2005). *The world is flat: A brief history of the twenty-first century.* New York: Farrar, Straus and Giroux.
> Kanigel, R. (1997). *The one best way: Frederick Winslow Taylor and the enigma of efficiency.* New York: Penguin.
> Parker, G. (2002). *Cross-functional teams: Working with allies, enemies, and other strangers.* San Francisco: Jossey-Bass.

On corporations as people:

> Hartmann, T. (2010). *Unequal protection: How corporations became "people"—and how you can fight back* (2nd ed.). San Francisco: Berrett-Koehler.

On how digital media can allow organization without institutions:

> Gee, J. P., & Hayes, E. R. (2010). *Women and gaming: The Sims and 21st century learning.* New York: Palgrave Macmillan.
>
> Shirky, C. (2008). *Here comes everybody: The power of organizing without organizations.* New York: Penguin.
>
> Shirky, C. (2010). *Cognitive surplus: Creativity and generosity in a connected age.* New York: Penguin.
>
> Wasik, B. (2009). *And then there's this: How stories live and die in viral culture.* New York: Viking.

CHAPTER 11

On creationism, intelligent design, and evolution:

> Dawkins, R. (2009). *The greatest show on earth: The evidence for evolution.* New York: The Free Press.
>
> Numbers, R. L. (1992). *The creationists: From scientific creationism to intelligent design* (Expanded ed.). Berkeley: University of California Press.

On the Anglo-Israel Story, Poole below is a classic source. Through the years many more sources have appeared and disappeared as the story waxes and wanes. See also http://www.angloisrael.info/ among many other websites devoted to the story. Henry Ford was a major proponent of the story:

> Baldwin, N. (2001). *Henry Ford and the Jews: The mass production of hate.* New York: PublicAffairs.
>
> Poole, W. H. (1879). *Anglo-Israel or, the british nation: The lost tribes of Israel.* Toronto: Bengough Bros.

For the text on the "stone of destiny":

> http://www.godswatcher.com/stone.htm

CHAPTER 12

On imagined kin groups:

> Anderson, B. (1983). *Imagined communities: Reflections on the origin and spread of nationalism.* London: Verso.
>
> Axelrod, R. H. (1984). *The evolution of cooperation.* New York: Basic Books.
>
> Barkow, J. H., Cosmides, L., & Tooby, J. (Eds.) (1992). *The adapted mind: Evolutionary psychology and the generation of culture.* New York: Oxford University Press.
>
> Ignatieff, M. (1994). *Blood and belonging: Journeys into the new nationalism.* New York: Farrar, Straus and Giroux.
>
> Ridley, M. (1997). *The origins of virtue: Human instincts and the evolution of cooperation.* New York: Viking.

On polarization:

> Bishop, B. (2008). *The Big Sort: Why the clustering of like-minded America is tearing us apart.* New York: Houghton Mifflin.

Pariser, E. (2011). *The filter bubble: What the Internet is hiding from you.* New York: Penguin.

On cultural politics over economic issues:

Bagent, J. (2007). *Deer hunting with Jesus: Dispatches from America's class war.* New York: Three Rivers.

Bagent, J. (2010). *Rainbow pie: A redneck memoir.* Carlton North, Victoria, Australia: Scribe Publications.

Frank, T. (2012). *Pity the billionaire: The hard-times swindle and the unlikely comeback of the right.* New York: Henry Holt.

Hacker, J. S., & P. Pierson (2010). *Winner-take-all politics: How Washington made the rich richer—and turned its back on the middle class.* New York: Simon & Schuster.

On the parable of the Good Samaritan:

Forbes, G. W. (2000). *The God of old: The role of the Lukan parables in the purpose of Luke's gospel.* New York: Continuum. http://episcopal.wordpress.com/2007/11/16 /parable-of-the-good-samaritan-an-exegesis/.

CHAPTER 13

On games and learning:

Gee, J. P. (2004). *Situated language and learning: A critique of traditional schooling.* London: Routledge.

Gee, J. P. (2007). *What video games have to teach us about learning and literacy* (2nd ed.). New York: Palgrave Macmillan.

Gee, J. P. (2007). *Good video games and good learning: Collected essays on video games, learning, and literacy.* New York: Peter Lang.

Gee, J. P., & Hayes, E. R. (2010). *Women and gaming: The Sims and 21st century learning.* New York: Palgrave Macmillan.

Gee, J. P., & Hayes, E. R. (2011). *Language and learning in the digital age.* New York: Routledge.

On humans optimizing for success:

Koster, R. (2004). *A theory of fun for game design.* Scottsdale, AZ: Paraglyph Press.

On artificial tutors:

Graesser, A. C., Chipman, P., & King, B. G. (2008). Computer-mediated technologies. In M. J. Spector (Ed.), *Handbook of research on educational communications and technology* (pp. 211-224). New York: Routledge.

Graesser, A. C., Lu, S., Jackson, G. T., Mitchell, H., Ventura, M., Olney, A., et al. (2004). AutoTutor: A tutor with dialogue in natural language. *Behavioral Research Methods, Instruments, and Computers,* 36: 180-193.

For "School of One":

http://schoolofone.org/

For the quote from "School of One" used in this chapter:

http://schoolofone.org/concept.html

On the Internet and customization:

Pariser, E. (2011). *The filter bubble: What the Internet is hiding from you.* New York: Penguin.

On the public sphere:

Habermas, J. (1989), *The structural transformation of the public sphere: An inquiry into a category of bourgeois society.* Cambridge, MA: MIT Press.
Sennet, R. (1974). *The fall of public man: On the social psychology of capitalism.* New York: Vintage Books.

CHAPTER 14

For the math problem at the opening of this chapter and a discussion of the problem:

Buonomano, D. (2011). *Brain bugs: How the brain's flaws shape our lives.* New York: W. W. Norton, pp. 7–8.

On humans, thinking, and tools:

diSessa, A. A. (2000). *Changing minds: Computers, learning, and literacy.* Cambridge, MA: MIT Press.
Latour, B. (1999). *Pandora's hope: Essays on the reality of science studies.* Cambridge, MA: Harvard University Press.
Pickering, A. (1995). *The mangle of practice: Time, agency, and science.* Chicago: University of Chicago Press.
Shapin, S. & Schaffer, S. (1985). *Leviathan and the air-pump.* Princeton, NJ: Princeton University Press.
Tomasello, M. (1999). *The cultural origins of human cognition.* Cambridge, MA: Harvard University Press.
Wertsch, J. V. (1998). *Mind as action.* Oxford: Oxford University Press.

On distributed cognition:

Hutchins, E. (1995). How a cockpit remembers its speeds. *Cognitive Science,* 19: 265-288.
Hutchins, E. (1995). *Cognition in the wild.* Cambridge, MA: MIT Press.
Salomon, G. (Ed.) (1997). *Distributed cognitions: Psychological and educational considerations.* New York: Cambridge University Press.

For our book on people designing in the Sims:

Gee, J. P. & Hayes, E. R. (2010). *Women and gaming: The Sims and 21st century learning.* New York: Palgrave Macmillan.

On the 2008 financial crisis:

> Johnson, S., & Kwak, J. (2010). *13 bankers: The Wall Street takeover and the next financial meltdown.* New York: Random House.
> Lewis, M. (2010). *The Big Short: Inside the doomsday machine.* New York: W. W. Norton.
> Lewis, M. (2011). *Boomerang: Travels in the new third world.* New York: W. W. Norton.

The quote from Alan Greenspan:

> Andrews, E.L. (2008, October 23). Greenspan concedes error on regulation. *The New York Times.* Retrieved from: http://www.nytimes.com/2008/10/24/business/economy/24panel.html?_r.

On Alan Greenspan:

> Sheehan, F. (2009). *Panderer to power: The untold story of how Alan Greenspan enriched Wall Street and left a legacy of recession.* New York: McGraw-Hill.
> Woodward, B. (2000). *Maestro: Greenspan's Fed and the American boom.* New York: Touchstone.

On pooling expertise:

> Parker, G. (2002). *Cross-functional teams: Working with allies, enemies, and other strangers.* San Francisco: Jossey-Bass.

CHAPTER 15

On meaning and the human desire for meaning:

> Bruner, J. (1986). *Actual minds, possible worlds.* Cambridge, MA: Harvard University Press.
> Coles, R. (1989). *The call of stories: Teaching and the moral imagination.* Boston: Houghton Mifflin.
> Frankl, V. E. (1959). *Man's search for meaning.* Boston: Beacon Press.
> Polanyi, M., & Prosch, H. (1975). *Meaning.* Chicago: University of Chicago Press.

On the Koch brothers:

> Press, B. (2012). *The Obama hate machine: The lies, distortions, and personal attacks on the President—and who is behind them.* New York: Thomas Dunne Books.

On argument and evidence:

> Kuhn, D. (1991). *The skills of argument.* Cambridge: Cambridge University Press.
> Kuhn, D. (2005). *Education for thinking.* Cambridge, MA: Harvard University Press.

On "modern" and "bush" consciousness:

> Berger, P., Berger, B., & Kellner, H. (1973). *The homeless mind: Modernization and consciousness.* New York: Random House.

Scollon, R., & Scollon, S. W. (1981). *Narrative, literacy, and face in interethnic communication.* Norwood, NJ: Ablex.

CHAPTER 16

On complexity and complex systems:

Barabasi, A.-L. (2002). *Linked: How everything is connected to everything else and what it means.* New York: Perseus.

Johnson, N. (2009). *Simply complexity: A clear guide to complexity theory.* Oxford: Oneworld.

Page, S. E. (2011). *Diversity and complexity.* Princeton, NJ: Princeton University Press.

On cane toads in Australia:

Weber, C. (Ed.) (2010). *Cane toads and other rogue species.* New York: Participant Media.

On our dying forests:

Nikiforuk, A. (2011). *Empire of the beetle: How human folly and a tiny bug are killing North American's great forests.* Vancouver, BC: Greystone Books.

On the root difference between liberals and conservatives:

Sowell, T. (1996). *The vision of the anointed: Self-congratulation as a basis for social policy.* New York: Basic Books.

On the importance of diversity in dealing with complexity:

Page, S. E. (2007). *The difference: How the power of diversity creates better groups, firms, schools, and societies.* Princeton, NJ: Princeton University Press.

CHAPTER 17

On democracy in Athens:

Ober, J. (1989). *Mass and elite in democratic Athens: Rhetoric, ideology and the power of the people.* Princeton, NJ: Princeton University Press.

On the social (inclusive "we") nature of our thinking:

Bakhtin, M. M. (1981). *The dialogic imagination.* Austin: University of Texas Press.

Bakhtin, M. M. (1986). *Speech genres and other late essays.* Austin: University of Texas Press.

Byrne, R. W., & Whiten, A. (1988). *Machiavellian intelligence: Social expertise and the evolution of intellect in monkeys, apes, and humans.* Oxford: Oxford University Press.

Clark, H. H. (1996). *Using language.* Cambridge: Cambridge University Press.

Fleck, L. (1979). *The genesis and development of a scientific fact.* Chicago: University of Chicago Press (orig. 1935).

Habermas, J. (1984). *Theory of communicative action, Vol. 1* (T. McCarthy, Trans.) London: Heinemann.

Hutchins, E. (1995). *Cognition in the wild.* Cambridge, MA: MIT Press.

Latour, B. (2005). *Reassembling the social: An introduction to Actor-Network-Theory.* Oxford: Oxford University Press.

Lave, J. (1988). *Cognition in practice.* Cambridge: Cambridge University Press.

Lave, J., & Wenger, E. (1991). *Situated learning: Legitimate peripheral participation.* Cambridge: Cambridge University Press.

Rogoff, B., & Toma, C. (1997). Shared thinking: Cultural and institutional variations. *Discourse Processes, 23:* 471-497.

Vygotsky, L. S. (1978). *Mind in society: The development of higher psychological processes.* Cambridge, MA: Harvard University Press.

Wenger, E. (1998). *Communities of practice: Learning, meaning, and identity.* Cambridge: Cambridge University Press.

Wertsch, J. V. (1985). *Vygotsky and the social formation of mind.* Cambridge, MA: Harvard University Press.

On the status syndrome and the effects of inequality:

Marmot, M. (2004). *The status syndrome: How social standing affects our health and longevity.* New York: Holt.

Pickett, K., & Wilkinson, R. (2011). *The spirit level: Why greater equality makes societies stronger.* New York: Bloomsbury Press.

CHAPTER 18

On Foldit, the protein folding video game:

http://fold.it/portal/

On "Minds" rather than just minds (using my terms):

Bazerman, C. (1989). *Shaping written knowledge.* Madison: University of Wisconsin Press.

Galison P., & Hevly B. (Eds.) (1992). *Big science: The growth of large-scale research.* Stanford, CA: Stanford University Press.

Jenkins, H. (2006a). *Confronting the challenges of participatory culture: Media education for the 21st century.* Chicago: MacArthur Foundation.

Knorr Cetina, K. (1992). The couch, the cathedral, and the laboratory: On the relationship between experiment and laboratory in science. In A. Pickering (Ed.), *Science as practice and culture* (pp. 113-137). Chicago: University of Chicago Press.

Latour, B. (1987). *Science in action.* Cambridge, MA: Harvard University Press.

Latour, B. (1999). *Pandora's hope: Essays on the reality of science studies.* Cambridge, MA: Harvard University Press.

Latour, B. (2005). *Reassembling the social: An introduction to Actor-Network-Theory.* Oxford: Oxford University Press.

Nielsen, M. A. (2012). *Reinventing discovery: The new era of networked science.* Princeton, NJ: Princeton University Press.

Pickering, A. (1995). *The mangle of practice: Time, agency, and science.* Chicago: University of Chicago Press.

Shapin, S., & Schaffer, S. (1985). *Leviathan and the air-pump.* Princeton, NJ: Princeton University Press.

Shirky, C. (2008). *Here comes everybody: The power of organizing without organizations.* New York: Penguin.

Steinkuehler, C. A., & Duncan, S. C. (2008). Scientific habits of mind in virtual worlds. *Journal of Science Education and Technology,* 17: 530-543.

Toffler, A., & Toffler, H. (2006). *Revolutionary wealth: How it will be created and how it will change our lives.* New York: Knopf.

CHAPTER 19

On "Mind Visions" and the humanities:

Bruner, J. (1990). *Acts of meaning.* Cambridge, MA: Harvard University Press.

Menand, L. (2010). *The marketplace of ideas: Reform and resistance in the American university.* New York: W. W. Norton.

Nussbaum, M. C. (2010). *Not for profit: Why democracy needs the humanities.* Princeton, NJ: Princeton University Press.

CHAPTER 20

On what I am here calling synchronized intelligence, see:

Gee, J. P., & Hayes, E. R. (2011). *Language and learning in the digital age.* London: Routledge.

Latour, B. (1999). *Pandora's hope: Essays on the reality of science studies.* Cambridge, MA: Harvard University Press.

Nielsen, M. (2012). *Reinventing discovery: The new era of networked science.* Princeton, NJ: Princeton University Press.

Pickering, A. (1995). *The mangle of practice: Time, agency, and science.* Chicago: University of Chicago Press.

On various forms of collective intelligence:

Howe, J. (2008). *Crowdsourcing: Why the power of the crowd is driving the future of business.* New York: Crown Business.

Ito, M., Baumer, S., Bittanti, M., Boyd, D., Cody, R., et al. (2010). *Hanging out, messing around, and geeking out: Kids living and learning with new media.* Cambridge, MA: MIT Press.

Jenkins, H. (2006b). *Convergence culture: Where old and new media collide.* New York: New York University Press.

Shirky, C. (2008). *Here comes everybody: The power of organizing without organizations.* New York: Penguin.

Shirky, C. (2010). *Cognitive surplus: Creativity and generosity in a connected age.* New York: Penguin.

Surowiecki, J. (2004). *The wisdom of crowds: Why the many are smarter than the few and how collective wisdom shapes business, economies, societies and nations.* Boston: Little, Brown.

Wasik, B. (2009). *And then there's this: How stories live and die in viral culture.* New York: Viking.

On affinity spaces:

Gee, J. P. (2004). *Situated language and learning: A critique of traditional schooling.* London: Routledge.

Gee, J. P., & Hayes, E. R. (2010). *Women and gaming: The Sims and 21st century learning.* New York: Palgrave Macmillan.

Gee, J. P., & Hayes, E. R. (2011). *Language and learning in the digital age.* New York: Routledge.

On The Nickel and Dimed Challenge:

All quotes are from The Nickel and Dimed Challenge Forum (BBS) thread. Unless otherwise noted, all quotes are from posts by Yamx. See The Sims 2 website for the full thread: http://thesims2.ea.com.

On Foldit and other related approaches to discovery and learning, see:

Nielsen, M. (2012) Chapter 7: "Democratizing Science." In *Reinventing discovery: The new era of networked science.* Princeton, NJ: Princeton University Press.

CHAPTER 21

On the increasingly collective nature of science:

Jones, B., Wuchty, S., & and Uzzi, B. (2007). Multi-university research teams: Shifting impact, geography, and stratification in science. *Science,* 316: 742-744.

Wuchty, S., Jones, B., & Uzzi, B. (2007). The increasing dominance of teams in the production of knowledge. *Science,* 316:1036-1039.

On the Polymath Project, Foldit, Galaxy Zoo:

Nielsen, M. A. (2012). *Reinventing discovery: The new era of networked science.* Princeton, NJ: Princeton University Press.

On brainstorming and the conditions for group creativity:

Lehrer, J. (2012). Groupthink: The brainstorming myth. Annals of Ideas. *The New Yorker.* March 5. Web only. http://www.newyorker.com/reporting/2012/01/30/120130fa_fact_lehrer#ixzz1nXNf8VXh.

Sawyer, K. (2007). *Group genius: The creative power of collaboration.* New York: Basic Books.

Sawyer, K. (2012). *Explaining creativity: The science of human innovation* (2nd ed.). Oxford: Oxford University Press.

On Building 20:

Brand, S. (1995). *How buildings learn: What happens after they're built.* New York: Penguin Group.

Lehrer, J. (2012). Groupthink: The brainstorming myth. Annals of Ideas. *The New Yorker.* March 5. Web only. http://www.newyorker.com/reporting/2012/01/30/120130fa_fact_lehrer#ixzz1nXNf8VXh (the quote from Lehrer comes from this source).

MIT Department of Electrical Engineering & Computer Science. MIT's Building 20: The Magical Incubator 1943-1998. http://www.eecs.mit.edu/building/20/.

MIT Department of Electrical Engineering & Computer Science. Stories about Building 20. http://www.eecs.mit.edu/building/20/anecdotes/index.html.

MIT News. Venerable Building 20, "A Building with Soul" October 30, 1996. http://web.mit.edu/newsoffice/1996/building-1030.html (this is where the phrase "building with soul" comes from).

On Amar Bose:

http://en.wikipedia.org/wiki/Amar_Bose:

CHAPTER 22

For more information on talk with adults and early vocabulary as key to later success throughout schooling, and the views on literacy expressed in this chapter, see:

Adams, M. J. (1990). *Beginning to read: Thinking and learning about print.* Cambridge, MA: MIT Press.

Beck, I., & McKeown, M. (1991). Conditions of vocabulary acquisition. In R. Barr, M. Kamil, P. Mosenthal, & P. D. Pearson (Eds.), *Handbook of reading research. Volume 2* (pp. 789-814). New York: Longman.

Biemiller, A. (2003). Oral comprehension sets the ceiling on reading comprehension. *American Educator,* 27.1: 23, 44.

Crowley, K., & Jacobs, M. (2002). Islands of expertise and the development of family scientific literacy. In G. Leinhardt, K. Crowley, & K. Knutson (Eds.), *Learning conversations in museums* (pp. 333-356). Mahwah, NJ: Lawrence Erlbaum.

Dickinson, D. K., Golinkoff, R. M., & Hirsh-Pasek, K. (2010). Speaking out for language: Why language is central to reading development. *Educational Researcher,* 39.4: 305-310.

Dickinson, D. K., & Neuman, S. B. (Eds.) (2006). *Handbook of early literacy research: Volume 2.* New York: Guilford Press.

Gee, J. P. (2004). *Situated language and learning: A critique of traditional schooling.* London: Routledge.

Gee, J. P. (2008). *Getting over the slump: Innovation strategies to promote children's learning.* New York: Joan Ganz Cooney Center.

Heath, S. B. (1983). *Ways with words: Language, life, and work in communities and classrooms.* Cambridge: Cambridge University Press.

Neuman, S. B. (2010). Lessons from my mother: Reflections on the National Early Literacy panel report. *Educational Researcher,* 39.4: 301-304.

Neuman, S. B., & Celano, D. (2006). The knowledge gap: Implications of leveling the playing field for low-income and middle-income children. *Reading Research Quarterly,* 41.2: 176-201.

Snow, C. E. (1991). The theoretical basis for relationships between language and literacy in development. *Journal of Research in Childhood Education,* 6.1: 5-10.

On the massive difference in hours of talk a richer child has heard over a poorer one before going to school, see:

Hart, T., & Risely, B. (1995*). Meaningful differences in the early experience of young American children.* Baltimore: Brookes.

For an example of the complex language involved in playing Yu-Gi-Oh, see the language on one card I got from a seven-year-old (there are thousands of Yu-Gi-Oh cards):

Cyber Raider
Card-Type: Effect Monster
Attribute: Dark | Level: 4
Type: Machine
ATK: 1400 | DEF: 1000
Description: "When this card is Normal Summoned, Flip Summoned, or Special Summoned successfully, select and activate 1 of the following effects: Select 1 equipped Equip Spell Card and destroy it. Select 1 equipped Equip Spell Card and equip it to this card." Rarity: Common

"Grit" is a term I took for my own uses from:

Duckworth, E. L., Peterson, C., Matthews, M. D., & Kelly, D. R. (2007). Grit: Perseverance and passion for long-term goals. *Journal of Personality and Social Psychology,* 92.6: 1087-1101.

On colleges and inequality, see:

Edsall, T. B. (2012). The reproduction of privilege. *New York Times,* March 12. http://campaignstops.blogs.nytimes.com/2012/03/12/the-reproduction-of-privilege/.

On the learning in violent video games and connections to brain plasticity, see:

Bavelier, D., & Green, C. S. (2009). Video game based learning: there is more than meets the eye. *Frontiers in Neuroscience,* special issue on Augmented Cognition, 3.1: 109.
Bavelier, D., Levi, D. M., Li, R. W., Dan, Y., & Hensch, T. K. (2010). Removing the brakes on adult brain plasticity: From molecular to behavioral interventions. *Journal of Neuroscience,* 30.45: 14964-14971.
Dye, M. W., & Bavelier, D. (2010). Differential development of visual attention skills in school-age children. *Vision Research,* 50: 452-459.
Green, C. S., Pouget, A., & Bavelier, D. (2010). Improved probabilistic inference, as a general learning mechanism with action video games. *Current Biology,* 20: 1573-1579.
Li, R., Polat, U., Scalzo, F., & Bavelier, D. (2010). Reducing backward masking through action game training. *Journal of Vision,* 10.14:33, 1-13.

Index

Abbey, Edward, 116
abstractions, 18, 38, 40, 43–4. *See also*
    generalizations
actor/simulators, 13
Adobe Photoshop, 124–5, 172
affinity spaces, 173–82, 188–9, 191, 197,
    202–3, 206, 210–14
Afghanistan, viii, 67
agency, human need for, 75–83, 107, 155,
    211
AIDS, 160, 188
Anglo-Israel Story, 97–101
argument and evidence game, 137–40
Armageddon, viii, 146
Armstrong, Garner Ted, 98
Armstrong, Herbert, 98
Assassin's Creed (video game), 214
associations, 23–7, 45, 49–58, 209–10

big questions, 143–7. *See also* complex
    questions
Birthers, 101
Bose, Amar, 194
Bose Corporation, 194
brainstorming, 193, 195
Brand, Stewart, 195
Buffett, Warren, vii,
Bufo marinus (cane toad), 142–3
bufotoxin, 142
Building 20 (MIT), 194–5
Bush, George W., 1, 69, 71
bush consciousness, 138–9, 212

Call of Duty (video game), 207
Chibi-Robo (video game), 113
Chomsky, Noam, 193–4
Christianity, 3–4, 36–7, 67–8, 98, 106,
    110–11, 118, 158, 209

circuit of reflective action, 14–19, 26, 30,
    72, 159, 161–2, 208
Civil War, American, 25–8
collective intelligence, 178–9, 192, 197,
    202, 208–9, 212, 214
college. *See* education: higher
comfort stories. *See* mental comfort stories
complex questions, 64–5. *See also* big
    questions
complex systems, 120, 128, 130–1, 141–7,
    160, 202, 213
complexity, 69, 76, 96–7, 141–7, 202,
    205–6, 213
confirmation bias, 2, 72, 211
conservatives, xiv-xv, 108, 137, 145–6
contextual thinking, 39–48
creationism, 96–7
creativity, 125, 153, 178–9, 193–6, 202,
    207, 211
Crossan, John Dominic, 37
crowdsourcing, 160, 178, 189
Curley, James Michael, 105

Darwinism. *See* natural selection
delayed gratification, 59–65
Deus Ex (video game), 113
digital literacy, 201–3
digital media, viii-ix, xi-xii, 6, 8, 54–5, 58,
    117, 198, 201–5, 208, 211, 214–15
digital tools, xiii, 116, 191, 197–201,
    208–15
distributed cognition, 122

economic collapse of 2008, 3, 5, 31, 127–9,
    140
economics, 128–31
education:
    affinity spaces and, 179–80, 213–14

agency and, 80–1
artificial tutors in, 114–15, 123
higher, x, xii-xiv, 5, 7, 56, 63, 78–82,
    87–91, 145–7, 179–80, 183, 194,
    204–5
inequality and, 204–5
Ivy League, 101
language and, 16–17, 68–9, 199–200
language of business used for, 68–9
real/genuine, ix, xii, 102, 164, 170,
    209
reform in, xi-xii, 144, 157, 207
status and, x, xiv, 204–5
video games and, xiii, 113–14, 208, 210,
    214
See also schools and schooling
Ehrenreich, Barbara, 182–3
Elder Scrolls, The (video game), 113
empirical game, 72–4, 161–6, 170, 210
evolution. See natural selection
experts and expertise, 128–31, 162–3,
    173–5, 179–80, 200–4, 211–12, 214

Facebook, 65, 117. See also social media
fear of suffering and death, 151, 160, 163
Foldit (game), 160, 188–9, 192, 206, 214
Ford, Henry, 98
Ford, John, 105
Fourteenth Amendment, 25–7
fracking, 127
From Dust (video game), 113

Galaxy Zoo, 192
Gates, Bill, vii
generalizations, 43–4, 47, 56. See also
    abstractions
global citizenship, 119–20
global warming, ix, xiv-xv, 3–4, 130, 143–4,
    146, 207
Good Samaritan (parable), 110–11
good taste, 212
Grand Theft Auto (video game), 113
Great Depression, 3, 128–9
Greenspan, Alan, 130–1
grit, 202
group discussion and brainstorming,
    193–5
Groups of One, 113–20, 211–12

Half-Life (video game), 113

Halo (video game), 113
Hayes, Elisabeth, 124
higher-order value-added approach to
    learning, 203
Homo sapiens, vii, 3
Hussein, Saddam, 1

"idiot," derivation of, 66
idiot savant, 21
if-then statements, 44–5
imagined kin groups, 103–13, 116
inequality, ix-x, xiii-xiv, 5, 7, 82, 155–8,
    160, 164, 204–7, 213
institutions, x-xi, 5–8, 83, 85–93, 129–31,
    141, 165, 211
intelligence:
    collective, 178–9, 192, 197, 202, 208–9,
        212, 214
    synchronized, 171–89, 195–6, 208, 214
intelligent design theory, 96–7
Iraq War, viii
islands of expertise, 200–1
Ivy League, 101

Jobs, Steve, 193

kick theory, 78–9
kin groups, imagined, 103–13, 116
King, Martin Luther, 209
knowledge communities, 93
Koch brothers, 136–8
Koran, 54

labor unions, x, 82, 108–9
language:
    actor/simulators and, 13
    context and, 44–7
    defined, 45
    education and, 16–17, 68–9, 199–200
    as a tool for making art, 68–70
    truth-seeking game and, 72–4, 210–11
    word meaning, 49–51
    See also linguistics
Lehrer, Jonah, 195
Lewis, Mark, 142
liberal arts, 170, 214
liberals, xiv-xv, 136–7, 145–6
lies and lying, 1, 54–5, 68, 152, 181–2
linguistics, xi, 42–5, 100–1, 116, 134, 147,
    193–5

mathematics, 46, 121–2, 164, 192, 207
meaning:
 circuit of reflective action and, 16–18
 defined, 134
 digital tools and, 198, 201–3
 experience and, 49–58
 human orientation for, 30–1, 75,
  133–40, 159, 171
 stories and, 27–38
 of words, 45–52
memory, human, 2, 21–8, 208–9
mental comfort stories, 29–38, 55, 65,
 72–5, 93, 95–7, 135, 139, 143, 152,
 160, 164, 181, 209
mentorship, importance of, 13–19, 159,
 176. *See also* TTK mentoring (talk,
 text, and knowledge mentoring)
Mind Visions, 167–70, 214
Minds, 165–72, 189, 196, 208, 214
mining skill, 212
Mother Nature, ix, 163

9/11, 1, 69
natural selection, 11, 14, 25, 42, 59, 78,
 96–7, 114, 118
New Age, 77, 192
Nickel and Dimed Challenge, 183, 206
*Nickel and Dimed: On (Not) Getting By in
 America* (Ehrenreich), 182–3
Nietzsche, Friedrich, 1

Obama, Barack, 1, 101, 104, 160
O'Connor, Edwin, 105
optimize, human urge to, 113–15, 120,
 124–7
Orwell, George, 1, 4, 6, 159

Pareto principle, 77–8
plug-and-play entities, humans as, 153,
 164–5, 167, 189
Pokémon (game), 201
Polymath Project, 192
poverty, 3–4, 36, 63, 67, 80, 109, 144, 152,
 154–8, 182–6, 198–200
Pseudo Empirical Stories, 95–103
*Public Committee Against Torture in Israel v.
 The State of Israel, The,* 71
public sphere, 118–20, 147, 174

QWERTY keyboard, 88–9

Reagan, Ronald, 26, 55
recession of 2008, 3, 5, 31, 127–9, 140
Rise of Nations (video game), 113

*Santa Clara County v. Southern Pacific
 Railroad,* 25, 27–8
savings and loan crisis, 5
scaffolding, 13–14. *See also* mentoring,
 importance of School of One, 115
schools and schooling:
 contextual thinking and, 39–40, 47–8
 as "frozen thought" institutions, 86
 as necessary but not sufficient, 199, 202
 problems with, 7, 16–18, 27, 47, 80–1,
  162–5, 195–6, 204–5
 See also education
Scollon, Ron, 138
Second Life (virtual world), 206, 209
self-deception, 1, 35, 54
September 11, 2001, 1, 69
shared interest groups, 116–18
Sims, The (life simulation video game), 78,
 124–5, 172–3, 177–8, 182–8, 206–7,
 210
smart human action, 12–14
social media, ix, xi, xiii, 6, 92, 188, 191,
 201, 203, 208, 211
 Facebook, 65, 117
 Twitter, 92
solidarity, human need for, 59–66, 75, 90,
 95, 158, 210
solidarity reference groups, 61–2, 64
status:
 affinity spaces and, 176–9
 Christianity and, 36–7, 158
 education and, x, xiv, 204–5
 human need for, 60–6, 75, 210
status reference groups, 61, 64
status syndrome, 79–80, 154–60
STEM (science, technology, engineering,
 and mathematics), x, xiii
storied truths, 180–2, 209
stories:
 defined, 29–30
 narratives vs., 29
 Pseudo Empirical Stories, 95–103
 See also mental comfort stories
survival of the fittest. *See* natural selection
synchronized intelligence, 171–89, 195–6,
 208, 214

Tabby Lou (Sims designer), 172–4, 180
theory building, 73–4
Thomas the Tank Engine (children's
    television program), 200
tools:
  affinity spaces and, 176–7, 179–80
  digital, xiii, 116, 191, 197–201,
    208–15
  humans as, 164–5
  humans as users of, 122–5, 164
  language as, 68
  limitations of, ix, 125–6, 191
  Minds and, 165–72
  synchronized intelligence and, 188–9
  user friendly, 125–8, 172, 179, 191,
    212
Tracy, Spencer, 105
trickle-down economics, 4, 109, 140, 152
tropism, 133
truth-seeking game (empirical game), 72–4,
    161–6, 170, 210
TTK mentoring (talk, text, and knowledge
    mentoring), 200–2, 208
Twitter, 92. *See also* social media

unions, x, 82, 108–9
universities. *See* education: higher
US Constitution, 25–7, 87

user friendly tools, 125–8, 172, 179, 191,
    212

video games:
  cheats and, 113–14, 184
  educational role of, xiii, 113–14, 208,
    210, 214
  first example of, 194
  role-playing and, 12
  solidarity and, 210
  spoilers and, xi
  TTK mentoring and, 201
  violence and, 54, 207
  See also individual video games

Waldman, Amy, 116–17
Wal-Mart, vii, 82
"What do YOU think WE should do?"
    game, 168–70, 214
Wikipedia, 197
winner-take-all world, 76–8, 80, 91, 110,
    178
Woodward, Bob, 130
words. *See* language
World of Warcraft (video game), 212

Yamx, 182–8
Yu-Gi-Oh (game), 201, 207–8